Strengthening Decentralisation through PRIs and SHGs

About the Author

Sujit Kumar Paul is a Social Scientist, obtained Master's and Ph.D. degree in Rural Development from Visva-Bharati (A Central University). He is also a development practitioner, researcher and resource person in the field of rural development. He has conducted several research projects funded by National and International Agencies. As prolific writer, he has published more than 100 research papers on various developmental issues in the National and International Journals of repute. He authored seven books. He also edited three issues of the International Journal of World Education, published by the Association for World Education, Denmark. Presently, Dr. Paul is working as Head in the Department of Lifelong Learning and Extension, Visva-Bharati (A Central University). He also served as Deputy Dean in the Institute of Rural Reconstruction of the same University. Dr. Paul visited different countries for academic, research and extension activities. He is closely associated with various Government and Non-Governmental Organizations, societies and associations in different capacities. He is the Vice President (International) of the Association for World Education— An International NGO with consultative status in the United Nations. Dr. Paul was awarded 'Bharat Shiksha Ratna Award' by the Global Society for Health and Educational Growth, New Delhi in 2015 and Mother Teresa Sadbhawana Award for his outstanding achievement in individual contribution for National Economic and Social Development in 2016.

Strengthening Decentralisation through PRIs and SHGs

Sujit Kumar Paul

CONCEPT PUBLISHING COMPANY PVT. LTD.
NEW DELHI-110059

ISBN-13: 978-93-86682-31-4

First Published 2018

Published and Printed by

Concept Since 1974

Concept Publishing Company Pvt. Ltd.
A/15-16, Commercial Block, Mohan Garden
New Delhi-110059 (India)
T: 25351460, 25351794, *F*: 091-11-25357109
E: publishing@conceptpub.com, W: www.conceptpub.com

Cataloging in Publication Data—Courtesy: D.K. Agencies (P) Ltd. <docinfo@dkagencies.com>

Paul, Sujit Kumar, 1970- **author.**
Strengthening decentralisation through PRIs and SHGs / Sujit Kumar Paul.
pages cm
Study conducted in Birbhum and Burdwan districts of West Bengal, India.
Includes bibliographical references and index.
ISBN 9789386682314

1. Decentralization in government—India—Bīrbhūm (District) 2. Decentralization in government—India—Barddhamān (District) 3. Panchayat—India—Bīrbhūm (District) 4. Panchayat—India—Barddhamān (District) 5. Self-help groups—India—Bīrbhūm (District) 6. Self-help groups—India—Barddhamān (District) I. Title.

LCC JS7025.B57P38 2018 DDC 320.8095414 23

Foreword

The decentralisation of power and decision-making processes from National and State to local bodies has become a major trend globally. Decentralisation, being a process that puts in place a structural arrangement for facilitating shared exercise of power among Central Government, State Government, local Government and local communities, is a wide and complex field allowing for community participation in governance and development. Centralized decision-making at National or State levels has been proven time and again to be unsuitable to local conditions. The "one size fits all" policy mechanisms have given way to the understanding that policies need to be tailored to the needs of local communities and should reflect the diversity embedded in these communities and the conditions faced by them. Local Government is that arm of the Government that lies closest to communities and decentralisation of power and resources, thus has the potential of increasing the community's access to the resources. The decentralised governance has been also considered as a mechanism of local self-government for promoting healthy and sustainable development. It is expected to facilitate effective people's participation, enhance degree of transparency and ensure greater accountability. Decentralised governance is assumed to provide more effective and competitive delivery of services at the grassroots level. Being closer to the people, decentralised governance is assumed to meet needs and preferences of the people.

In recent time, local self-governance has given its emphasis on decentralised community engagement, is touted for being a much more flexible and democratic way to deal with community problems and requirements in a right-based framework. The most important actors in this new approach of local governance have been Panchayati Raj Institutions (PRIs) and Self-Help Groups (SHGs) that have carved out new arenas for these different forms of socio-political engagement. Operating in the spaces between formal Governmental structures and the community, PRIs and SHGs have grown as the major agents for decentralised governance and sustainable development. In particular, PRIs and SHGs have enhanced public involvement in decision-making and at the same time increased the quality and legitimacy of decision-making.

Dr. Sujit Kumar Paul has made an in-depth study on the role of Panchayati Raj Institutions and Self-Help Groups in strengthening decentralisation process and has made many valuable suggestions for further strengthening the grassroots governance system. Dr. Paul has attempted to provide a holistic picture of the decentralisation process with a special reference to Panchayati Raj Institutions and Self-Help Groups. It is well understood that after the formation of SHGs, the participation of women in every aspects of PRIs has developed a lot. All the chapters in this book provide a comprehensive analysis and understanding of various dimensions of decentralization process. The author has brought his considerable academic expertise and practical experiences in the field to present this volume a coherent set of arguments dealing with both theoretical and empirical aspects of decentralisation, PRIs and SHGs. The thoughts and experiences of Dr. Paul are lucidly exposed in this publication. This book will be of assistance to students, social scientists, policy-makers, public administrators and development organizations who are involved with the local self-governance and micro-level planning; to reflect on issues related to decentralisation.

Chandra Shekhar Ghosh
MD and CEO
Bandhan Bank Limited
Kolkata

Preface

Decentralisation is not unique in India, but a global trend. Most developing countries are embracing decentralisation whether in Latin America, Europe or East Asia. Decentralisation is a worldwide phenomenon as it ensures political stability and more effective and efficient service delivery. It has been considered as a mechanism of local self-government for promoting healthy and sustainable development. It is expected to facilitate effective people's participation, enhance degree of transparency and ensure greater accountability. Decentralised governance is assumed to provide more effective and competitive delivery of services at the grassroot level. Being closer to the people, decentralised governance is assumed to meet needs and preferences of the people. Hence, the decentralisation of power and decision-making processes from National and State to Local bodies has become a major trend globally. The establishment of strong and accountable systems of governance at grassroots level will encourage a more equitable distribution of state-provided resources, which can be directed towards poor and vulnerable groups. An underlying hypothesis here is that democratic participation will yield strong mechanisms of accountability, which in turn, will improve the distribution of benefits to groups that are traditionally marginalized by market and state.

India is not an exception to this trend. India has been experimenting with the decentralised governance process for quite some time. Over time it has been realised that centralised decision-making at National and State levels to be unsuitable for local conditions and policies need to be customized to the need of the local communities and should reflect the diversity embedded in these communities and situations faced by them. So, that, the local self-governance has become the arm of the Government that lies closest to the communities as well as increase the community access to resources. The grassroots initiatives from different states of India provide insights into the participation of local communities in decentralized decision-making and local self-governance.

Following the same trend, West Bengal has been one of the forerunners in installing a 3-tier Panchayati Raj System for rural local governance in India. The present generation Panchayats in the State started its journey in 1978, i.e. 15 years ahead of the 73rd Amendment of the Constitution of India. Ever since their inception, the State has demonstrated strong commitment to rural decentralization by ensuring regular elections to PRIs, entrusting them with increasing responsibility of implementing various rural development programmes and making the development bureaucracy part of PRIs. The State also ensured adequate representation of the socially backward classes—Scheduled Castes (SCs), Scheduled Tribes (STs) and women in PRIs for their involvement in the process of socio-economic development. West Bengal is one of the states which have achieved success to some extent in implementing decentralised plans and programmes. It has devolved many powers to the PRIs and recently to SHGs for strengthening decentralization and promoting sustainable development.

In recent time, local self-governance has given its emphasis on decentralized community engagement, is tourted for being a much more flexible and democratic way to deal with community problems and requirements in a right-based framework. The most important actor in this new approach of local governance has been Self-Help Groups (SHGs) that have carved out new arenas for these different forms of socio-political engagement. Operating in the spaces between formal Governmental structures and the community, these activities emphasize the growing importance of SHGs as a major agent for decentralised governance and sustainable development. In particular, SHGs have enhanced public involvement in decision-making and at the same time increased the quality and legitimacy of decision-making within a right-based framework.

Further, the active involvement of grassroots women in local self-governance and decentralization process has been promoted in West Bengal through Self-Help Groups (SHGs), in turn builds ownership over local developments as well as the leadership capabilities of women. The SHGs advocate for effective functioning of the decentralization process in West Bengal by enabling women and marginalized communities to engage in the participatory planning and local self-governance.

In this present book attempts have been made to assess the role of Panchayati Raj Institutions in strengthening rural decentralisation in West Bengal. How the Self-Help Groups are taking active role in local self-governance for strengthening decentralization process has also been studied. Attempts have also been made to discuss the structure of Panchayati Raj Institution in West Bengal, scenario of decentralisation and people's participation, constrains affecting decentralisation and some policy measures.

On whole, the book gives a holistic picture of the status of decentralisation in West Bengal with a special reference to Panchayati Raj Institutions and Self-Help Groups. This book will be very helpful to the students, researchers, teachers, academicians, development workers, planners, policy-makers and various development organizations interested in Panchayati Raj Institution, decentralisation and Rural Self-Governance. The book will extremely be useful for the students of Developmental Studies, Rural Management, Social Work, Sociology, Public Administration, Economics, Political Science, Geography, Journalism and Mass Communication and the like.

Sujit Kumar Paul
Department of Lifelong Learning and Extension
Institute of Rural Reconstruction
Visva Bharati (A Central University)
Sriniketan-731236
Birbhum, West Bengal
Email: skpaulrd@gmail.com

Acknowledgements

Decentralized governance has been conceived as a mechanism of local self-government for promoting healthy and sustainable development. It facilitates effective people's participation, enhance degree of transparency and ensure greater accountability. It provides more effective and competitive delivery of services at the grassroots level. In West Bengal, Panchayati Raj Institutions have demonstrated strong commitment to rural decentralization by ensuring regular elections, implementing various rural development programmes and making the development bureaucracy part of governance. Further, SHGs have also strengthened decentralized governance through building ownership over local developments and the leadership capabilities of women as well as improve their participation in decision-making process at grassroots level.

It has been a great opportunity for me to undertake the present research work entitled "Strengthening Decentralization in Rural Bengal through Panchayati Raj Institutions and Self-Help Groups: Some Emerging Issues." The present volume is the outcome of Research Project funded by the University Grants Commission. I am grateful to the University Grants Commission for their constant coordination and cooperation. This research work is made possible by their financial support. I am also grateful to the Department of Panchayat and Rural Development, Government of West Bengal; Block Development Offices, Government of West Bengal; Gram Panchayat Office, District Rural Development Cell, Birbhum and Burdwan, ISGP Cell for their administrative support.

I would like to express my sense of gratitude to the Gram Panchayat Members, Pradhans, and other respondents for their constant cooperation and support. I am also grateful to the University authority (Visva Bharati) for giving me the opportunity to conduct the research. I would like to acknowledge the support and help extended by Shri Anindya Mitra, my Research Scholar and Project Fellow to complete this book. I am thankful to Anindita Gupta and Soumen Sarkar for helping me to complete this book. I am thankful to my wife Dr. Kakali Paul for her constant encouragement, support and cooperation and for the rounds of discussions that we had on the subject towards completion of this book. I am also grateful to my daughter Nilormi for kindly sparing the time for completing the book. I have no words to express my gratitude to my parents, who inspired and encouraged me in every moment to complete this work. I am extremely grateful to Shri Chandra Shekhar Ghosh, MD and CEO, Bandhan Bank Limited for writing the Foreword for this book. It will be my pleasure to have suggestions, comments and remarks from the users of this publication for bringing about improvements in future publications.

Sujit Kumar Paul

Contents

List of Tables and Figures

Tables

Figures

1
Introduction

Decentralised governance has been conceived as a mechanism of local self-government for promoting healthy and sustainable development. It is expected to facilitate effective people's participation, enhance degree of transparency and ensure greater accountability. Decentralised governance is assumed to provide more effective and competitive delivery of services at the grassroots level. Being closer to the people, decentralised governance is assumed to meet needs and preferences of the people (Crook and Sverrisson, 2001; Bardhan and Mukherjee, 2000). The case for democratic decentralisation is also predicated upon the notion that greater participation in local political affairs will improve the quality and reach of Government services, particularly ones aimed at improving the lives of poor and politically marginal groups in society (De Souza, 2000). For proponents of democratic decentralisation, a central challenge of improving the delivery of public services becomes one of 'crafting' (Ostrom, 1990) institutions which can maximize participation in political life. In the context of poverty reduction, access to the (myriad) resources and benefits that Governments provide is associated with systems of governance that empower poor and vulnerable groups in society.

Although, there is of course great variation among cultures, countries and regions, we can identify a number of roles that Governments typically play in poor and predominantly rural areas:

- One is the provision of public goods, such as universal education and healthcare;

- Second is the provision of divisible goods, such as irrigation, agricultural extension and credit;
- Third is the determination and enforcement of laws regulating key economic inputs, such as land, labour and capital; and
- Fourth and critical element is the recognition and protection of rights allowing for organization, association and entitlement in the eyes of the state.

All of these, it is worth emphasizing, are problematic in the sense that they require systems of governance which ensure that public resources are being delivered efficiently and effectively (Johnson and Start, 2001).

However, there are some scholars who have expressed reservation about the efficacy of decentralised governance (Prud'homme, 1995; Tanzi, 1995). Prud'homme argues that decentralised governance promotes inefficiency and scope for corruption due to an influence of interest groups and discretion of local officials. The long tenure of officials at the same place makes it easier to establish unethical relationships with the local people. Tanzi also argues that decentralisation promotes personalism and reduces professionalism. Personalism breeds corruption as officials pay greater attention to individual citizen's needs and disregard public interest, thereby defeating the philosophy of decentralised governance. However, the notion that improving participation through decentralisation will necessarily lead to improvements in people's well-being is not entirely consistent with documented evidence. A recurring theme that emerges from a sizeable body of literature is the relatively weak correlation that exists between democratic decentralisation and poverty reduction (Blair, 2000; Crook and Manor, 1998; Crook and Sverrisson, 2001; Golooba-Mutebi, 2000; Manor, 1999; Moore and Putzel, 1999; Rahman, 2001; World Bank, 2000d). In one respect, this reflects the difficulty of establishing a clear and rigorous link between changes in governance and improvements in well-being (Rahman, 2001). It also suggests a more sober conclusion about the ways in which democratic decentralisation is thought to affect the quality and availability of local economic opportunity. As Crook and Sverrisson's cross-country comparison (2001) concludes,

> "The notion that there is a predictable or general link between decentralisation of Government and the development of more

> 'pro-poor' policies or poverty-alleviating outcomes clearly lacks any convincing evidence. Those who advocate decentralisation on these grounds, at least, should be more cautious, which is not to say that there are not other important benefits, particularly in the field of participation and empowerment."

Even the most successful forms of democratic decentralisation have been unable to overcome economic and political disparities, both within and among regions. This, in part, highlights the problem of raising public revenue in rural areas, in which economic surplus (and therefore taxable revenue) is typically poor. Decentralisation can also pose new problems of coordination and planning. As the Kerala experience has shown (Ghatak and Ghatak, 2002) too much devolution can lead to major duplications of effort and gaps among different Government agencies.

Finally, there is a problem of local elite capture. As many studies (e.g. Blair, 2000; Crook and Sverrisson, 2001; Drèze and Sen, 1996; Manor, 1999; Moore and Putzel, 1999) have pointed out, one of the dangers of devolving authority is that it simply empowers local elites and, worse, perpetuates existing poverty and inequality. Whether, the introduction of democratic principles—on its own—would overcome the historical and cultural factors that perpetuate political inequality is somewhat doubtful (Luckham *et al.*, 2000; Moore and Putzel, 1999). This, in turn, highlights the challenge of encouraging democracy in rural areas in which large numbers of people are dependent upon small numbers of local, powerful elites. It also highlights the challenge of encouraging 'empowerment' without addressing the rights and entitlements (particularly ones governing land and property) that underlie political structures in rural areas.

Where the spoils of Government intervention are particularly good, one can predict with reasonable confidence that the costs of ensuring equitable distribution and of discouraging local corruption will be high. This is notoriously true of rural infrastructure projects, such as road building (Rao, 2000) or irrigation (Wade, 1985), in which markets for primary inputs, labour and public regulation (Wade, 1985) are strong. Here, the corruption of local administrative bodies will depend on a number of factors:

- the ease of procuring spoils from the programme;
- the ability to avoid detection and/or sanction;

- the amount of money involved (i.e. some departments and programmes are more 'wet' than others); and
- systems of accountability, which would ideally expose and sanction behaviour of this kind.

This last factor is worth highlighting, both because it can be affected by public policy and because it is the misallocation or 'corruption' of public resources that often justifies the strongest calls for democratic decentralisation (e.g. Drèze and Sen, 1996; World Bank, 2000a).

Perhaps the strongest argument in favour of decentralisation is the idea that the establishment of strong and accountable systems of governance will encourage a more equitable distribution of state provided resources, which can be directed towards poor and vulnerable groups. An underlying hypothesis here is that democratic participation will yield strong mechanisms of accountability, which in turn, will improve the distribution of benefits to groups that are traditionally marginalized by market and state.

Moreover, the whole idea of decentralised governance is based upon some key factors like people's participation, accountability, transparency, and fiscal transfers (Braun and Grote, 2002; Tanzi, 2001; Romeo, 1999; Crook and Manor, 1998; Litvack *et al.,* 1998). These are interlinked and their effects on development cannot simply be measured. The critique of decentralisation is valid in those regions of the world where poverty and a dysfunctional democracy are rampant for various reasons. A large part of literature talks about issues of quality of citizens' participation and broader questions of democratic control. The critical democratic theorists have noted that the predominant mode of social organizations is not a vertical relationship of authority between selfish individuals and the supra state, but a series of horizontal associations embodying groups of individuals who are capable of regulating and expressing themselves as members of a community, rather than as self-promoting individuals (Roy Chowdhury, 1996).

Decentralised governance may be effective in some parts of the world, where people are active, vigilant, and participative. In such societies, civil society groups assume far greater roles in educating people and, ultimately, people themselves seek greater accountability (fairness) from elected members and officials in meeting their immediate needs. On similar lines, recently the theory of social capital has been receiving increasing attention and it has begun to generate a remarkable consensus regarding the role and importance of communities and local organisations in making decentralised governance effective (Sangita, 2002; Sundaram, 1997; Putnam, 1993; Slater and Watson, 1993).

Matching with the global trend, developing countries often initiate decentralised governance to promote development. India is not an exception to this trend. India has been experimenting with the decentralised governance process for quite some time. After India attaining Independence Mahatma Gandhi—father of the nation—strongly favoured far larger role for Panchayats as small republics, enjoying complete political autonomy. He was of firm belief that such an institutional arrangement provides opportunity for villagers to involve in planning, programme implementation and thereby play catalytic role in achieving faster development of village India. Article 40 was added to the Constitution due to Gandhi's insistence (Mathur, 1988; Manor, 1997). The block as a Centre of Community Development (CD) came into existence throughout the country in 1952. However, CD was replaced by the Panchayati Raj Institutions (PRIs) on the basis of Balwant Rai Mehta Committee Report in 1959 with a view to ensure people's involvement in development programmes. These institutions could not be stabilized due to irregular elections, inadequate powers, poor finances and lack of political will. The broad framework for decentralised governance has been laid down in India under the 73rd Constitution Amendment Act. This has ushered in a greater degree of uniformity in the structure (three-tier), composition (reservation for SC, ST and women), powers and functions (financial and planning) of these institutions with the objective of achieving faster social and economic development. The three-tier structures of the PRIs are Zilla Panchayat at the district level, Taluk Panchayat at the intermediate levels and Gram Panchayat at the village level. The 73rd Constitutional Amendment Act has given an impetus to Panchayats for promoting development in terms of infrastructure, education, health and poverty alleviation in rural India.

Further, with the passing of 73rd Constitutional Amendment Act in 1992, a new system of decentralised governance was brought into being. This institutional arrangement promised an alternative to the hitherto followed bureaucratic mechanism. Instead of strengthening the PRIs in true spirit, the Union/State Governments from time-to-time initiated various programmes without making the PRIs effective.

There are several parallel programmes in implementation which are directly funded by Union/State Governments and monitored by State Government officials. These actions undermined the role of PRIs. Empirical evidences from various Indian States have shown that the decentralisation exercises have succeeded, to some extent, in a few States such as West Bengal, Karnataka, Kerala, Maharashtra and Madhya Pradesh. If one has to understand the dilemma of decentralised governance, is needed to understand the nature of political process, political institutions, local organizations and their temperment towards the development.

Evolution of Decentralisation Concept in India

India is huge with many states having a population of more than 50 million, dwarfing most sovereign countries in the world. To democratically govern a country of this size requires several tiers of Government. Even though decentralisation has been an issue of concern in India for over a century, until recently there were generally only two federated tiers of Government—Central and State. This section summarizes the process leading to the 73rd Constitutional Amendment and its key features. During pre-Independence, all efforts were towards administrative decentralisation only. The first attempt was after the 1857 Mutiny with the British administration coming under severe financial pressures. Initially, the focus was on municipalities. The Resolution on Local Self-Government of 1882 set out principles of decentralisation which many believe have influenced the debate to date. The resolution recognized the twin considerations of local Government: (i) administrative efficiency, and (ii) political education; and sought to promote these. However, the resolution met with resistance, and what evolved in spite of various subsequent committees, such as the Royal Commission on Decentralisation (1907), the Report of Montagu and Chelmsford on Constitutional Reforms (1918), and the Government of India Resolution (1918) etc., was a hierarchical administrative structure-based on supervision and control that still pervades much of the rural space in India. After Independence the scenario was changed and rural self-governance got special priority but its actual implementation took more decades. The debates in the Constituent Assembly on Panchayati Raj were more fundamentally grounded. There were two differing view points—that of Gandhi and of Ambedkar. The fundamental difference in philosophies of these two thinkers was on parliamentary democracy—Ambedkar believed the unit of development should be the individual while Gandhi believed the unit of development should be the village. A compromise was forged and in 1948, PRIs found place in the non-justifiable part of the Constitution.

India has been experimenting with the decentralised governance practices for quite some time. In the Indian context, decentralisation enjoyed a traditional name 'Panchayat'. Mahatma Gandhi was inspired by an idyllic view of the village life and the village organization and formulated his ideas as a *sine qua non* for alternative polity of a free India. He observed that India lives in its villages and its development process will start with village and villagers. Gandhi emphasized on the supremacy of the people and insisted in the people's democracy as sovereignty at the grassroots which he called "panchayat".

Gandhi says, "My idea of Village *Swaraj* (panchayat) is that it is a complete republic, independent of its neighbours for its vital wants and yet inter-dependent for many others in which dependence is a necessity. Thus, every village's first concern will be to grow its own food crops, and cotton for its cloth. It should have a reserve for its cattle, recreation and playgrounds for its adults and children. Then, if there is more land available, it will grow useful money crops. The village will maintain a village theatre, school and public hall. It will have its own water works ensuring clean supply. Education will be compulsory up to the final basic course. As far as possible every activity will be conducted on cooperative basis. There will be a compulsory service of village guards, who will be selected by rotation from the register maintained by the village. The Government of village will be conducted by the panchayat of 5 persons elected annually by the adult villagers, male and female, both possessing minimum prescribed qualifications. These will have all the authority and jurisdiction required. This panchayat will be legislature, judiciary and executive combined, to operate for its year of office. Any village can become such a republic today without much interference" (*Harijan*, 26th July, 1942). His idea was to establish such a society where every individual got maximum freedom and opportunity to develop personality and character to the maximum. Therefore, he stated that decentralisation was essential for true democracy, in which everyone can participate in the decision-making and implementation processes (Islam, 2003).

However, Gandhi's plan of decentralisation failed to win acceptance in the operative scheme of the Constitution of India. Soon after Independence the urban and the rural elite and their representatives in politics had disdained for Panchayats. They had started looking at elite dominant bureaucratic system as the British ruled in India. The Drafting Committee of the Constitution of India effortlessly did exclude panchayat in the Constitution. Since, Ambedkar, Chairman of the Drafting Committee of the Constitution had a different view of the Indian rural society, who argued in the Constituent Assembly that "village communities have survived surely on a low, on a selfish level. I hold that these village republics have been the ruination of India. I am, therefore, surprised that those who condemn provincialism and communalism should forward as champions of the village. What is the village, but a sink of localism, a den of ignorance, narrow mindedness and communalism" (Constituent Assembly debates 4th November, 1948). In his point of view, it would be dangerous to give power to the panchayat, as he thought that it may control rural power structure, which would work to the detriment of the Harijans and the rural poor. Although, Gandhi looked at village panchayat as mechanism of all kinds of development, very few of his followers agreed with such views. Even Pandit Nehru chiefly supported the view of Ambedkar, and expressed that no progress can be made from the village, as villages are backward intellectually and culturally. Gandhi insisted on the inclusion of the panchayat in the revised draft. Finally, Panchayats gained a provision in the Directive Principles of State Policy, which is not mandatory. Power was given to the State that if the State wants could empower Panchayats. As Article 40 says that, "the State should take steps to organise village Panchayats and endow them with such powers and authority as may be necessary to enable them to function as units of self-government".

In spite of this, Pandit Nehru also realized the importance of decentralised governance in India when he started leading a nation like India. He says, "India will progress only, when the people living in villages become politically conscious. The progress of our country is bound up with the progress in our village. If our villages make a progress, India will become a strong nation and nobody will be able to stop its onward march if you flinch from your determination and get involved in mutual quarrels and petty factions, you will not be able to succeed in your mission."

Prime Minister Nehru inaugurated the Community Development Programme (CDP) that was launched under First Five-Year Plan of India in the year 1952. CDP was initiated mainly for promoting development in rural India under the bureaucratic system without taking cognizance of Gandhi's idea of Panchayats. During the implementation period it was observed that the goal of the CD was not successful because of lack of people's participation. At this point, it was so important to know to what degree this challenge had been met. A study team was appointed under the Balwant Rai Mehta Committee in 1957 to examine the creativity for improving economic and social conditions in the rural areas. The Committee's view was that without an institute at the village level, which could represent the entire community, assume responsibility and provide the necessary leadership, evoke people's initiative and mobilize their voluntary and spontaneous participation for promoting development, the real success would not come about at all. The team favoured democratic decentralisation through the setting up of PRIs to community. Its recommendation works should be was that, "public participation is organized through statutory representative bodies". The Committee viewed at establishing three-tier Panchayati Raj Systems throughout the country through necessary legislation in States and Union Territories. The Committee also attempted to translate Article 40 of the Constitution and remarked that Panchayti Raj System acts as a means of involving people and their representatives in development programmes of the Government (Report of the Committee, 1959). The Prime Minister Jawharlal Nehru inaugurated Independent India's First Panchayati Raj on 2nd October, 1959 in Rajasthan. After long ages it was observed that Panchayat system suffered from a number of weaknesses and another study team headed by Asoka Mehta Committee was set-up in 1977. The Committee viewed that PR system was not only meant for decentralisation of powers and people's participation but it was also supporting rural development and strengthening the planning process in the micro-level (1978). It was marked as turning point in the concept and practice of PRIs.

Again, a Committee chaired by Dantwala (1978-83) viewed decentralised block level planning since the centralized planning strategy had failed to provide rural employment and ameliorating the conditions of the rural poor.

Furthermore, a Committee was set-up in 1982 chaired by Hanumantha Rao, which viewed that unless planning was made from the lower level the desired result might not have been achieved, there should have been decentralised planning process in district level and participation of people through democratic institutions for promoting the development programmes.

Later the G.V.K. Rao Committee was set-up in 1980, which viewed that strengthening of Zilla Parishad and District level Planning, as well as a better integration of block and lower level planning with lower level PRIs (integrating administrative structure with PR institution) was essential for rural development.

Of late, the 73rd and 74th Constitutional Amendment Act saw the birth of a new era in decentralised governance in India. This has brought out uniformity in the structure (three-tier), composition (reservation for SCs, STs and women), powers and functions (finances and planning) of these institutions to achieve economic and social development.

The inducement behind the 73rd Amendment Act was to make Panchayats as good governance or an effective mechanism for economic development and social justice at grassroots-level. This Act has brought forth a genuine spirit of democratic decentralisation in the country. The Acts have ushered in-change by providing wide-ranging powers and functions to local-level constitutional bodies and ordinary people for ensuring participation in planning and implementation for effective and efficient development. The important initiatives have been envisaged for the people's participation are as follows:

- Preparation of plans for economic development and social justice;
- Implementation of schemes for economic development;
- The power and function of Gram Sabha for reservoir of people's power;
- Regular elections to the Panchayats; and
- Proportional seat reservation for Scheduled Castes, Scheduled Tribes and women.

In consonance with the 73rd Amendment Act, 1992, different State Governments have initiated new Acts on decentralisation. Like other States GOWB also has introduced new Amendment Act, 1994 on decentralisation. However, West Bengal had a long history of democratic decentralisation since 1977.

1882: The Resolution on Local Self-Government.
1907: The Royal Commission on Decentralisation.
1948: Constitutional debates between Gandhi and Ambedkar on Gram Swaraj, 'self-rule'.
1957: Balwant Rai Mehta Commission—an early attempt to implement the Panchayat structure at district and block (samiti) levels.
1963: K. Santhanam Committee—recommended limited revenue raising powers for Panchayats and the establishment of State Panchayati Raj Finance Corporations.
1978: Asoka Mehta Committee—appointed to address the weaknesses of PRIs, concluded that a resistant bureaucracy, lack of political will, ambiguity about the role of PRIs, and élite capture had undermined previous attempts at decentralisation, recommending that the District serve as the administrative unit in the PRI structure. Based on these recommendations, Karnataka, Andhra Pradesh and West Bengal passed new legislation to strengthen PRIs.
1985: G.V.K. Rao Committee—appointed to address weaknesses of PRIs, recommended that the Block Development Office (BDO) should assume broad powers for planning, implementing and monitoring rural development programmes.
1986: L.M. Singhvi Committee—recommended that local self-government should be constitutionally enshrined, and that the Gram Sabha (the village assembly) should be the base of decentralised democracy in India.
1993: The 73rd Amendment to the Constitution of India—PRIs at district, block and village levels are granted constitutional status. The Gram Sabha is recognised as a formal democratic body at the village level. The 74th Amendment, granting Constitutional status to municipal bodies, is passed soon after.
1996: The Adivasi Act—Powers of Self-government are extended to tribal communities living in 'Fifth Schedule' areas.

Fig. 1.1: Milestones in Indian Decentralisation

Decentralisation at State Level

Bengal, the erstwhile province in British India, had a long tradition of working of the statutory decentralisation. The diverse experience of running these rural bodies was inherited by West Bengal, a truncated part of old Bengal province since Independence and the new State has been experimenting with different types and methods of rural self-government since then (Mukhopadhyay, 1977). The rural administration of Bengal till 1957 was governed by three pre-independence Acts: (1) The Village Chowkidari Act of 1870; (2) The Bengal Local Self-Government Act of 1885; and (3) The Bengal Village Self-Government Act of 1919.

In the British period, the villagers of Bengal were acquainted with the idea of Panchayat primarily in 1870 through the Village Chowkidari Act. It may be observed that this panchayat had no Panchayati Raj Institutions and Rural Development semblance with the ancient panchayat system that existed in India in different forms in the provinces of India in the pre-British and even in the early period. The Chowkidari Act was purely of British make and its scope was extremely restricted. These Panchayats appointed by the District Magistrates, were merely an agency for the assessment and collection of a local tax, which was levied for the support of the village police without having anything to do with the management of affairs of immediate interest to the villagers (Mukherjee, 1974).

The Bengal Local Self-Government Act of 1885 established a network of rural local bodies at three levels of the District Board, the Local Board and the Union Board. The District Board had jurisdiction over a whole district. The local Board was meant for each sub-division and the Union Committees for selected areas within the sub-division. The main functions of District Board were maintenance and improvement of roads and other communications, primary education, health and sanitation, veterinary work, construction and maintenance of rest house, administration of ponds and ferries and relief of suffering in time of famine and serious distress. The function of Local Board was care and maintenance of village roads, management of ponds and charge of ferries. The function of Union Committee was management and control over ponds, control over village roads, sanitation and supply of water. The Act of 1885 provided for a District Board for each district and a Local Board for every sub-division of a district and fixed their term of office at four years. These bodies were to be constituted by the Government on the basis of informal election. In most cases the names of persons nominated by the Government used to be made known to the village folk in a meeting presided over by the sub-divisional officer. And the people invariably were expected to approve those names.

The Local Board had no independent authority and jurisdiction of its own. The Local Boards in the district were designed to act as the agents of the District Board for undertaking the public works and duties assigned to them by the District Board at its direction. Consisting of not less than six members, the two-thirds of the Local Board's members had to be elected by the people directly on the basis of a restricted franchise, and the remaining one-third to be

Bengal on October 2, 1964, the date being the birthday of Mahatma Gandhi (Mukherjee, 1974).

Even though the above said Act facilitated decentralisation, in practice it was merely playing lip services to the idea of people's participation. Meanwhile, the then Congress Government in the State went through a crisis (1965-66) of an unprecedented nature. The Congress Party was defeated and a United Front dominated by the Left Party came to the power in West Bengal in 1967 General Election. The new Ministry introduced a comprehensive Panchayat Bill in the Legislative Assembly. But, before this Bill was enacted, Front Government went out of office in 1970. When a new Congress led coalition Government came to the power it promised a new panchayat system in Bengal. At last, the West Bengal Panchayat Act was passed in 1973 (Ghosh, 2000). However, the then Government took no steps to implement them. Elections were not held regularly. The Anchal and the Gram Panchayat elections had been due for periods varying from ten to fifteen years in 1977. Again, The Congress Government went out of office in West Bengal in 1977. The CPIM-led Left Front Government (LFG) came into power in Bengal and proceeded to pass a series of Amendment Acts of 1973 (Webster, 1992). Thus, major amendments to the Panchayat Acts were made in 1992, 1994, and 1997. The immediate purpose of the 1994 amendment was to bring the State Act in conformity with the Constitutional Amendment and in fact provisions of the 1992 Amendments, particularly provisions relating to reservation of seats, were made in conformity with the Constitutional Amendment.

West Bengal is one of the fore-runners in installing a 3-tier Panchayati Raj System (PRI) for rural local governance in India. The present generation Panchayats in the State started their journey in 1978, i.e. 15 years ahead of the 73rd Amendment of the Constitution of India. Ever since their inception, the State has demonstrated strong commitment to rural decentralisation by ensuring regular elections to PRIs, entrusting them with increasing responsibility of implementing various rural development programmes and making the development bureaucracy part of PRIs. The State also ensured adequate representation of the socially backward classes—Scheduled Castes (SC), Scheduled Tribes (ST) and women in PRIs for their involvement in the process of socio-economic development.

That rural poverty declined in the State from 73 per cent in 1973-74 to 32 per cent in 1999-2000, that annual growth rate of foodgrain production was recorded at 6.5 per cent between 1981 and 1991 and that the highest rate of growth of wages was recorded between 1979-80 and 1992-93 is mostly attributed to the effective role of PRIs in the successful land reforms and in organizing the poor and augmenting their social and economic opportunities through various programmes. It is acclaimed that West Bengal Panchayats showed the way and inspired the Constitutional Amendment.

While the Panchayat system in West Bengal attracted even world-wide attention, some critics have observed the "concepts of Panchayats being institutions of self-governance" still "either missing or dimly perceived". Some others observe that PRIs function more as part of the delivery system of the State Government rather than as institutions of self-governance. The State Government itself identified areas in PRI functioning which needed systemic improvements, e.g. (i) institutionalization of bottom-up planning approach; (ii) intensification of people's participation and of local-level organizations in PRI functioning; (iii) convergence of PRIs with all other development agencies; and (iv) greater accountability of the development bureaucracy to PRIs; and the like.

The State Government, always open to new ideas, brought about need-based reforms in the Panchayat system from time-to-time from the very beginning. Some unique features are—

(a) *Gram Sansad* at village-level/*Gram Panchayat* (GP)-level, Block *Sansad* at Block-level/*Panchayat Samiti* (PS)-level and *Zilla Sansad* at District-level/*Zilla Parishad* (ZP)-level;
(b) District Council at each headed by the leader of the opposition;
(c) *Gram Unnayan Samiti* at the *Gram Sansad* level;
(d) Institutional involvement of opposition members in the Standing Committees of ZP and PS and in the Finance and Planning Sub-Committee of GP;
(e) Determination of principles of subsidiarity for each tier of Panchayats;
(f) Mapping of activities to be performed by three tier Panchayats falling under 28 subjects (out of 29) listed in the Eleventh Schedule of the Constitution of India;
(g) Empowering the Standing Committees and Sub-Committees to prepare and implement their own work plan and budget;

(h) Opening Panchayat Window in the State Budget by the Departments who have substantial flow of fund to Panchayats;

(i) Annual self-evaluation of all the three-tier Panchayat bodies through score-based schedules for assessment of their performances and providing incentive grant to the best performing GP in each Block, to the best performing PS in each District and to the best performing ZP in the State separately under two heads—(1) institutional functioning and good governance, and (2) mobilization of revenue and utilization of resources on the basis of validated scores of self-evaluation; and

(j) Double entry system of accounting for all the three tier Panchayats.

The PRIs in the State have grown over the years with more spontaneity and has made positive impact in order to achieve economic development and secure social justice for all. However, even now there is a long way to go for the West Bengal Panchayats to really become proper people's institution as vanguard of holistic development of rural people. This document visions such institutions and sets out strategy to accomplish the vision. (Roadmap for Panchayat in West Bengal: A Vision Document of Department of Panchayat and Rural Development, Government of West Bengal, 2009).

73rd and 74th Constitutional Amendment Act, 1992

Only in 1992, with the 73rd Constitutional Amendment, were local Governments in rural areas at the district, block and village-levels, the PRIs, made an effective reality all over India. The 73rd Constitutional Amendment is based on a political ideal—decentralised democracy. In it citizen's participation is seen as key in both decision-making and effective service delivery. This goal of reclaiming the State by the citizen has become important at this stage of India's development, not just because the bureaucracy and political class have reduced the State to a rent-seeking state, but also because the state's delivery mechanisms are showing signs of atrophy. The 73rd Constitutional Amendment Act (CAA) was passed on December 22, 1992, on the basis of general consensus. After ratification by more than half of the State Assemblies and after obtaining the assent of the

President the Act came into force on 24 April, 1993.There are some radical features in the Act (Mahipal, 1997). The 73rd Constitutional Amendment gives village, block and district-level bodies a Constitutional status under Indian Law (World Bank, 2000a). They try to address some of the problems encountered by PRIs in previous years, by—

(i) granting PRIs Constitutional status;
(ii) empowering socially and economically disadvantaged groups, i.e. *Dalits* (*Dalits* are broadly Scheduled Castes), Adivasis (Adivasis are Scheduled Tribes), and women;
(iii) ensuring free, fair, and regular elections;
(iv) keeping terms fixed;
(v) identifying a list of items which would come under the jurisdiction of PRIs; and
(vi) Addressing the issue of PRI finance.

Some of the provisions of the new Act are mandatory in nature, which are to be followed by all the states.

Mandatory Provisions

1. Constitution of Panchayats: According to the Central Act, there shall be a three-tier system of Panchayats in all states: at the village, intermediate and district levels. However, in states having a population of less than 20 lakh, the intermediate level may not be constituted.

2. Composition of Panchayat: All the seats in a Panchayat shall be filled by persons chosen by direct election from territorial constituencies in the Panchayat area. Such elections shall be conducted under the supervision, control and direction of the State Election Commission, comprising the State Election Commissioner appointed by the State Government. The Chairperson of the Panchayat at the intermediate level shall be indirectly elected by and from amongst the elected members of the Panchayats.

3. Reservation of Seats: Seats shall be reserved for both Scheduled Castes (SC) and Scheduled Tribes (ST) in every Panchayat. The number of such seats shall be, as far as possible, in proportion with the percentage of their population to the total population. Such seats may be allotted by rotation to different constituencies in a Panchayat. Again, one-third of these reserved seats will be further reserved for women from these castes and tribes. Similarly, in case of general seats also, one-third of them shall be reserved for women belonging to any class or category. Such seats will also be allotted by rotation to different constituencies in a Panchayat. Such reservations will also apply to the offices of chairpersons on a rotation basis.

4. Duration of Panchayats: A Panchayat shall have a term of five years and if it is dissolved for any reason, fresh elections shall be held within six months from the date of such dissolution. In case the remainder of the period is less than six months, it shall not be necessary to hold any election for constituting the Panchayat for such period. A Panchayat constituted following the dissolution of its predecessor as above, shall continue only for the remainder of the period for which the dissolved Panchayat would have continued.

5. State Finance Commission: The Governor of a State is to constitute a State Finance Commission within one year of the Act coming into force and thereafter every fifth year. The Commission is to review the financial position of the Panchayats and make recommendations to the Governor in the following respects:

(a) The principles which should govern—
   (i) The distribution of the proceeds of the taxes, duties, tolls, fees levied by the State between itself and the Panchayats and the allocation among the Panchayats at all levels, their respective shares of such proceeds;
   (ii) The determination of the taxes, tolls, duties and fees which may be assigned to or appropriated by the Panchayats;
   (iii) The grants-in-aid to Panchayats from the Consolidated Fund of the States;
(b) The measures needed to improve the financial position of the Panchayats; and
(c) Any other matter referred to the Finance Commission by the Governor in the interest of sound finance of the Panchayats.

The Central Finance Commission (CFC) is also required to make recommendations to the President as to the measures needed to augment the Consolidated Fund of a State to supplement the resources of the Panchayats in the State on the basis of the recommendations made by the State Finance Commission.

6. *District Planning Committee*: The provision for constituting the District Planning Committee was made under the 74th

Constitutional Amendment Act, 1992. Accordingly, there shall be a District Planning Committee at the district-level to consolidate the plans prepared by the *Panchayats* and municipalities and to prepare a draft development plan for the district as a whole.

The subject Panchayati Raj Institutions belongs to the State List in the Indian federal system. Therefore, the Central Act has left a large area for the State legislatures to fill in. Suitable provisions were to be made in the Acts passed by them for the purpose; keeping in mind the overall objectives spelt out in the Central Act. Some other provisions are discretionary in nature where the States are given some choice in their implementation.

Source: The 73rd Constitutional Amendment Act, 1992.

Discretionary Provisions are Listed below

1. Nomenclature of the Panchayats at different levels.
2. Nomenclature of the Chairpersons at different levels.
3. Size in terms of population and area for determination of Panchayats at village and intermediate levels.
4. Powers and functions of the Gram Sabha.
5. Composition of the Panchayats at different levels: Provided that the ratio between the population of the territorial area of a Panchayat at any level and the number of seats in such Panchayat to be filled by election shall, so far as practicable, is the same throughout the State.
6. To provide or not for the representation of:
   (a) the Chairpersons of village Panchayats in the Panchayats at the intermediate level, and of the intermediate level Panchayats at the district-level Panchayat;
   (b) the members of the Lok Sabha and the members of the State Legislative Assembly representing constituencies that comprise wholly or partly a Panchayat area at levels other than the village level;
   (c) the members of the Rajya Sabha and the members of the State Legislative Council where they are registered as electors.
7. The mode of election of the Chairperson of a Panchayat at the village level.
8. The manner in which the seats of the members of the Panchayats at different levels shall be reserved for scheduled

castes/tribes and women, provided that the number of seats shall be allotted by rotation to different Panchayats at each level.

9. The manner in which the offices of the chairpersons at different levels shall be reserved for scheduled castes/tribes and women: Provided that the number of offices reserved shall be allotted by rotation to different Panchayats at each level.
10. To provide or not for reservation of seats in favour of backward class in any Panchayat or offices of chairpersons in the Panchayats at any level.
11. To endow the Panchayats at various levels with such powers and authority as may be necessary to enable them to function as institutions of self-government and to make provisions for the development of powers and responsibilities upon Panchayats at the appropriate level with respect to:
    (a) the preparation of plans for economic development and social justice; and
    (b) the implementation of schemes for economic development and social justice entrusted to them, including those in relation to the matters listed in the 11th Schedule to the Constitution.
12. To decide the taxes, duties, tolls and fees for which a Panchayat is authorised and also lay down the procedure and limits for the same.
13. To decide limits and the conditions of the taxes, duties, tolls and fees levied and collected by the State Government but assigned to the Panchayats.
14. To decide the amount of grants-in-aid provided to the Panchayats from the Consolidated Fund of the State.
15. To authorise the Panchayats at different levels to create a fund for crediting all money received by or on behalf of the Panchayats and also for the withdrawal of such money.
16. To provide for the composition of the Finance Commission, the qualifications this shall be requisite for appointment as members thereof and the manner in which they shall be selected. The Commission shall determine their procedure and shall have such powers in the performance of their functions as the legislature of the State by law confers on them. The Governor shall cause every recommendation made

by the Commission under this article together with an explanatory memorandum as to the action taken thereon to be laid before the State Legislature.

17. To make provisions with respect to the maintenance of accounts by Panchayats and the auditing of such accounts.
18. To determine the conditions of service and tenure of office of the State Election Commissioner and to make provision with respect to all matters relating to or in connection with election to the Panchayats. It is provided that the State Election Commissioner shall not be removed from his office except in like manner and on the like grounds as a judge of the High Court. This condition of service of the State Election Commissioner shall not be varied to his disadvantage after his appointment. The Governor, when so required by the State Election Commission, shall make available such staff as may be necessary for the discharge of the functions conferred on it.
19. To make provision with respect to all matters relating to, or in connection with elections to the Panchayats.
20. To make provisions with respect to:
    - (a) the composition and functions of the District Planning Committee;
    - (b) the manner in which the office of the Chairperson of the District Planning Committee shall be filled, provided that not less than four-fifths of the total number of members of the committee shall be elected by and from amongst the elected members of the Panchayat at the district level and of the municipalities in the district in proportion to the ratio between the populations of rural and urban areas.

At the village level, the most important provisions relating to participation and accountability are those governing reservations and the Gram Sabha. Under the 73rd Constitutional Amendment one-third of all seats must be reserved for women. Likewise, reservations for Scheduled Castes (SCs) and Scheduled Tribes (STs) are made in proportion to their population. At the village-level, the Gram Sabha, which constitutes all eligible voters within a Gram Panchayat area, is meant to serve as a principal mechanism for transparency and accountability. Among its principal functions are:

- to review the annual statement of accounts;
- to review reports of the preceding financial year;
- to review and submit views on development programmes for the following year; and
- to participate in the identification of beneficiaries for some Government schemes.

This last provision is particularly important because it confers substantive authority over an area that is particularly prone to misallocation and corruption (Sections 3 and 4). As Jha (2000) has argued, "The 73rd and 74th Constitutional Amendments . . . are designed to promote self-governance through statutory recognition of local bodies. The latter are expected to move away from their traditional role of simply executing the programmes handed down to them by higher levels of Government and to formulate and implement their own programmes of economic development and social justice."

In short, the 73rd Constitutional Amendment covers many areas that would enable the Panchayats to improve the lives and well-being of poor and vulnerable groups. Moreover, it contains specific provisions that guarantee the participation of traditionally excluded groups, such as women, SCs and STs, and transparency for local institutions such as the Gram Panchayats and the Gram Sabha. However, as Mukherjee (1999) has argued, the ambiguity surrounding the concept of 'Self-government' and the substantial power that still rests with the State Governments have prevented most States from devolving any substantive power to the Panchayats. Such findings are consistent with a wider literature on the problems most commonly associated with decentralisation in India (e.g. Crook and Manor, 1998; Jha, 1999; Mathew, 2001; Mukherjee, 1999; Oommen, 1999; World Bank, 2000).

Under 73rd and 74th Constitutional Amendments a series of ideal conditions under which local institutions have been shown to be more accountable to poor and politically marginal groups in society. These were:

- active participation among broad elements of society, including voting, campaigning, attending meetings, running for office, lobbying representatives etc.;
- fiscal and political support from higher level authorities within Government; and

- the existence of competitive political parties whose legitimacy depends at least in part on the support of the poor.

In order to consider these hypotheses in relation to India's decentralisation process, it is first necessary to establish whether the Constitutional changes that transpired in 1993 were in fact decentralisation. The scholarly literature on Panchayati Raj tends to move in two fairly incongruous directions. One, which is firmly grounded in the liberal democratic paradigm, argues that the 73rd Constitutional Amendment did indeed create the conditions for decentralisation in India, and that this was a positive development.

Although there is some disagreement about whether and to what extent the reforms have been implemented, the general consensus within this thought is that the 73rd Constitutional Amendment was a positive step for Indian decentralisation and that the only factor preventing successful devolution is the failure to implement fully the terms and conditions of the 73rd Constitutional Amendment. A second thought is decidedly more critical of decentralisation in general and the 73rd Constitutional Amendment in particular. A central assertion that underlies this second school is that the reforms put in place in 1993 are largely cosmetic, and that the ultimate distribution of power and resources in rural areas is dependent on the pre-existing pattern of social inequalities created by caste, religion, class, gender and other forms of rural domination.

Using the conventional classification of "political, administrative and fiscal decentralisation", the World Bank's three-volume study of Indian decentralisation (World Bank, 2000) ranks India "among the best performers" internationally in terms of political decentralisation, but "close to the last" in terms of administrative decentralisation. Most States have held at least one round of elections since 1993. Reservations allowing the participation of women, Scheduled Castes and Scheduled Tribes have been respected. Finally, voter participation has been high. The World Bank study goes on to argue that although Indian States and the Union Government have been willing to recognise the Panchayats, to hold elections and to respect stipulations governing reservations for Scheduled Castes (SCs), Scheduled Tribes (STs) and women, they have been unwilling to vest them with sufficient "administrative control over significant functions or fiscal autonomy," (World Bank, 2000). In most States, Panchayats have been handed a wide array of responsibilities without the necessary fiscal and administrative resources.

In its assessment of Indian decentralisation, the Task Force on Devolution of Powers and Functions upon Panchayati Raj Institutions (MoRD, 2001) found that "most of the States" had satisfied only the basic requirements relating to the transfer of functions, functionaries, funds and financial autonomy to the Panchayats.

Vyasulu (2000) finds that State Governments have devolved little finances and fiscal powers to the Panchayats. Instead, many have established "parallel bodies" as a channel for development funding. Self-Help Groups (SHGs) connected to the Janmabhoomi programme in Andhra Pradesh and the Rajiv Gandhi Watershed 'Missions' in Madhya Pradesh are two illustrations of this trend.

Similarly, Oommen's (1999) comparison of 12 Indian States concludes that the Conformity Acts have generally "been an exercise in amending existing Panchayat legislation for the sake of satisfying the mandatory provisions of the 73rd Constitutional Amendment." In particular, he raises the following concerns:

- Village Panchayats have been delegated functions "without adequate administrative, financial and technical support", (1999);
- With the exception of Kerala and West Bengal, Panchayats lack discretionary powers over spending and staff;
- There is insufficient clarity and differentiation of functions among Panchayats and other levels of Government;
- States reserve the right to assign or withdraw functions to and from the Panchayats by "executive fiat", (1999);
- Panchayats at all levels have inadequate powers of taxation; and
- Panchayats lack autonomous budgeting powers.

Again, the question of fiscal autonomy is a matter of some debate. George Mathew has argued that Panchayats do not necessarily need their own revenues to operate effectively. Access to 'guarded' or 'fenced' transfers from higher level authorities can serve this purpose, so long as the Panchayats have the autonomy to decide how the money gets spent. Others, such as Oommen (1999) have argued that political autonomy is directly dependent on the ability to raise and spend public resources and fiscal autonomy cannot be built into a regime of grants-in-aid. PRIs can play a genuine role in local development and self-rule only if they enjoy some degree of fiscal autonomy. This attribute is clearly more than relying on untied funds and rests on innovative resource mobilization, including project-tied loans, public contribution and the like.

Leaving aside the problem of raising revenues in poor areas, there is also a problem of inter-Governmental transfers. As Jha (2000) has argued, the State Finance Commissions (SFCs) have encountered difficulties in assessing the financial needs of local bodies, reflecting both a lack of clear guidelines governing the function of SFCs and a dearth of reliable information on sub-district revenues and incomes (Jha, 2000). For the Panchayats, this has reinforced a situation in which local bodies (particularly village-level Panchayats) have been handed vast responsibility with insufficient authority to raise and spend revenues and resources.

Again, the political structures created during Independence and the political dynamics that unfolded in the 1970s and 1980s have combined to create a political environment that has been particularly hostile to Panchayati Raj. However, there are exceptions to this rule, and the exceptions can tell us something about the ways in which decentralisation can work in this relatively inhospitable climate.

Crook and Manor (1998) argue that decentralisation has helped to counteract the types of top-down processes that have traditionally sheltered public officials from scrutiny and accountability in India. The 73rd Constitutional Amendment contains a number of provisions that aim to counterbalance patterns of inequality and discrimination in rural India. Theory, reservations and the Gram Sabha provide an important means of ensuring that marginal groups are incorporated into local politics and that representative's act in a way that is consistent with their formal responsibilities and the plural interests of their constituents. In practice, however, neither appears to have lived up to this (rather lofty) ideal. Studies of decentralisation have consistently highlighted the fact that the 73rd Constitutional Amendment and earlier attempts at decentralisation have failed to prevent a local (and primarily landed) elite from controlling local Panchayats. Micro-level studies have shown that Gram Sabha often fails to fulfil their role as deliberative bodies or as a mechanism for accountability (Alsop *et al.*, 2000; Deshpande and Murthy, 2002; Nambiar, 2001). This is partly attributed to low levels of participation among the electorate as well as the non-cooperation of local officials. Examples of the latter include officials delaying or postponing Gram Sabha meetings, officials were not attending Gram Sabha meetings, and, more generally, official decisions having no bearing on decisions reached during the Gram Sabha (Crook and Manor, 1998; Deshpande and Murthy, 2002; Nambiar, 2001). Explanations for poor participation in the Gram Sabha include (e.g. Alsop *et al.*, 2000; Nambiar, 2001):

- Limited benefits of participation;
- Opportunity costs, particularly on the part of very poor groups;
- Fear of disrupting existing patron-client relations;
- Corruption;
- Agenda fixing;
- Factionalism; and
- Fear of exclusion from community.

The World Bank's study of 53 villages in Rajasthan and Madhya Pradesh (Alsop *et al.*, 2000) found that gender and education were important determinants of political participation, measured in terms of campaigning, attending rallies, supporting a candidate, influencing voters, contacting a public representative, and attending Gram Sabhas. Even when there are reservations to ensure that marginal groups have a place in the Panchayat system, there is evidence to suggest that these formal institutions have been usurped by more informal patterns of domination and power. Reservations for women, for instance, are notoriously prone to corruption by male relatives, excluded from formal participation by their lack of scheduled status (Vyasulu and Vyasulu, 1999). Similar patterns have been observed among SCs and STs, whose economic well-being is dependent on the patronage of local elites. Such findings highlight the difficulty of transposing a formal model of democracy onto societies in which power and politics are still determined by highly informal systems of inequality and domination.

Self-Help Group and SGSY Programme

Self-Help Group (SHG) is a group of homogeneous people who can develop their socio-economic condition by their own help. According to Alka Srivastava (2006), "A Self-Help Group is a socially and economically homogeneous group of 10-20 poor people voluntarily coming together to achieve common goals." In India this concept is not older one. We can find the concept of SHG in rural India in the form of foodgrain storage practice. The origin of SHGs is from the brainchild of Grameen Bank of Bangladesh, which was founded by Mohammed Yunus. SHGs were started and formed in 1975. In India, NABARD initiated SHG in 1986-87. But the real effort was taken after 1991-92 from the linkage of SHGs with the banks. A SHG is a small economically homogeneous affinity group of the rural poor voluntarily coming together to save small amount regularly, which are deposited in a common fund to meet members emergency needs and to provide collateral free loans decided by the group (Jha, 2000). Self-Help Groups have been recognized as useful tool to help the poor and as an alternative mechanism to meet the urgent credit needs of poor through thrift. SHG is a media for the development of saving habit among the women (S. Rajamohan, 2003). SHGs enhance the equality of status of women as participants, decision-makers and beneficiaries in the democratic, economic, social and cultural spheres of life (Jain, 2003).

The people who have lack of Power, Opportunity, Outlook and Resource may be called as poorest of poor. These poor people are the main target group for the Self-Help Group formation. Upliftment of their socio-economic condition it is necessary to achieve Power, Opportunity, Outlook and Resource and it is possible when they become under a single umbrella. The main objective of Self-Help Group formation is reduction of poverty by generating income through entrepreneurship development. Beside this SHG formation has some objectives which are:

- To make a habit of group work by increasing self-reliance and self-dependency.
- Improvement in thinking, decision-making power for equal right and equal distribution.
- To sort out the local problem and make plan for income-generation and proper implementation of that plan.
- To create the saving habit for capital formation and free from the money indebtedness.
- Free from superstition by eradicating of illiteracy and dissemination of light of education.
- To raise voice against all kinds of violence, de-addiction, any kind of illegal work and also to create awareness about health, education, sanitation etc.

Swarnajayanti Gram Swarozgar Yojana (SGSY)

The SGSY Scheme is operative from 1st April, 1999 in rural areas of the country. This programme replaces the earlier self-employment and allied programmes, like IRDP, TRYSEM, DWCRA, SITRA, GKY, MWS etc. This programme offers the perfect balance of credit and subsidy. It aims at establishing a large number of micro-enterprises in the rural areas. SGSY is conceived as a holistic programme of micro-enterprise where self-employment is generated through self-help groups formation, their capacity-building, planning of activity clusters, infrastructure build up, technology, credit and marketing. The Scheme has been funded by the Centre and the States in the ratio of 75:25 and implemented by Commercial Banks, Regional Rural Banks and Co-operative Banks. Other Financial institutions, Panchayati Raj Institutions (PRIs), District Rural Development Agencies (DRDAs), Non-Governmental Organisations (NGOs), Technical Institutions in the district, have been involved in the process of planning, implementation and monitoring of the Scheme. NGO's help may be sought in the formation and nurturing of the Self-Help Groups (SHGs) as well as in the monitoring of the progress of the *Swarozgaris*. According to Vanitha Chethan and B. Krishna Murthy "the SGSY has a definite aim of improving the family incomes of the rural poor and, at the same time, providing for flexibility of design at the grassroots level to suit the local needs and resources." Selection of key activities will be with the approval of the Panchayat Samitis at the block level and the DRDA/Zilla Parishad at the district-level. As many as possible, Panchayats are involved for covering key activities. The beneficiaries are known as *"Swarozgaris"*. There are some fixed objectives of this scheme which are:

- To uplift the rural poor who are belonging to BPL category within a definite period and trained them for sustainable income generation by creating micro-enterprises.
- To improve the skills of the rural poor for effective utilization of resources.
- To improve the economic status of rural poor through self-employment.
- To improve the economic and social status of rural women by involving them in SHGs.

- To establish micro-enterprises in the rural areas in large scale to utilize the potentiality of the rural poor for their own development.
  Source: Reserve Bank of India, 2010.

Gram Sabha at Gram Panchayat-level identify the families belonging to Below Poverty Line (BPL). The DRDAs through the Panchayat Samitis implement the programme. The process of planning, implementation and monitoring would integrate banks, other financial institutions, the PRIs as well as technical institutes in the districts.

Self-Help Group and Decentralisation

Rapid growth of Self-Help Groups (SHGs) is occurring in the last decade of India. SHGs have begun to contribute in improving the economic conditions of the poor. By joining SHG, women become more socially and economically empowered. SHGs are improving the conditions of poor by savings and credit. Through credit obtain from SHG; poor families have made protection from various vulnerabilities like poverty. In the recent past SHGs have come out from its actual shape and play a key role in the grassroots governance. The Self-Help groups became an interface between the development process and the number of Government and elected institutions at the grassroots level, particularly the Panchayati Raj Institutions. The efficacy of these Self-Help Groups (SHGs) has been considerably enhanced through a symbiotic relationship with the Panchayati Raj Institutions. The key to this is to integrate these existing groups with the democratically elected and empowered Panchayats when the required devolution of power, functions and authority to them took place. In West Bengal, establishment of a system through which the SHGs and the PRIs interface efficiently, has been experienced and is successful, because both these institutions have the same mandate and objectives, i.e. ushering people-centred development and through it to empower the disempowered. In the present context SHGs became an important agent of decenttalization as it has been incorporated into the grassroots governance system and as well as the development process.

Scope/Rational of the Study

West Bengal has demonstrated sustained commitment to decentralisation, regularly holding panchayat (local) elections for over 25 years and with vibrant Panchayati Raj Institutions (PRIs), which, along with successful land reforms, are credited with significant poverty reduction in the State in 1980s. Panchayats have been particularly important in the implementation of poverty alleviation schemes, which enabled West Bengal to reduce its rural poverty profile from 73 per cent in 1973-74 (highest among all states) to 32 per cent in 1999-2000. However, in recent years, West Bengal's progress in reducing poverty has slowed down. To reach the rural poor more effectively, and regain the momentum for rural development, West Bengal, in common with many other states and countries in the region, has reaffirmed its commitment to strengthening rural decentralisation. Rural decentralisation is seen as an end in itself, conferring an improved governance environment which empowers the rural poor to participate fully as citizens and stakeholders, governing their own development, and holding Government accountable for the delivery of infrastructure and services. However, it is also a means to an end: strong participatory and pro-poor decentralised local governance is a necessary condition for identifying and responding effectively to the development needs of the poorest and most marginalised rural women and men.

Government of West Bengal has taken some positive steps to further strengthen rural decentralisation. These include framing of acts and rules for formation of Gram Unnayan Samiti at the Gram Sansad level and Upa-samitis at GP-level; giving additional responsibilities to *Artha-Sangstha-Unnayan-O-Parikalpana Sthayee Samitis* at block and ditrict level; formation of Block Sansad and District Sansad at block and district-level respectively; and inclusion of members from Opposition Political parties in all *Sthayee Samitis*. For these reforms, the WB Panchayat Act was amended [WB Panchayat (Amendment) Act, 2003]. For implementation of this Act in reality framing of rule is pending finalisation. The main objectives of these amendments are enhancement of transparency and accountability of Panchayats to people, institutionalization of inclusiveness of people in development and planning process, enhancement of upper tier Panchayat's transparency and accountability to lower tier Panchayats and institutionalization of people's active participation in planning process in reality.

There are so many studies done by various scholars on efficiency of decentralised planning, people's participation in PRI, involvement of women in the development process and the like. Most of these studies are macro-level based on secondary data and main concentration was given on decentralisation. But the realities of the sustainable decentralisation with linkages between PRIs and SHGs are yet to be studied. The success of decentralised planning is very important for strengthening the sustainable decentralisation programme in future. Another important thing is, this study also concern with the exploration of the SHGs, PRIs and Rural Development.

Objectives of the Study

In the past two decades, two interventions in India have changed the scenario of rural governance system. One is the 73rd and 74th Constitutional Amendments, which makes it mandatory for a one-third reservation of seats in local self-governing bodies, and the other is, the women Self-Help Groups which combines the access to low-cost financial services with a process of self-management and development for the women. In one hand decentralisation and local self-governance have been incorporated and strengthened in place of centralized decision-making and on the other hand women empowerment have been done through Self-Help Group (SHG) movement. However, the present study has some specific objectives which are as follows:

1. To study the role of PRIs and SHGs for strengthening rural decentralisation.
2. To enumerate the way of the preparation and implementation of micro-level plans and people's participation in the planning process.
3. To study the perception and attitude of the elected members of PRIs in regard to devolution and delegation of powers to grassroots level.
4. To study the efficacy of SHG members *vis-à-vis* non-SHG members in decentralisation process.
5. To find out the changing scenario of decentralisation in PRIs after the SHG movement.

6. To study the socio-cultural and political constraints, which are hindering for strengthening the decentralisation process.
7. To suggest some appropriate policy measures for making effective micro-level plans as well as implementing mechanisms.

Limitation of the Study

Due to time limitations and shortage of other resources the present study has some limitations which are:

- The Present study is limited to the Birbhum and Burdwan District of West Bengal only.
- Lack of availability of materials in the Government office and Gram Panchayats.
- Lack of availability of data regarding planning, Gram Sabha and Gram Sansad and financial aspects.
- Lack of Cooperation among the Gram Panchayat officials and members were the major constrains for collecting data.
- The West Bengal Panchayat election was held on July 2013 after a delay of six months from its scheduled time and new Panchayat Body was developed during September 2013 to October 2013. This highly affected the PRIs administrative structure and officials were not ready to facilitate. This highly affected the field survey.
- The unstable political conditions of rural West Bengal also affected the study.
- Shyness and less participation of villagers had enhanced the period of fieldwork (survey time).
- Mathematical errors and inconsistency in the data available with the departments as well as plan documents have created another serious limitation in the processing of data.

References

Alsop, R., Krishna, A. and Sjoblom, D. (2000), Are Gram Panchayats Inclusive? Report of a Study Conducted in Rajasthan and Madhya Pradesh, Background Paper No. 3 of the World Bank's unpublished *Overview of Rural Decentralisation in India*, Volume 3.

Bardhan, P. and Mookherjee, D. (2000), *Decentralising Anti-Poverty Programme in Developing Countries*. De Ivery. Retrieved from www.httpi/ lglobetrotter.berkeley.edu/macarthur/inequallty/papers/decdelpov.pdf.

Blair, H. (2000), Participation and Accountability at the Periphery: Democratic Local Governance in Six Countries, *World Development* 28 (1): 21–39.

Braun, F.V. and Ulrike, G. (2002), Does Decentralisation Serve the Poor, Ed. by Ahmed Ehtisham and Vito Tanzi, *Managing Fiscal Decentralisation*, London: Routledge Publications.

Crook, R.C. and Manor, J. (1998), *Democracy and Decentralisation in South Asia and West Africa,* Cambridge: Cambridge University Press.

Crook, R.C. and Sverrisson, A.S. (2001), 'Decentralisation and Poverty Alleviation in Developing Countries: A Comparative Analysis or, is West Bengal Unique?" IDS Working Paper 130, Brighton: Institute of Development Studies.

Deshpande, S.V. and Venkatesha, Murthy, G.B. (2002), Pressures from Below: Decentralised Governance in Karnataka, *Economic and Political Weekly*, 4, May.

Drèze, J. and Sen, A. (1996), *India: Economic Development and Social Opportunity*, New Delhi: Oxford University Press.

Ghatak, M. and Ghatak, M. (2002), Recent Reforms in the Panchayat System in West Bengal: Towards Greater Participatory Governance, *Economic and Political Weekly*, 5, January, pp. 45-58.

Ghosh, B. (2000), *Status of Panchayati Raj in the States and Union Territories of India*, New Delhi: Indian Institute of Social Sciences and Concept Publishing Company.

Golooba-Mutebi, F. (2000), Reassessing Participation in Uganda, paper presented at the conference, *New Institutional Economics, Institutional Reform and Poverty Reduction,* Development Studies Institute, London: School of Economics and Political Science, 7-8 September.

Government of West Bengal (1973), The West Bengal Panchayat Act, 1973, As modified up to the 1st November, Government of West Bengal.

Government of West Bengal (1994), The West Bengal Panchayat Amendment Act, 1994, Government of West Bengal.

Islam, Md. N. (2003), Decentralised Governance and Development: A Gandhian Vision, *Gandhi Prasang*, V (2): 63-68.

Jha, S. (2000), Fiscal Decentralisation in India: Strengths, Limitations and Prospects for Panchayati Raj Institutions, Background Paper No. 2, World Bank Unpublished, *Overview of Rural Decentralisation in India*, Volume 3.

Johnson, C. and Start, D. (2001), *Rights, Claims and Capture: Understanding the Politics of Pro-Poor Policy*, ODI Working Paper 145, London: Overseas Development Institute.

Litvack, J., Ahmed, J. and Richard, B. (1998), *Rethinking Decentralisation in Developing Countries,* Washington, DC: The World Bank.

Luckham, R., Goetz, A.M. and Kaldor, M. (2000), *Democratic Institutions and Politics in Contexts of Inequality, Poverty, and Conflict: A Conceptual Framework*, IDS Working Paper 104, Brighton: Institute of Development Studies.

Mahipal (1997), Panchayati Raj in India: Issues and Challenges, *Kurukshetra*, 97(8).

Manor, J. (1999), *The Political Economy of Democratic Decentralisation, Directions in Development Series*, Washington DC: World Bank.

Mathew, G. (2001), Panchayat Elections: Dismal Record, *Economic and Political Weekly*, 20, January, pp. 183-84.

Mathur, K. (1988), Panchayati Raj, Democracy and Politics in India, A Paper Presented on ICSSR Seminar on India since Independence, December 26-30.

Moore, M. and Putzel, J. (1999), Politics and Poverty: A Background paper for the World Development Report 2000/1, Brighton: Institute of Development Studies.

Mukherjee, S. (1974), *Local Self-Government in West Bengal*, Calcutta: Dasgupta and Company (Private) Limited.

Mukhopadhyay, A. (1977), *The Panchayat Administration in West Bengal: A Study of West Bengal's Unhappy Utopia*, Calcutta: The World Press Private Ltd.

Nambiar, M. (2001), Making the Gram Sabha Work, *Economic and Political Weekly*, 18, August.

Oommen, M.A. (1999), Panchayat Finance and Issues Relating to Inter-governmental Transfers, in S.N. Jha and P.C. Mathur (eds.) *Decentralisation and Local Politics: Readings in Indian Government and Politics*, London: Sage Publications, 142-72.

Ostrom, E. (1990), *Governing the Commons: The Evolution of Institutions for Collective Action*, Cambridge: Cambridge University Press.

Panchayat and Rural Development Department (P&RD Department), Government of West Bengal (GoWB); (2008), *Annual Administrative Report 2008-09*, P&RD Department, GoWB, Kolkata, WB.

Panchayat and Rural Development Department (P&RD Department), Government of West Bengal (GoWB), (2008), *SRD Annual Report 2007-08*, P&RD Department, GoWB, Kolkata, WB.

Panchayat and Rural Development Department (P&RD Department), Government of West Bengal (GoWB), (2009), *Roadmap for Panchayat in West Bengal: A Vision Document*, P&RD Department, GoWB, Kolkata, WB.

Panchayat and Rural Development Department (P&RD Department), Government of West Bengal (GoWB), (2010), *Information on West Bengal Panchayats: Their Members and Functionaries*, P&RD Department, GoWB, Kolkata, WB.

Prud'home, R. (1995), The Dangers of Decentralisation, *The World Bank Research Observer*, 10 (2): 201-20.

Putnam, R.L. and Raffaella, Y.N. (1993), *Making Democracy Work: Civic Tradition in Modern Italy,* Princeton, NJ.: Princeton University Press.

Rahman, H.Z. (2001), Re-thinking Local Governance Towards a Livelihood Focus, *PPRC Policy Paper,* Dhaka: Power and Participation Research Centre.

Rao, G.B. (2000), Strengthening of Panchayats: Beyond Contractor's Role, Paper presented at the Workshop on *Role of Panchayati Raj Institutions in Natural Resource Management*, 2 and 3 February, New Delhi.

Romeo, L. (1999), Systems Experimentation in Support of Decentralisation Reforms: Reflections on Local Development Funds, *Regional Development Dialogue*, 20 (2): 134-57.

Roy Chowdhury, S. (1996), Rethinking Co-Operation: Towards a Non-Essentialist Conception, *National Seminar on Rediscovering Co-Operation*, Institute of Rural Management, Anand (November): 1-10.

Sangita, S.N. (2002), Institute for Self-Governance of Community Forestry Resources: Experiences from Three Indian States, Bangalore: ISEC (IDPAD Project).

Slater, R.P. and Watson, J.R. (1993), Decentralised Planning and the Anti-Poverty Programmes, Some Possible New Direction, Ed. By Hooja, Rakesh and B. Yerram Raju, *Decentrallsed Planning in Multilevel Framework*, New Delhi: Rawat Publications.

Sundaram, K.V. (1997), *Decentralised Multilevel Planning, Principles and Practice: Asian and African Experiences*, New Delhi: Concept Publishing Company.

Tanzi, V. (1995), Fiscal Federalism and Decentralisation: A Review of Some Efficiency and Economic Aspects, Ed. by Michael Bruno and Boris Pleskovic, *Annual World Bank Conference on Development Economies*, Washington DC: The World Bank.

Tanzi, V. (2001), Pitfalls on the Road to Fiscal Decentralisation, Working Paper, No. 19, Washington D.C: Carnegie Endowment for International Peace.

UNDP (2003), *The Human Rights Based Approach to Development: Towards a Common Understanding among the UN Agencies*: UNDP, New York.

Vyasulu, V. (2000), *Decentralisation, Democratisation, Finances, and the Constitution: Reflections Based on Local Reality*, Paper prepared for the Panel on Decentralisation of the National Commission to Review the Working of the Constitution.

Wade, R. (1985), The Market for Public Office: Why the Indian State is not better at Development, *World Development*, 13(4): 467-97.

Webster, N. (1992), *Panchayati Raj and Decentralisation of Development Planning in West Bengal*, Calcutta: K.P. Bagchi & Company.

World Bank (2000), *Overview of Rural Decentralisation in India,* Volume II: *Approaches to Rural Decentralisation in Seven States,* Unpublished Report, World Bank.

World Bank (2000), *Multi-State Study of Panchayati Raj Legislation and Administrative Reform*, Vol. 3, Background Paper 1: De Souza, Peter, 2000. New Delhi, India.

World Bank (2000), *Overview of Rural Decentralisation in India,* Vol. 1, September 27, 2000, New Delhi, India.

2
Conceptual Framework

Evolution of PRIs

India has a long history of tradition local governments, going back to more than 4000 years. This institution has survived numerous political changes and upheavals in the ancient and medieval periods till the advent of the British Raj. With the coming of the colonial administration, the patterns of the working of the local bodies underwent marked changes. The present pattern of urban and rural bodies reflects a distinct impact of colonial period. The modern structure of Panchayati Raj in India is evolved through a long historical phase.

Village administration was also a significant part of the Ancient Indian Political System. During the Vedic age, the Aryans had built-up small villages and the administration of the area was looked after by the village councils. A system of giving taxes also prevailed in the ancient society. Taxes such as *Pali*, *Sulk* and *Bhaga* were collected from the people. The revenue was spent for the benefit of the subjects. The presence of local self-governance has found in '*Veda*', '*Upanishads*' and other old manuscripts. The Concept of Panchayat has originated from the word *'Panch-Ayat'* or a group of five persons selected by the villagers. Basically, it indicates the system through which rural people are governed. The word '*Panchayatan*' been found in old Sanskrit scriptures, which means a group of five persons, including some spiritual man. The concept of "*Panch Parameshwar*" is found in ancient manuscript. Terms like '*Samiti*' and '*Sabha*' were found in *'Rig Veda'*. *Sabha* and *Samiti* were the democratic structure at the local level or village level and the king used to get the approval of '*Sabha*' and '*Samiti*' regarding certain functions and decisions (Joshi, R.P. and Narwani, G.S., 2002). In the later Vedic period, the *Samiti* disappeared as a popular assembly while the *Sabha* sank into a narrow body corresponding to the kings Privy Council (Singh Raj, 1996). In *Rig Veda* and *Atharva Veda* there are references to the ancient nature of Panchayats. This system was started by the king 'Prithee'. Administration of village was administrated under the supervision and guidance of *Mukhiya* in great extent reference as "*Gramin*" is obtained in Vedic literature. It is called "*Grambhojak*" in *Jatakkathas*. Volumes, inscriptions, copper-plates and notes of tourists from Vedic age to ancient age refer "*gramin*" in various different world. In this way, it was known by different names in different regions of India. It is referred as "*Gramin*" in North India, "*Munund*" in Telangana, "*Mahattak*" in Uttar Pradesh and "*Gramukut*" and "*Gavunda*" in South India. Names may be differed but he was the main officer of village. Generally, rank of "*Gramin*" was hereditary but in case of non-worthiness of heir, the rank of "*Gramin*" was allocated to worth member of his family. "*Gramin*" was the administration and military head of village. His main duty was to maintain peace and defence against external force, administration and to collect taxes. The office of the village headman (*Gramani*) indicates the emergence of the village as a unit of administration.

Again according to a 10th Century '*Sukha Neetisar*' in ancient India members of the Panchayat was elected by the common man. Panchayats were given utmost respect. Disbursement of land, collection of taxes, law enforcement was under its full control. Panchayat used to come to the rescue of villagers during the time of emergency. The head of Panchayat was seen as a man of justice. The elder son of the head used to inherit his father. This way Indian rural society from the ancient period had Panchayat system which worked in a traditional manner. Mentions of village administration are also found during the fourth century B.C. when republican federation existed in the society of India. The city of Vaishali had Panchayat for administering justice and courts. The republican character of the polity of Vaishali lasted for thousands of years.

The existence of Panchayat system in Epic ear had been found in two great epic—*Ramayana*' and '*Mahabharata*'. The administration was divided into '*Pur*' (city) and '*Janapad*' (villages). The village peoples were called *Janapadi* in those days. The villages were termed as their size, i.e. '*Gram*' (village); '*Maha Gram*' (big village); *Ghosh* (group of Villages). The existence of *Mandi* (local market) is also found in the *Ramayana*. In *Ramayana* of Valmiki, there are references to the *Ganapada* (village federation) which was perhaps a kind of federation of village republics (Ghosh, R. and Pramanik, A.K., 1999). The local bodies were called as *Shreni* and *Nigam*. The system of governance was divided into the rule of king (*Raj-Tantra*), the rule of people (*Praja-Tantra*) and rule of the wise men (*Vidvat-Tantra*) or educated and knowledgeable person (Joshi, R.P. and Narwani, G.S., 2002).

Panchayats were so powerful during the *Mahabharata* period that even king could not interfere in their working. They were called *Gana* or *Sabha*. Although, the system during that period was autocratic, even then the king has to except the decision of the members of the *Sabhas* on *Panchayats*. As per the *Mahabharata*, over and above the villages, there were units of 10, 20, 100 and 1,000 village groups. *Gramik* was the chief official of the village. *Dashap* was the chief of ten villages. *Vishya Adhipati*, *Sath Gram Adhyaksha* and *Sahasra Gram Pati* were the chief of 20, 100 and 1,000 villages respectively (Joshi, R.P. and Narwani, G.S., 2002). Existence of local self-governance had been also found in *Manu Smriti* as well as in Chanakya's *Arthashastra*. In *Manu Smriti* and Chanakya's *Arthashastra* the head of the village was called *Gramik*. Chanakya established Panchayats in villages and they had all powers to deal with issues relating to social and religious behaviour. They could interfere and express their opinion in the day-to-day affairs of the *Sabha*. The village panchayat enjoyed a lot of autonomy. Most of the religious, cultural, and economic activities were handled with care and efficiency by them. During the Mauryan period (322 to 195 B.C.), Gram Panchayat existed and were well organized. Village life was run by the Panchayats. They also worked as administrative units. Villagers used to organize works of public utility and recreation, settle disputes, and act as trustees for the property of minors. But, they had not yet evolved regular councils. The village council appeared to have evolved into regular bodies in the Gupta period. They were known as *Panchamandalas* in Central India and *Gramajanapadas* in Bihar (Altekar, A.S., 1997). In Chandragupta Maurya's regime, the decentralisation of powers was adopted as administrative policy. The smallest unit of the governance was village and head of the village known as *'Gramik'*. The villagers elect *Gramik*. The term like '*Gram sabha*', *Gram Janpad* and '*Panch Mandali*' are also found from the record of Gupta period. Village governance is also found in the Shukracharya's "*Neeti Shastra*". Self-governance in the villages was also developed by the Chola.

During the medieval and Mughal periods, village bodies were the pivot of administration. In India after the 10th Century, when influence of Muslim started increasing, there was a change in the traditional face of Panchayats. But new rulling system did not change outwardly. Tughlaqs had instructed his men especially not to interfere in the working of Panchayats and also not to harm them. In the Mughal period, particularly in the regime of Sher Shah, the villages were governed by their own panchyats. Each Panchayat comprised village elders who looked after the interest of the people and administered justice and imposed punishment on defaulters. The headman of the village, a semi-government official, acted as a coordinator between the village panchayat and the higher administrative hierarchy. Akbar accepted this system and made it an indispensable part of civil administration. In this period, each village had its own panchayat of elders. It was autonomous in its own sphere and exercised powers of local taxation, administrative control, justice and punishment (Ghosh, R. and Pramanik, A.K., 1999). But during the Mughal period, because of innumerable battles and of, the exploitation by land revenue officials, there was a decline in the power of Panchayats. The system of providing justice directly by the Muslim rulers was another reason for the decline of this system. This was a very crucial period for the existence of Panchayats. The Mughals introduced elaborate administrative machinery with a hierarchy of officials, particularly in the field of revenue. The Mughal local administrative system lasted over centuries. It was with the collapse of the Mughal stronghold, the British established their hegemony in India.

To a large extent, however, the modern idea of the panchayat, its nature and its functions, derives from the image of the Indian Village Community conjured-up in the writings of Sir William Jones, Hector Munro, Mountstuart Elphinstone, John Malcolm and a variety of other colonial authors in the late eighteenth and early nineteenth centuries. References to Panchayats and Janapadas in ancient Vedic texts, translated into English for the first time by orientalist scholars, played a part in persuading.

British officials found it as an elemental unit of Indian society and politics. Its most succinct and influential expression may be found in Charles Metcalfe's defence of the Mahalwari system of revenue settlement adopted in the newly ceded and conquered territories of the North-Western Province (later UP). Describing the fortified villages which sprung-up around Delhi in the years after the collapse of Mughal power in 1761. Metcalfe wrote to the 1832 Select Parliamentary Committee on the East India Company's charter in brilliantly evocative terms:

> "The village communities are little republics, having nearly everything they can want within themselves and almost independent of any foreign relations. They seem to last where nothing else lasts. Dynasty after dynasty tumbles down; revolution succeeds to revolution; Hindoo, Pathan, Mogul, Mahratta, Sikh, English, are all masters in turn; but the village community remains the same.... This union of the village communities, each one forming a separate State in itself, has, I conceive, contributed more than any other cause to the preservation of the people of India through all the revolutions and changes which they have suffered, and is in a high degree conducive to their happiness, and to the enjoyment of a great portion of freedom and independence" (Dewey, C.J., 1972).

The British came to India as traders. The primary focus of the British Raj was much to do with trade and little to do with governance and development. The local governments were hardly their first priority. The British Government was much more interested in the creation of 'controlled' local body instead of local governance. In the British period centralized administration established instead of decentralised administrative system. Colonial administrators controlled over the area by their own employees. Gram Sabha based Panchayat system gets abolished day-by-day after starting civil court and criminal court by the colonial ruler. Development of road connectivity, water communication in rapid way by the British Government it was very easy for them to rule the whole country from central. But in course of time, British Government constituted institute for village administration. It is a true and historical fact that local self-governance in India, as a representative institution, was developed by the British (Mathew, 1995).

It was Lord Mayo, the then Viceroy of India (1869 to 1872), who felt the need to decentralise powers in order to bring about administrative efficiency and in the year 1870 introduced the concept of elected representatives in the urban municipalities. The revolt of 1857 that had put the imperial finances under considerable strain and it was found necessary to finance local service out of local taxation. Therefore, it was out of fiscal compulsion that Lord Mayo's resolution on decentralisation came to be adopted. The beginning of local governance can be presumed from 1687, when the Madras City Corporation was established. The subsequent history was summarized as following category:

1. *1687-1881*: Local Government was established to share the burden of resources of the Central and Provincial Governments.
2. *1882-1919*: Local Government was seen as local self-government.
3. *1920-1937*: Local Government was established in the provinces and people's representatives were controlling the provincial administration also.
4. *1938-1947*: Local Government was in the State of rejuvenation and reconstruction (Maheswari, R.S., 1971).

The major events and initiative by the British Government are described briefly.

Establishment of Bombay (1726) and Calcutta Municipal Bodies (1773)

The Bengal Chowkidar Act of 1870: The Bengal Chowkidar Act of 1870 marked the beginning of the revival of the traditional village panchayat system in Bengal. The Chowkidar Act empowered District Magistrates to set-up Panchayats of nominated members in the villages to collect taxes to pay the chowkidars or watchmen engaged by them.

Famine Commission (1880): The 1880 Famine Commission also indicated the necessity of the local bodies at the village-level for famine relief work (Maheswari, R.S., 1971).

Ripon Resolution (1882): Lord Ripon made remarkable contribution to the development of Local Government. In 1882, he abandoned the existing system of local Government by the officially nominated people. According to his local self-government plan, the local boards were split into smaller units to achieve greater efficiency. In order to ensure popular participation, he introduced an election system for the local boards.

The Government resolution of 18th May, 1882, stands as a landmark in the structural evolution of local governments. It provided for local boards consisting of a large majority of elected non-official members and presided over by a non-official chairperson. This is considered to be the *Magna Carta* of local democracy in India. This resolution proposed the establishment of rural local boards where two-third of whose membership was composed of elected representatives. He brought in the concept of self-government in urban municipalities. He is treated as the founding father of urban local Government. Ripon's resolutions followed a series of Committees, Commissions and Acts in this line. To stimulate the candidature of man of standing, courtesy title of '*Rai Bahadur*' and '*Rai Saheb*' were allowed to Indian members during their term of services on local bodies (Maheswari, R.S., 1971). During 1883-85, the local self-government acts were passed in many provinces. Local boards could be superseded in case of abuse of powers. The British bureaucracy did not think of Indians as mature and experienced enough for local self-government. Hence, Lord Curzon subsequently opposed such liberalism and increased government control over such local bodies (Maheswari, R.S., 1971).

The Royal Commission: In 1906, Dadabhai Naoroji, the President of Congress accepted the "Self-Government" as the political goal for the country. Royal Commission constituted by the Government in 1907 on decentralisation and in 1909 released its reports. The Royal Commission reported on decentralisation that paucity of funds and caste and religious disputes were the main obstacles in effective functioning of local bodies. The Commission recommended "it is most desirable alike in the interest of decentralisation in order to associate people with the local tasks of administration that an attempt should be made to constitute and develop village Panchayat for the administration of local village affairs." The Royal Commission on Decentralisation in 1909 elaborated further the principles of Ripon resolution. But this remained merely on paper. Ripon's scheme did not make much progress in the development of local self-government institutions.

Montagu-Chelmsford Reforms of 1919: Montagu-Chelmsford reforms were passed in the year 1919. This reform transferred the subject of local government to the domain of provinces. The reform also recommended that as far as possible there should be a complete popular control in local bodies and the largest possible independence for them, of outside control. By 1925, eight provinces had passed Village Panchayat Acts. However, these Panchayats covered only a limited number of villages with limited functions (Stephen, F. and Rajasekaran, 2001). But this reform could not get much result as far as democratization of Panchayats was concerned and lead to a lot of organizational and fiscal constraints.

Simon Commission (1930): In 1930, evaluation of the implementation of self-governance was done by Simon Commission. It reported that except Uttar Pradesh, Bengal and Madras, they did not find any progress in the rural areas. The condition of the local bodies deteriorated between 1919 and 1930. Hence, it was suggested by the Simon Commission to increase the control of the State over these local bodies.

Government of India Act (1935): Government of India Act (1935) is considered as another important stage in the evolution of Panchayats in British India. With popularly elected Government in the provinces, almost all provincial administrations felt duty bound to enact legislations for further democratization of local self-government institutions, including village Panchayats. Although, the popular Government in the provinces governed by the Congress vacated office following the declaration of Second World War in 1939, the position as regards local Government institutions remained unchanged till August 1947, when the country attained independence.

Even though the British Government did not have interest in the village autonomy, they were forced to do so, in order to continue their rule in India and moreover to meet financial necessities. The Indian rural democracy had flourished till the arrival of British. It received a setback during the British rule. Self-contained self-sufficient village communities and their Panchayats ceased to get substance. They were replaced by formally constituted institutions of village administration. In the highly centralized system of British rule, village autonomy seems to have lost.

Panchayati Raj Institutions in Post-independence Period: The Village Panchayats were a part of the ideology of Indian National Movement. Gandhiji had given the idea of '*Gram Swaraja*': "The

Government of Village will be conducted by the panchayat of five persons annually elected by the adult villagers, male and females, possessing minimum prescribed qualifications. These will have all the authority and jurisdiction required. Since, there will be no system of punishment in the accepted sense, the panchayat will be legislature, judiciary and executive combined to operate for its year of office. Any village can become such republic today.... Here, there is perfect democracy-based on individual freedom. The individual is the architect of his own government."

So, the task of strengthening Panchayati Raj System fell on the Government of India formed after Independence. It was clear that India a country of villages, had to strengthen village Panchayats to strengthen democracy. Mahatma Gandhi who strongly believed in *Grama Swaraj* pleaded for the transfer of power to the rural masses. According to him, the villages should govern themselves through elected Panchayats to become self-sufficient. But surprisingly, the draft Constitution prepared in 1948 had no place for Panchayati Raj Institutions. Gandhi severely criticized this and called for immediate attention. It is, thus, that panchayat finds a place in the Directive Principles of the State Policy. A compromise was forged and in 1948, PRIs found place in the non-justifiable part of the Constitution as Article 40 which reads as under:

> "The State shall take steps to organize village Panchayats and endow them with such powers and authority as may be necessary to enable them to function as units of self-government."

During the early independent phase, Mahatma Gandhi conceptualized the Village Panchayats as the primary grassroots level democratic unit and people's participation was considered as necessary so that India's perception as a welfare State could be fulfilled. According to Gandhiji "Grater power of the panchayat, the better for the people as true democracy."

The first organized effort to tackle the problem of rural India was made through Community Development Programme in 1952 and National Extension Service in 1953. The programme was based on an integrated approach to the various aspects of rural development. The objectives were to promote self-help and self-reliance among the rural people, to generate a process of integrated social, economic and cultural change with the aim of transforming social and political life of the villagers. This programme was intended to bring socio-economic development of the rural masses on democratic lines, but failed to take off along the expected lines due to the absence of an effective instrument for people's participation. The programme was more or less bureaucratic and excessively politicized. SDO-*cum*-BDO fulfilled the local demands like road drinking water wells, panchayat ghars, school building etc. All schemes were treated as Government Schemes rather than people's programme (Joshi, R.P. and Narwani, G.S., 2002).

Committees, Commissions and Five Year Plans

The debates in the Constituent Assembly on Panchayati Raj were more fundamentally grounded. There were two differing viewpoints—that of Gandhi and of Ambedkar. The fundamental difference in philosophies of these two thinkers was on parliamentary democracy—Ambedkar believed the unit of development should be the individual while Gandhi believed the unit of development should be the village. Gandhi said in the issue of the *Harijan* of July 26, 1942 that—"My idea of village *swaraj* is that it is a complete republic, independent of its neighbours for its vital wants, and yet interdependent for many others in which dependence is a necessity. Thus, the village's first concern will be to grow its own food crops and cotton for its cloth. It should have a reserve for its cattle, recreation and playground for adults and children.... The village will maintain a village theatre, school and public hall. It will have its own waterworks ensuring a clean water supply. This can be done through controlled wells or tanks. Education will be compulsory up to the final basic course. As far as possible every activity will be conducted on a co-operative basis. There will be no caste, such as we have today with their graded untouchability. Non-violence with its technique of *satyagraha* and non-cooperation will be the sanction of the village community.... The Panchayat of five persons annually elected by the adult villagers, male and female, possessing minimum prescribed qualifications will conduct the Government of the village. These will have all the authority and jurisdiction required. Since, there will be no system of punishments in the accepted sense, this Panchayat will be the legislature, judiciary, and executive combined to operate for its year in office. Any village can become such a republic without much interference." While Dr. B.R. Ambedkar said in the Constituent

Assembly Debates in November 1948, that "It is said that the new Constitution should have been drafted on the ancient Hindu model of a State and that instead of incorporating Western theories the new Constitution should have been raised and built upon village Panchayats and District Panchayats... They just want India to contain so many village governments. The love of the intellectual Indians for the village community is of course infinite if not pathetic... I hold that the village republics have been the ruination of India. I am therefore surprised that those who condemn provincialism and communalism should come forward as champions of the village. What is the village, but a sink of localism, a den of ignorance, narrow-mindedness and communalism? I am glad that the Draft Constitution has discarded the village and adopted the individual as its unit." (Panth, A.H. and Bohra, O.P., 1995).

The Indian National Congress emphasized the issue of *Swaraj*, and organized movements for Independence under the leadership of Mahatma Gandhi. There was no idea among the top leaders about the status to be assigned to the local self-government. Dr. B.R. Ambedkar opposed the idea of Gandhi's Village *Swaraj*. He believed that the village represented regressive India, a source of oppression. During the drafting of the Constitution of India, Panchayati Raj Institutions were placed in the non-justiciable part of the Constitution, the Directive Principles of State Policy, as Article 40. After Independence, Panchayati Raj had to go through various ups and downs. To strengthen the local bodies of our country and after the Independence, the Constitutional Assembly discussed the matter and at last the Constitution of India placed the issues in the Directive Principles of the State Policy and mandated that "Organization of village Panchayats—The State shall take steps to organize village Panchayats and endow them with such powers and authority as may be necessary to enable them to function as units of self-government." (Constitution of India, Directive Principles of State Policy, Article 40). So, the Constitution of India was failed to provide guidance on how to develop the PRIs. This responsibility fell to a series of National Committees that addressed issues of implementation of the Constitutional mandate.

The First Five Year Plan recognized the need for a disaggregated planning exercise through a process of democratic decentralisation incorporating the idea of a village plan and of District Development

Councils. But the First Five Years Plan failed to bring about active community participation and involvement of the people in the Planning processes, which included Plan formulation, implementation and monitoring.

During Second Five Year Plan, Prime Minister Jawaharlal Nehru inaugurated the Community Development Programme (CDP) on 2nd October, 1952 under the major influence of the Etawah Project undertaken by the American expert, Albert Mayer. Community Development sought to motivate the rural people to take community-based approach for the improvement of the economic and social condition of their life. The Government was expected to provide general guidance and technical-*cum*-financial assistance in some blocks in a phased manner. The Community Development Programme was followed by the National Extension Service in 1953. Some National Extension Service (NES) blocks were earmarked as the lowest unit of administration. But unfortunately, both the programmes were failed due to wastage of funds, corruption, malpractices and favouritism. That failure compelled the National Development Council to appoint a committee headed by Balwant Rai Mehta in 1956 to critically review the CDP and NES and suggest measures for effecting economy and improving efficiency in implementation of schemes. At the same time, the Planning Commission also recommended that Village Panchayats should be strengthened and given the responsibility for taking over development administration.

The Balwant Rai Mehta Committee believed that community development would only be effective when the community was involved in the planning, decision, and implementation process. The Committee suggested that the basic unit of democratic decentralisation was to be at the block (*samiti*) level since the area of jurisdiction of the local body should neither be too large nor too small. The block was large enough for efficiency and economy of administration, and small enough for sustaining a sense of involvement in the citizens. Further, the Zilla Parishad (ZP) should play an advisory role. The Committee focused on the rural sector and recommended that the functions of PRIs should cover the development of agriculture in all its aspects, the promotion of local industries and other services such as drinking water, road building etc. Balwant Rai Mehta Committee studied the Community Development Projects and the National Extension Service and the team felt that there should be a single representative and vigorous democrartic institution to take charge of all aspects of development work in the rural areas. The Committee suggested the concept of democratic decentralisation should be based on planning and implementation of CDP and NES. The main recommendations of this Committee were as under:

- Suitable administrative decentralisation for effective implementation of development programmes.
- Place decentralised administrative system under the effective control of elected representatives of people.
- Development block covering about 100 villages and having a population of a hundred thousand should coincide with taluka/tehsil/sub-district unit.
- There should be three-tiers—Zilla Parishad at the district-level to replace the District board, Panchayat Samiti at the block-level and the Gram Panchayat at the village-level.
- Panchayats should work under the overall supervision of the Panchayat Samiti, which would include their representatives.
- The three-tier Panchayati Raj system would be vested with power and functions. Resource will largely be devolved upon the Panchayat Samiti—the intermediate tier. The Panchayat Samiti will play a primary role in rural development process.
- Looking at the diversity of the socio-economic conditions, some States might modify the proposed system. They may prefer devolution of powers to the district level body.
- Composition of the Panchayati Raj bodies should be representative of all sections of people, by and large.
- Dynamic attitude should be adopted towards the functioning of the proposed new setup. Further, devolution of powers, functions and resources from the State Government should be done in future, looking to the success of the scheme.
- Effective training of people's representatives at the three tiers of the local bodies was also stressed.
- People's representatives would plan the community development and allied programmes as well as direct and supervise their implementation by the bureaucracy. Hence, they should develop the knowledge and attitude essential for it. Seminars, workshops and conferences and training course should be arranged adequately.

(*Source*: R.P. Joshi and G.S. Narwani, 2002).

The National Development Council also agreed most of the recommendations of 1958. The Government of India convinced all the States to adopt participatory approach for rural development. The PRI structure was introduced in most parts of the country as a result of the Balwant Rai Mehta Report. However, it did not develop the requisite democratic momentum and failed to cater to the needs of rural development. Reasons for this were: (i) political and bureaucratic resistance at the State level to sharing of power and resources with the local level institutions; (ii) the takeover of these institutions by the rural elite who cornered a major share of the benefits of the various welfare schemes; (iii) the lack of capability at the local level; and (iv) the absence of political will of the grassroots leaders.

The Third Five Year Plan (1961-1966) re-emphasized decentralised planning in various sectors, while the absence of proper planning mechanism resulted in poor planning process.

The K. Santhanam Committee in 1963 was appointed to look solely at the issue of PRI finances. Its recommendations have influenced the thinking and the debate to date on following issues:

- The Panchayats should have special powers to levy special tax on land revenues, home tax etc.
- People should not be burdened with huge taxes.
- All grants and subventions at the State-level should be consolidated and untied.
- A Panchayat Raj Finance Corporation should be set up which would look into the financial resources of PRIs at all three levels, provide loans and financial assistance to these grassroots level Governments and also provide support for non-financial requirements of villages.
  (*Source*: A.H. Panth and O.P. Bohra, 1995).

These issues have been debated over the last three decades and have been taken-up by the State Finance Commissions.

The Fourth Five Year Plan (1969-1974) again emphasized on shifting towards district planning. The Planning Commission also took interest in helping the States in initiating decentralised planning. However, a very little progress was made towards decentralising the planning process during the Fourth and Fifth Five Year Plans.

The Asoka Mehta Committee was set-up when the Janata Party Government came to power at the Centre in 1977 to examine the functioning of PRIs and to suggest measures for making decentralised planning effective. The Asoka Mehta Committee was appointed in 1977 to find out the weakness of Panchayati Raj Institution. It was decided to appoint a high-level committee under the chairmanship of Asoka Mehta to examine and suggest measures to strengthen PRIs and decentralised planning process. The Committee made the following recommendations:

- More genuine and effective devolution of powers to Panchayati Raj Institutions should take place. The district is a viable administrative unit for which planning, co-ordination and resource allocation is feasible and technical expertise is available.
- PRIs as a two-tier system, with Mandal Panchayat at the base and Zilla Parishad at the top. Because Zilla Parishad had better resource and leadership.
- Well qualified civil servants should be appointed for better administration at both Zilla Parishad and Mandal Panchayats.
- Below the Mandal Panchayat, there should be a village committee including the weaker sections of people. Representation of SCs and STs in the election to PRIs on the basis of their population.
- Political parties should take part in the elections of PRIs.
- A Panchayati Raj Finance Commission should be set-up to fulfil the district demands to implement plans. Besides that the PRIs should also develop their own resources of funds by collecting taxes.
- The District-level panchayat should prepare the district-level plans and those plans should be implemented with incorporation of Mandal Panchayat.
  (*Source*: R.P. Joshi and G.S. Narwani, 2002).

The States of Karnataka, Andhra Pradesh and West Bengal passed new legislation-based on this report. But 1978 onwards was an unstable period in State politics, and Panchayati Raj Institutions were unable to develop their own political dynamics.

The Sixth, Seventh and Eighth Five Year Plans were again emphasized on district planning within a multi-level planning framework. But proper administrative arrangements were not made to facilitate this process and there was also a lack of technical expertise and financial devolution in the successful process of democratic decentralisation.

The GVK Rao Committee was appointed in 1985 to again revisit the obstacles in the way of effective PRIs. It recommended that PRIs at the district level and below be assigned responsibilities for planning, monitoring and implementation of rural development programmes and that the block development office should be the spinal cord of rural development.

More thinking on PRIs was initiated by the *L.M. Singhvi Committee in 1986*. The *Gram Sabha* (village assembly) was considered the base of decentralised democracy. The PRIs were to be viewed as institutions of self-government which would facilitate the participation of the people in the process of planning and development. It recommended that local self-government should be constitutionally recognized, protected and preserved by the inclusion of a new chapter in the Constitution. It also viewed with dismay the irregularity of elections and engaged with the issue of the role of political parties in Panchayat elections, stating that a non-involvement should be consensual rather than through legislative fiat. The role of political parties in Panchayats has since then divided the advocates of PRI into two camps. On the one side are those such as Jayaprakash Narayan, writing within the Gandhian tradition of partyless democracy, who saw " 'self-government through faction-fighting will not be self-government but self-ruination', and on the other are those such as Asoka Mehta who support the involvement of political parties since it enables candidates, from weak economic backgrounds, to effectively compete with the backing of a strong organization" (Wadhwani, M. and Mishra, S.N., 1996).

Sarkaria Commission was inquiring about federal structure and Centre-State relations. But anyway this Commission had made a comment on PRIs. That is, the local bodies are not functioning effectively, because elections to these bodies were superceded and also the Panchayat Raj laws are not uniform across the states. Constitutional status for PRIs was opposed by the *Sarkaria Commission*. But the idea gained momentum in the late 1980s especially because of the endorsement by the late Prime Minister Rajiv Gandhi who introduced the 64th Constitutional Amendment Bill in 1989. Rajiv Gandhi's commitment to the PRI route to rural development seems to have emerged through a series of workshops he had as Prime Minister with District Collectors, where he got a sense of the insensitivity of District Administration and of wastage of funds for rural development. The 64th Constitutional Amendment Bill caused much anxiety among opposition parties because they perceived it to support the partisan agenda of Rajiv Gandhi and it was defeated in the Rajya Sabha.

Various other committees were instrumental for the design of rural decentralisation in India, namely on decentralised planning (Mahapatra, 2012). The Planning Commission in 1966 issued guidelines for District Planning. The M.L. Dantwala Group of the Planning Commission issued guidelines in 1978 for Block-level Planning. The report of the Economic Advisory Council of the Prime Minister on "Decentralisation of Development Planning and Implementation in the States" was issued in 1983, and the Working Group on District Planning of the Planning Commission issued its report in 1994. The concern with decentralised planning stemmed from "the slow rate of benefits flowing from the infrastructure already built-up", as indicated by the slow growth of productivity, and (...) insufficient percolation of benefits to the poor and the socially disadvantaged sections, despite the proliferation of several poverty alleviation programmes (Rao, H.C., 1989). Centralized planning, it was felt, had not solved the "basic problems of poverty, unemployment and inequality."

In the Ninth Plan, democratic decentralisation became effective with the enactment of the 73rd and 74th Constitutional Amendment Acts. Most of the State Governments/UTs have enacted enabling legislations for three-tier system by providing political power with adequate representation from the weaker sections and women. In case of some UTs only a two-tier structure has been recommended. Most of the States have formed State Election Commissions and State Finance Commissions (SFCs) as stipulated.

At present, Panchayati Raj Institutions have Constitutional entities. The State Governments have to implement the three-tier Panchayats with adequate powers and authority to enable them to function as institutions of local self-government. The Eleventh Schedule has identified 29 subjects which have to be brought under the Panchayats. The Panchayati Raj Institutions are able to undertake the responsibility entrusted to them both financial and functional. It is necessary not only to ensure flow of funds to them from the States and from the Central Government *via* the Centrally Sponsored Schemes (CSS), but also to give them independent revenue collection

Table 2.1: Decentralisation—Chronology of Attempts and Committee Reports

Year	*Item*	*Ideas and Concepts*
First Plan 1951-56	Community Development Blocks	To break-up the planning exercise into national, state, district and local community levels.
Second Plan 1956-61	District Development Councils	Drawing-up of village plans and popular participation in planning through the process of democratic decentralisation.
1957	Balwant Rai Mehta	Village, block, District Panchayat institutions established.
1967	Administrative Reforms Commission	Resources to be given local variations accommodated, purposeful plan for area.
1969	Planning Commission	Formulated guidelines; detailed the concept of the district plan and methodology of drawing up such a plan in the framework of annual plans, medium-term plans and perspective plans.
1978	Prof. M.L. Dantwala	Block-level planning to form link between village and district-level planning.
1983-84	CSS/Reserve Bank of India	Strengthen District Level Plan/District Credit Plan.
1984	Hanumantha Rao Committee	Decentralisation of functions, powers and finances; Setting-up of district planning bodies and district planning cells.
1985	G.V.K. Rao Committee	Administrative arrangements for rural development; District Panchayat to manage all development programmes.
1986	L.M. Singhvi Committee	The Gram Sabha (village assembly) was considered the base of decentralised democracy; local self-government should be constitutionally recognized.
Ninth Plan	73rd and 74th Constitutional Amendment Act	Democratic decentralisation became effective; local governments in rural areas became an effective reality all over India.

powers that they can generate their own fund. The State Finance Commissions were set-up with the objective of making the Panchayats financially viable. While resource mobilisations by Panchayati Raj Institutions are generally limited, it is imperative to provide PRIs with revenue-raising powers of their own in order to reduce their financial dependency on the Central and State Governments. There are taxes which can be collected by local bodies. On the other side, grants for specific schemes entrusted to the Panchayats will be given to them by the State Government. Funds from Centrally Sponsored Schemes will also be in the form of a grant but those would not be a part of the untied grants. Sixteen per cent of the net proceeds of all taxes collected by the State in a year will be transferred to local bodies. Some other taxes like entertainment tax will be handed over to the local government. The three-tier Panchayati Raj Institutions have been empowered to raise taxes, levies and tolls to increase their incomes. An untied grant to Panchayats by sharing of tax and non-tax revenues and the flow of programme funds to the Panchayats has been mandated.

According to the recommendations of the Tenth Finance Commission these elected local bodies would receive ₹ 5381 crore as grant-in-aid to supplement their resources over a four-year period from 1996-97. However, the Eleventh Finance Commission considers this issue that the State Governments may ask for more resources provided that their elected bodies are by then functioning well and are able to plan and implement various development works entrusted to them. Along with financial autonomy, functional autonomy of the Panchayati Raj Institutions also is clearly delineated. Even in respect of the 29 subjects identified in the Eleventh Schedule it is necessary for the State Governments to clearly identify what would be done by the three-tiers of Panchayats at their own level. Detailed instructions and guidelines would have to be issued by the concerned departments. Some States like Gujarat, Maharashtra, Karnataka, Kerala, Tripura, and West Bengal have already been issued the detailed instructions. One major task of the PRIs is the preparation of plans for economic and social development. The district development plans would have to be prepared by the District Planning Committee (DPC) which is mandated. But in many States the DPCs have not been set up. Gram Sabha would be responsible to prioritize and selection of beneficiaries for various programmes and schemes. In this way, the people's participation can be ensured. Thereafter, village level plans will have to be prepared which would be incorporated in the intermediate plans and finally merged into a district plan. The village level Panchayat is responsible to look after the roads, sanitation, drinking water etc. at the village-level. The intermediate level would be responsible for Primary Education, Women and Child Welfare and Employment Generation Activities. At the Zilla Parishad level drinking water, rural roads, secondary education and the district component of employment would be implemented. The DPCs should not only consolidate plans from below but also should take decisions on the development of the district within the available resources.

Panchayati Raj Institutions became the safeguard for the weaker section of our society. The 73rd Constitutional Amendment Act provides for reservation for Scheduled Castes/Scheduled Tribes in every panchayat in the proportion of the population in the panchayat area. On the other side one-third of the seats would have to be reserved for women in every tier of PRIs. In the process of democratic decentralisation, people can be involved through their elected representatives. Gram Sabha is a platform for empowerment of the weaker section of our society and also fulfil their urgent needs. For this, more powers have to be vested in the Gram Sabha who has the authority to sanction and disburse benefits in open meetings. But this is not enough for people's participation at Gram Sabha meetings. Steps have to be taken to ensure that maximum people can attend Gram Sabha meetings and make the PRIs in actual people's institutions.

Concepts and Operational Definitions

Decentralisation: In a single word, Decentralisation is a process where the decision-making dispersed and governance come closer to the people. It is the process of redistributing or dispersing functions, powers, people or things away from a Central location or authority. While decentralisation, especially in the governmental sphere, is widely studied and practiced, there is no common definition or understanding of decentralisation. The meaning of decentralisation may vary in part because in different ways it is applied. Concepts of decentralisation have been applied to group dynamics and management science in private business and organizations, political science, law and public administration, economics and technology (*Wikipedia*). The term 'decentralisation' embraces a variety of concepts which must be carefully analysed in any particular country/ state. As per the definition given by World Bank in 2002, Decentralisation is a process through which authority and responsibilities for some substantial government functions are transferred from Central Government to intermediate and local governments, and often also to communities. In other way, Decentralisation can be usefully understood as a political process whereby administrative authority, public resources and responsibilities are transferred from Central Government agencies to lower-level organs of government or to non-governmental bodies (Craig Johnson, February, 2003). Through decentralised process government has wider range of control, and a bottom-up decision-making from the grassroots people. On the other way it may be said that Decentralisation is the transfer of the locus of power and authority either from upper-level to lower-level or to other units or organizations. This may be political, administrative and fiscal or financial.

Political Decentralisation: Political Decentralisation refers at one level to the extent to which political institutions map the multiplicity of citizen interests onto policy decisions (Inman and Rubinfeld, 1997). Political Decentralisation transfers policy and legislative powers from Central Governments to autonomous, lower-level assemblies and local councils that have been democratically elected by their constituencies (World Bank, 2000). Political decentralisation is also known as democratic decentralisation. The word 'democratic' derived from 'democracy' is considered as one of the best forms of government because it ensures liberty of thought, expression, belief, faith and worship, equality of status and opportunity, fraternity as well as the right to participate in political decision-making. Under political decentralisation people are drawn into decision-making process through empowerment. It signifies transferring of power and responsibilities from Central Government to autonomous and local tiers that have been democratically elected by their constituencies.

Fiscal/Financial Decentralisation: Fiscal decentralisation accords substantial revenue and expenditure authority to intermediate and local governments (World Bank, 2000). Dispersal of financial responsibility is a core component. If local governments and private organizations are to carry out decentralised functions effectively, they must have an adequate level of revenues, either raised locally or transferred from the central government, as well as the authority to make decisions about expenditures. "The establishment of effective and transparent financial management is at the core of any effort to reform the public sector.... To be genuinely supportive of a decentralisation process, the basic characteristics of a system for decentralised financial management should include: (a) transparency of allocation; (b) predictability of the amounts available to local institutions; and (c) local autonomy of decision-making on resource utilization. In contrast with the widespread practice of *ad hoc* grants driven by politics, the allocation of resources should be based on transparent formulas. Also, unlike the typical unpredictability of most central-to-local transfer mechanisms prevailing in developing countries, the process should provide local institutions with an up-front indication of how much money will be available in the next multi-year planning cycle. This makes local strategic planning possible and provides a financial ceiling that makes such planning a meaningful exercise and an opportunity for local communities to take autonomous decisions on the use of limited resources."

Functional Decentralisation: Functional Decentralisation refers to transferring subject specific functions to local tiers. Generally, functional refers to something able to fulfil its purpose or function; decentralisation is no exception (World Bank, 2000). In functional decentralisation, the issues are transfer of functions and inter-tier demarcation of functions in order to enable them to discharge their functional role.

Administrative Decentralisation: Administrative Decentralisation places planning and implementation responsibilities in the hands of locally situated civil servants and these local civil servants are under the jurisdiction of elected local governments (World Bank, 2000). It is the transfer of responsibility for the planning, financing and management of public functions from the Central Government to the local government. The three major forms of administrative decentralisation—deconcentration, delegation, and devolution—each have different characteristics. Administrative decentralisation is concerned with how political institutions, once determined, turn policy decisions into allocative (and distributive) outcomes through both fiscal and regulatory actions. The political decision to devolve powers from Central Government, for example, can only get translated into actual powers being shifted if subnational governments have the fiscal, political, and administrative capacity to manage this responsibility (Litvack, J., Ahmad J., Bird, R., 1999).

Decentralised Governance: "Decentralising governance, from the Centre to regions, districts, local governments/authorities and local communities, can be an effective means of achieving critical objectives of the Sustainable Human Development (SHD) vision—improved access to services and employment, increased people participation in decisions affecting their lives, and enhanced Government responsiveness" (UNDP, 1997). United Nations also stated that "Today, throughout the world there is a broad-based movement towards greater decentralisation. At the same time, however, there is still real debate about whether decentralised governance can be an effective means of achieving the critical objectives of sustainable human development: improved and more equitable public access to services and employment, increased popular participation and enhanced government responsiveness. Consequently, there is an increasingly urgent need to review the structure and processes of local governance in light of the growing recognition that good local governance is a *sine qua non* for improved national governance."

Devolution: According to UNDP, Devolution is "The first type of autonomous lower-level units, such as provincial, district, local authorities that are legally constituted as separate governance bodies. The transfer of authorities to such units is often referred to as devolution and is the most common understanding of genuine decentralisation. Through devolution, the Central Government relinquishes certain functions or creates new units of government that are outside its direct control. Federal states are by definition devolved, though the extent of legally defined and shared powers devolved by the federal government to lower level governmental units can be quite limited. Devolution in its purest form has certain fundamental characteristics. First, local units of government are autonomous, independent and clearly perceived as separate levels of Government over which central authorities exercise little or no direct control. Second, the local governments have clear and legally recognized geographical boundaries within which they exercise authority and perform public functions. Third, local governments have corporate status and the power to secure resources to perform their functions. Fourth, devolution implies the need to "develop local Governments as institutions" in the sense that they are perceived by local citizens as organizations providing services that satisfy their needs and as governmental units over which they have some influence. Finally, devolution is an arrangement in which there are reciprocal, mutually beneficial, and coordinate relationships between Central and local governments. In other words, Devolution is a type of administrative decentralisation. When governments devolve functions, they transfer authority for decision-making, finance, and management to quasi-autonomous units of local government. In a devolved system, local governments have clear and legally recognized geographical boundaries over which they exercise authority and within which they perform public functions. It is this type of administrative decentralisation that underlies most political decentralisation. Devolution is the transfer of power from a large to a smaller jurisdiction. Devolution is an administrative type of decentralisation. When governments devolve functions, they transfer authority for decision-making, finance, and management to quasi-autonomous units of local government with corporate status. Devolution usually transfers responsibilities for services to local governments that elect their own elected functionaries and councils, raise their own revenues, and have independent authority to make investment decisions.

Delegation: As per UNDP delegation is "semi-autonomous lower-level units, such as urban or regional development corporations to whom aspects of governance are delegated through legislation or under contract. This is a fairly common variant of decentralisation that stops short of devolution, but involves significant delegation of authorities and responsibilities. Delegation refers to the transfer of government decision-making and administrative authority and/or responsibility for carefully spelled out tasks to institutions and organizations that are either under government indirect control or semi-independent. Most typically, delegation is by the Central Government to semi-autonomous organizations not wholly controlled by the government but legally accountable to it, such as state owned enterprises and urban or regional development corporations". Delegation is a more extensive form of decentralisation. Through delegation Central Government transfers responsibility for decision-making and administration of public functions to semi-autonomous organizations not wholly controlled by the Central Government, but ultimately accountable to it. Delegation may be vertical or horizontal transfer of limited executive, but not decision-making authority from an administrative service to local government or private companies. Delegation is a more extensive form of decentralisation. Through delegation Central Government transfer responsibility for decision-making and administration to semi-autonomous organizations not wholly controlled by the Central Government, but ultimately accountable to it. Governments delegate responsibilities when they create public enterprises or corporations, housing authorities, transportation authorities, special service districts, semi-autonomous school districts, regional development corporations, or special project implementation units.

De-concentration: As per UNDP, "the third type is sub-ordinate lower-level units or sub-units, such as regional, district or local offices of the Central Administration or service delivery organization. These units usually have delegated authority in policy, financial and administrative matters without any significant independent local inputs. This type of arrangement is most often referred to as deconcentration and involves very limited transfer of authority. It involves the transfer of authority for specific decision-making, financial and management functions by administrative means to different levels under the same jurisdictional authority of the Central Government. This is the least extensive type of administrative decentralisation and the most commonly found in developing countries." De-concentration—which is often considered to be the weakest form of decentralisation and is used most frequently in unitary states-redistributes decision-making authority and financial and management responsibilities among different levels of the Central Government. De-concentration or administrative decentralisation is the vertical decentralisation of the power to Act, but not to decide or ultimately control within the administrative or technical institute. This is regarded as the weakest form of decentralisation. It redistributes decision-making authority and financial and management responsibilities among different levels of the National Government. It can merely shift responsibilities from Central Government officials to the local officials, or it can create strong field administration or local administrative capacity under the supervision of Central Administration.

Deregulation: Deregulation is the lifting or regulations previously imposed by a public authority. Deregulation reduces the legal constraints on private participation in service provision or allows competition among private suppliers for services that in the past had been provided by the government or by regulated monopolies. In recent years privatization and deregulation have become more attractive alternatives to governments in developing countries. Local governments are also privatizing by contracting out service provision or administration.

Divestment or Privatization: According to UNDP, Divestment or Privatization "refers to units external to the formal governmental structure (non-governmental or private), such as NGOs, corporations and companies. While sometimes included in discussions of decentralisation, the nature of these transfers is not level-specific, i.e. transfers could occur at the same level, which is often the central one. These phenomena are best not treated as forms of decentralisation, but of divestment. Divestment occurs when planning and administrative responsibility or other public functions are transferred from government to voluntary, private, or non-governmental institutions. In some cases, governments may transfer to "parallel organizations" such as national industrial and trade associations, professional or ecclesiastical organizations, political parties, or cooperatives—the right to license, regulate or supervise their members in performing functions that were previously controlled by the government. In other cases, governments may shift responsibility for producing goods or supplying services to private organizations, a process often called privatization". So, Privatization is the transfer of the ownership and/or management of resources, and/or the transfer of the provision and production of goods and services, from the public sector to private entities (commercial or non-profit). Privatization can range in scope from leaving the

Table 2.2: Level of Decentralisation

Type of Unit to which Authority is Transferred	*Aspect of Governance Transferred or Shared*			*Generic Name*
	Political (policy or decision-making)	*Economic or financial resource management*	*Administration and service delivery*	
Autonomous lower-level units	Devolution	Devolution	Devolution	Devolution
Semi-autonomous lower-level units	Delegation	Delegation	Delegation	Delegation
Sub-ordinate lower-level units or sub-units	Directing	Allocating	Tasking	Deconcentration
External (non-Governmental) units at any level	Deregulation	Privatization	Contracting	Divestment

Source: UNDP, Decentralised Governance Programme: Strengthening Capacity for People-Centred Development, Management Development and Governance Division, Bureau for Development Policy, September 1997.

provision of goods and services entirely to the free operation of the market to "public-private partnerships" in which government and the private sector cooperate to provide services or infrastructure. Privatization cannot in the real sense be considered equivalent to decentralisation.

Top Down and Bottom-up Approach: Top-down planning approaches describes the conventional procedure of systematic surveys on the basic of which plans are devised centrally and worked out in detail by professional staffs to meet goals that are also decided centrally. Implementation is again typically the responsibilities of line ministries or other government agencies. Bottom-up planning approaches describe that type of planning which is initiated locally and processed through the active participation of the community. The pooled experience and local knowledge of the land users and local technical staff are mobilized to identify the development project on priority basis, then draw up the plans and implement them.

People's Participation: According to UNDP (1993), "Participation means the people are closely involved in economic, social, cultural and political processes that affect their lives." Therefore, participation is a process by which the beneficiaries influence the direction and execution of a development programme to enhance prosperity in terms of income, personal growth, self-reliance or other values that they cherish.

'Participation' is one of those words that can be interpreted in many different ways—it can mean finding something out and proceeding as originally planned; it can mean developing processes of collective learning that change the way that people think and act. The many ways that organizations interpret and use the term participation can be resolved into six distinct types. These range from passive participation, where people are told what is to happen and act out predetermined roles, to self-mobilization, where people take initiatives largely independent of external institutions.

Good Governance: The term 'governance' was first used in France in the 14th Century where it meant "a set of Government". Governance is "the process of decision-making and the process by which decisions are implemented (or not implemented)". The World Bank reinvented it, in different context, as "a new approach to development". The concept of "Good Governance" was formulated

Table 2.3: A Typology of Participation

Typology	*Characteristics of Each Type*
Passive Participation	People participate by being told what has been decided or has already happened. Information being shared belongs only to external professionals.
Participation by Consultation	People participate by being consulted or by answering questions. Process does not concede any share in decision-making, and professionals are under no obligation to take on board people's views.
Bought Participation	People participate in return for food, cash or other material incentives. Local people have no stake in prolonging technologies or practices when the incentives end.
Functional Participation	Participation seen by external agencies as a means to achieve their goals, especially reduced costs. People participate by forming groups to meet predetermined objectives.
Interactive Participation	People participate in joint analysis, development of action plans and formation or strengthening of local groups or institutions. Learning methodologies used to seek multiple perspectives, and groups determine how available resources are used.
Self-Mobilization and connectedness	People participate by taking initiatives independently to change systems. They develop contacts with external institutions for resources and technical advice they need, but retain control over how resources are used.

Source: UNDP, 1993.

by World Bank (1992) as the "Manner in which power is exercised in the management of a country's economic and social resources for development". Good governance, in modern democracy, means democratization of governance. In participatory democracy people elect their leaders to govern them. But governance is not the monopoly of elected leaders. Good governance is characterized by transparency and accountability. People are biggest stakeholder in governance; they have a critical and crucial role to play. So, it is imperative that people must have the right to know about the activities of the government. Good governance aims at enhancing the "quality of life" and involves governing process which strives for maximum good for the maximum number of people.

The issue of good governance in Panchayat administration is gradually emerging as a key issue in the sphere of rural development, because failure in the rural governing system will result into spread of corruption, inadequate availability of basic services for the rural poor, and failure in tackling rural poverty. On the other hand, good governance will minimise corruption, the views of minorities will be taken into account, the voices of the most vulnerable in society will be heard in decision-making, and the rural administration will be responsive to the present and future need of the rural population. So, the need of rural good governance lies at the heart of rural decentralisation process. Panchayat, being nearer to the people it serves, has every potential to act as a model administrative unit of rural good governance. In the process of government functioning, e-governance is the application of ICT for good governance and to bring 'SMART' governance (Simple, Moral, Accountable, Responsive and Transparent).

Fig. 2.1: The Basic Characteristics of Good Governance

Source: Annual Administrative Report 2008-09. WB: P&RD Department, GoWB.

Theories of Decentralisation

Decentralisation is not unique in India, but a global trend. Most developing countries are embracing decentralisation whether in Latin America, Europe or East Asia. Decentralisation is a world-wide phenomenon for at least two reasons: (a) need for political stability—decentralisation means a dispersion of formal political power to elected local-level politicians. This dispersion of power is a global trend (*Source*: World Development Report 1999-2000). Political scientists suggest that this is an outcome of the declining credibility of the centralized state. Groups and jurisdictions that have historically been denied power now demands it, and governments are increasingly reluctant to oppose this demand with force. In a fundamental sense, decentralisation is a strategy to maintain political stability; and (b) more effective and efficient service delivery (Oates, 1972). There are many theories which advocate decentralisation for development of more efficient and effective rural governance system. Among those major theories are: (i) Fiscal Federalism, (ii) Neo-Classical Economic Theories of Public Choice, (iii) Public Administration and Public Finance, (iv) Political Economy, and (v) Social Capital.

(i) Fiscal Federalism

Fiscal federalism refers to the structure of financial and broader relationships between central and subordinate levels of government. The process of altering the structure of fiscal federalism by devolving powers to lower levels of government is generally known as fiscal decentralisation. The history of fiscal federalism in modern India goes back to the Government of India Acts of 1919 and 1935. While the Act of 1919 provided for a separation of revenue heads between the Centre and the provinces, the 1935 Act allowed for the sharing of Centre's revenues and for the provision of grants-in-aid to provinces. It was assumed that federalism is supposed to bring about political and fiscal decentralisation to realize administrative and economic efficiency in the delivery of public goods. So, optimal allocation of powers and responsibilities amongst governments at various levels in a federation is very significant and ever relevant. As a subfield of public economics, fiscal federalism is concerned with "understanding which functions and instruments are best centralized and which are best placed in the sphere of decentralised levels of government"

(Oates, 1999). In other words, it is the theory of how competencies (expenditure side) and fiscal instruments (revenue side) are allocated across different (vertical) layers of the administration. An important part of its subject matter is the system of transfer payments or grants by which a Central Government shares its revenues with lower levels of Government. Fiscal federal approach spells out that local level planning system provides cost effective public services, because it considers local preferences more carefully than the Central Government (Oates, 1972).

Fiscal federalism in India unlike in many rich countries has to satisfy the competing demands to deliver a number of essential and basic socio-economic services. As a paramount objective, fiscal federalism is expected to enable the national and sub-national governments to operate in such a way that leads to efficiency in the use of resources—not only in terms of the quality of services provided by the various levels of government but also in terms of creating the environment in which all economic agents use resources efficiently (Rangarajan, 2004). It analyses the system of sharing tax revenues and public expenditure commitments between central and subnational governments. Under decentralised fiscal system, the local jurisdiction collects all taxes from various local sources and according to these collections, it undertakes developmental programmes for the people (Rao, 2002). It also shares tax revenues and public expenditure between richer areas and poorer areas. Although, there has been drawback that it makes macro-economic policies more difficult. The analysis of fiscal federalism is used only to understand the system of sharing tax revenues and the commitment of public expenditure between Central and Sub-national Governments (Prud'home, 1995). But recently this approach is facing a new challenge due to changing political scenario. It is clear that political environment is important in determining contours of fiscal federalism. After Independence, there was a single and same party rule at the Centre and in almost all States for many decades. There are now telltale signs that India is moving away from an era of cooperative federalism towards competitive federalism, due to multi-party polity, and predominance of regional parties at the State-level, and coalition Governments at the Centre. The existence of competition brings-in the importance of transaction cost of coordinating policies and their implementation: (a) vertically between different levels of Government, and (b) horizontally between different units within each of the levels. Many challenges, therefore, lie ahead for fiscal federalism in the country.

(ii) Neo-Classical Economic Theories of Public Choice

Public choice theory can be useful in analyzing the benefits and costs of decentralising the provision of some public services, especially those for which user charges can be levied or for which criteria of exclusion can be developed. It also can be helpful in determining the feasibility of deregulation and privatization and in changing the rules for renewable natural resource use (Nicholson, 1981). Public choice theory is a branch of economics that developed from the study of taxation and public spending. It was developed by James Buchanan and Gordon Tullock to explain how public decisions are made. It involves the interaction of the voting public, the politicians, the bureaucracy and political action committees. As James Buchanan artfully defined it, public choice is "politics without romance". The wishful thinking it displaced presumes that participants in the political sphere aspire to promote the common good. In the conventional "public interest" view, public officials are portrayed as benevolent "public servants" who faithfully carry out the "will of the people". In tending to the public's business, voters, politicians, and policy-makers are supposed somehow to rise above their own parochial concerns. Public choice takes the same principles that economists use to analyze people's actions in the market place and applies them to people's actions in collective decision-making. In other words, public choice is an application of neo-classical economic tools (self-interest and utility maximization) to explain political behaviour.

Public Choice theory assumes that the voter is a customer and the politician is a businessman. Public Choice school holds the view that the people are aware of their needs, and therefore, people's involvement in planning and implementing will be more effective and efficient (Russel and Nicholson, 1981; Mueller, 1989). Hence, the theory proposes to allow them to make choices about services, taxes and other policies. Again, the problem is that the public choice theorist is not much concerned with improving the capacity of government institutions for facilitating effective services which may not be achieved by market mechanism. Public choice approach can be useful in understanding the nature of goods and services. It analyses the cost and benefits of decentralisation. The main limitation of public choice approach is that it is too much rationalistic and suggests narrow prescriptions (Oppenheimer, 1981). Further, rational voters do not vote, and that when rational candidates compete for the votes of rational voters, there is no equilibrium outcome (Ledyard, 1984). This is because the behaviour of people is different from one another. The prediction of rational behaviour always may not be authentic.

The main limitations of public choice theories are their overly rationalistic assumptions and narrow prescriptions (Oppenheimer, 1981). There are strong disagreements among proponents of public choice theory about definitions of concepts and terms (Ostrom, 1986); assumptions and conditions (Baker, 1976); the ability to test theoretical constructs (Moe, 1984) and whether the discipline is sufficiently advanced to allow for empirical testing in developing countries (Hite, 1984). The disagreements are particularly strong over whether or not public choice theories can be used in institutional analyses. Ostrom (1986) points out that "little agreement exists on what the term 'institution' means, whether the study of institutions is an appropriate endeavour, and how to undertake a cumulative study of institutions".

(iii) Public Administration and Public Finance (Maddick, 1963; Leonard and Marshall, 1982; Cheema and Rondinelli, 1983; Conyers, 1983)

Policy analysts using public administration and finance theories take a different perspective on decentralisation than neoclassical economists using public choice theories. As discussed in the "Decentralisation and local autonomy for participatory democracy", presented at the 6th Global Forum on Reinventing Government towards Participatory and Transparent Governance, Professor James Katorobo thought that "decentralisation involves the transfer of political, administrative and fiscal authority from the Central Government to the authorities and the sub-national governments". The significance of public administration and public finance lies in the fact that it provides better services to local people according to their needs (Conyers, 1983:99; Cheema and Rondinelli, 1983; Leonard and Marshel, 1982; Maddik, 1963).

Public finance is the study of the role of the government in the economy (Gruber, Jonathan, 2005). It is the definitive branch of Economics which assesses the government revenue and government expenditure of the Public Authorities and the adjustment of one or the other to achieve desirable effects and avoid undesirable ones (Jain, P.C., 1974). Collection of sufficient resources from the economy in an appropriate manner along with allocating and use of these resources efficiently and effectively constitute good financial management. Resource generation, resource allocation and expenditure management (resource utilization) are the essential components of a public financial management system. The public finance focused heavily on identifying the sources of local government revenue, assessing the equity and strength of these revenue sources, dependence of local government on Central Government transfers, revenue generation and financial management, and examining mechanisms to stimulate greater local resource mobilization.

While, 'Public Administration' is concerned with the implementation of government policy, and is an academic discipline that studies this implementation and prepares civil servants for working in the public service (*Wikipedia*). In the realm of public administration there is a renewed interest in decentralisation. It is called 'New Development Administration'. It aims at ensuring and institutionalizing people's participation through the process of decentralisation. Decentralisation in public administration is the basis for solving problems which is not done by officials appointed by the Centre, but by those elected by the electoral body. More specifically, in the decentralised administrative system, the administration of the interests of local administration is conducted by freely elected authorities from and by the mass of citizens of that community, which have, according to constitutional rules, their financial and autonomous decision-making power. In the case of decentralisation, the state does not assume the burden of administration alone, but splits it in certain levels, with other categories of persons such as local communities. According to legal provisions (Art. 2 letter 1 from the framework Law on Decentralisation 195/2006), decentralisation is the transfer of administrative and financial powers from the Central Government to the local government or private sector required to meet local interests.

The public finance theorists have not dealt with the issues like improving resource utilization, performance of voluntary organizations or private firms etc. The public finances and public administration approach is concerned mainly with macro-economic issues. It analyses organizational arrangements and financial instruments.

(iv) Political Economy

Neither approach mentioned above alone offers a comprehensive theoretical or methodological solution to determining how decentralisation should be carried out, but both can contribute important concepts and guidelines for designing and implementing decentralisation policies. While an integrated political economy framework of decentralisation can draw a clear picture on the useful concept and identifies the factors that should be considered by policy analysts because of its components which include the analysis of: (a) local goods and services and their users; (b) alternative financial and organizational means of providing services; (c) feasible institutional arrangements for service delivery; (d) socio-economic and political conditions affecting the design of policy and the implementation of programmes; and (v) feasible policy interventions and instruments that can provide guidance for policy formulation project and programme design, financial and technical assistance and programme evaluation.

For the past few decades, experiments in decentralisation and federalization have been developing in India. Many of the powers previously in the hands of the Central Government or its de-concentrated structures have been transfered to lower government layers. Additionally, local governments are gradually emerging as development actors. Whatever, the reasons for decentralisation, the transfer of new functions to local governments can be substantive, at least in intent. The Political Economy of Decentralisation in India offers a new policy-oriented implementation model.

It is a greater model theory, which has experienced that institutional and financial arrangements have an impact on the cost efficiency of delivery of services (Rondinelli, *et al.*, 1989). It includes significant factors like political, administrative, financial, social, organizational, local resources, technical assistance and so on. In decision-making process political conditions (creative and systematic thinking of leaders and political stability) are considered very significant which affect the implementation of decentralised governance. Political economy implies that useful relationships among the interest groups are necessary for policy-making and implementation. Even in non-democratic countries decisions are made not only by rational calculation but also by political bargaining and negotiation (Rondenelli, *et al.*, 1989). The most common political rationale for decentralised governance is that it is assumed as good governance which is very much closer to the people (Inman and Rubinfeld, 1997; World Bank, 1997). It accommodates pressure of regional autonomy, and sustains heterogeneous society. The economic rationale for decentralised governance is to improve the 'competitiveness' of governments by satisfying the wishes of citizens and cost efficiency in delivery services (Breton, 1996; Salmon, 1987). Nevertheless, it is not very clear whether political economy can identify local needs and satisfy people in a society where society is based on a certain hierarchy. Again, there is debate as to whether politics and economics will go together or economy will go simply.

(v) Social Capital

All the above discussed theories are generally based on macro-level study. These theories have not only explained phenomenon but also have not identified the causal mechanisms and processes of grassroots-level institutions or decentralised governance. Perhaps, they have identified the perspective of decentralisation in a macro-level not in a micro-level. Decentralisation is a process of development which performs better in a certain socio-political matrix. It has been also argued that any single element of democracy is not sufficient to ensure local government's responsiveness to people's needs and wants (World Bank, 2000).

Keeping this in the view, recently, the theory of social capital has been receiving increasing academic attention from all the social science disciplines, and it has begun to generate a remarkable consensus regarding the role and importance of social organization in effective and efficient decentralised governance and development. Social capital is conceived as a bilateral and multilateral relationship between neighbours, and a third person or an actor (organization) which binds both the person and actor to meet the level of satisfaction of various dimensions of human needs. It is understood in two dimensions, i.e. trust (cognitive) and network (structural or institutional). Trust is understood as a spontaneous relational tie between different actors in society, and network as a channel of relationships between different actors involved in different actions. These two together ensure better coordination and reciprocity such that outcome is the optimal.

Putnam (1993) establishes social capital as a critical contribution to the development field by drawing on the broader evaluation of institutional performance across Italy's 20 regions. Putnam (1993) describes social capital as a feature of social organization, such as trust norms, and networks, that can improve the efficiency of society by facilitating coordinated actions. His views on social capital as a set of "horizontal association" among people who have an effect on the productivity of the community. Here, norms and networks are empirically associated and they have important economic consequences. So, the main argument of social capital is that it facilitates cooperation and coordination for the mutual benefit of the members of association. He refers to how the rotating credit association is more a simple economic institution, and is a mechanism strengthening the overall solidarity. These associations are groups of friends and neighbours who typically meet monthly, each person contributing to a central fund which is then given to one of the members until each of the members received the amount. These associations become important aid institutions for economic development. Trust and network are playing here a crucial role to overcome the dilemma of collective action. Putnam emphasizes, therefore, that trust and network (horizontal association or self-help groups) could produce effective decentralised governance.

However, some scholars have expressed their doubts about the effect of social capital. It has been argued that it is not always a successful universalistic outcome, it may produce negative effects for different purposes (Woolcock and Narayan, 2000; Furstenberg and Hughes, 1995:589). Of late, Harriss (2002) has published a meticulous critique of Putnam's work on social capital. Harriss's explication is that social capital is an anti-politics machine. This may be because of the World Bank's special attention to social capital which made social capital a momentous discourse.

Apart from this, Harriss puts forth several arguments on this issue. He believes that redistribution of resources may have a significant part to play both in facilitating local organization as well as assisting political and economic development which Putnam totally appears to have ignored. An example, from his work in West Bengal where redistribution of resources has been undertaken fits in well here. Harriss reveals that the successful socio-economic change which was observed in 1980s in West Bengal was not the only effect of the agrarian reform programmes of the Left Front Government, but also many related issues such as commitment (political), coordination and cooperation between poor people, landowner and local institutions, and particularly mass movement of grassroots people (1993). This justifies the importance of local organizations (self-help groups) or institutions (Gram Panchayats) and the people (landless, labour and sharecropper and marginal and middle class peasant, and middle class intellectual). It shows that politics can only be a means but not an end. Similarly, Bhattacharyya (1998) from his empirical study argues that social capital ensures effective governance performance.

Further, Heller (1996) argues that the 'synergy' of the state and the class mobilization in Kerala has produced two forms of social capital: Redistribution and class coordination which result in turn Kerala's successful development. Heller gives an incompatible picture whether civic engagement is responsible for Kerala's development or political redistribution. If redistribution and class base politics have become an important factor in Kerala's case, as argued by Heller then it may ignore the truth of the civic tradition of nineteenth century in Kerala which played a crucial role for socio-economic changes in Kerala. It is, therefore, the institutional value that should come forth in development at grassroots-level (Islam, 2003).

Therefore, social capital can be a useful theory to analyze processes of effective decentralised governance. It is practicable because social capital not only brings back many of the theoretical insights from the classics like Marx, Weber, Durkheim, and Simmel but also make sense to link the micro with the macro level in social and political analysis (Blomkvist and Swain, 2001). It may help policy-makers to explain social phenomenon in coherent and systematic form, which is more important before finalizing any policy for grassroots-level. Social capital may also promote development at grassroots level very fast. It is not merely a demand for institution building, but also a reality to building "pro-poor institution" to reach the poor more effectively.

Decentralisation Governance: Evolution of the Concept

First Generation Strategies—Genesis: Decentralisation emerged as the concept of devolution of power to the people when there was no adult franchise in the Western world. The British system of local government found in South Asia, Africa, Australia and North America which conceptualized as a devolved local self-government with characteristics of a representative elected council and citizens' participation. Whereas in Europe, North and West Africa and South America, decentralisation has been distinguished by deconcentration, executive dominance and rigid hierarchy. Decentralisation is conceptualized as a deconcentrated administrative organ for relieving administrative congregation, since over-centralized governance did not have a way to find out what needs to be done for different places, and what needs and desires of the people are to be met. From this close association with the people of a particular area arose a detailed understanding not only of their needs, but also of the long-term potentialities of that area. The planning of this potential development can be carried out in far greater detail and with a great deal of understanding by the people of the area who are particularly and primarily concerned with its welfare.

Second Generation Strategies—Middle Era: In 1962, one UN study phrased the problem. Decentralisation of government relieves members of the legislature and of the national executive from involvement in many purely local issues, frees key officials from onerous and detailed tasks and increases the speed and effectiveness of the administration at all levels; decentralisation is especially important in developing countries where rapid expansion of public services greatly increases the number of government transactions and consequently the hindrances and wasted efforts resulting from over-centralization of controls' (UN, 1962).

Nevertheless, with time and population growth, the State increasingly faced varied problems like widespread unemployment, poverty, and disease, leaving the administration crippled and ineffective because of its inherent maladies. From this backdrop, the scholars of classical public administration looked for answers to questions, how can administration offer effectiveness, cost efficiency and equity in the delivery of services. Also, they began to find out the ways and means of re-orienting traditional public administration to be relevant to its time. This new thinking was called New Public Administration as it sought "to enhance change and change for increasing social equity" which would augment its objectives relevance, topicality, good management, efficiency, economy, cultivation of virtues, and promotion of social equity. The New Public Administration in its search for a changeable structure tends, therefore, to modify centralized administration or bureaucratic organizational form with decentralisation, devolution, projects, contracts, sensitivity training, reorganization, confrontation, and client involvement. Contemporarily, the literature on New Development Administration talks about ensuring and institutionalizing people's participation through the process of decentralisation. Decentralisation, thus, results in political elasticity by means of devolution: legal establishment of locally elected political authorities and deconcentration: transfer of allocative and implementable decisions to local authorities. This new avatar of Development Administration was based on the experiences of such welfare-oriented governments whose development strategies failed miserably. These experiences were, first, due to the governments' limited capabilities, and therefore, people and civil society should be brought in as alternative and complementary institutions/mechanisms for augmenting development processes. Secondly, ecological considerations are vital, when formulating development strategies. Finally, popular participation must be politically sanctioned to ensure allocative and implementable decision-making.

Therefore, New Development Administration as a decentralisation mechanism implies giving every citizen an opportunity to actively participate in constructive public work, besides the franchise in a democracy. It also refers to participation in specific action by which the citizen registers her/his involvement in public affairs to achieve a particular objective. In its initial stage, the reinvented concept of decentralisation was most significant for activating a variety of development functions, ranging from peoples' involvement to better management of grassroots development. The trends, which dominated the thinking and the application aspects, were very crucial at this stage, as these act as the guiding posts for the concerted development of the idea of 'Decentralised Governance'. The trends were first, 'top down' to 'bottom-up' approach in development. Second, for encouraging and ensuring stakeholders' participation in development process and finally, institutionalizing 'self-reliance' in development strategies.

Third Generation Strategies—Modern Way: In this modern era of the 'administrative state', many writers have voiced concern over the problem of responsiveness of the administrative state to the norms of democratic procedures. To safeguard individual liberties against bureaucratic or arbitrary abuse, an increase in people's vigilance and participation in politics is necessary. Modern states consider assigning each person's needs equal weight in policy deliberations in an effort to make as broad as feasible the opportunities for people to participate in the decisions that affect them (Sharkansky, 1991).

Political scientists unanimously agree on the fact that the main utility of extensive public participation in politics is to ensure that the stakes of the privileged do not prevail over the interests of the majority. To guard against such possibilities, adequate measures of public accountability and ventilation of public grievances should exist besides avenues of citizens' participation in governance. By decentralising, the state apparatus opens new channels for popular participation inside the political system. The idea of decentralisation is closely identified with the creation of democratic units as well as effective and efficient administrative structures at the grassroots levels (Haque, 1997; Schonwalder, 1997; Smith, 1985; Friedman, 1983). Moreover, the contemporary 'communitarian' concerns are also similar. There is an increasing demand to bring in people and local communities for more participatory and direct action-oriented democracy. Communitarians believe that under the New World order of market individualism, social and political power is concentrated even more in those in command of material wealth. What lies at the heart of the communitarian objection to market individualism is the latter's alleged cancerous effect on community life. Human beings who are in control of more economic resources than others are able to set the agenda for everyone from a privileged bargaining position. They can make substantial private 'donations' to those in the government; they can distort public opinion by buying control of the media; they can subdue all those who are dependent on the employment, investment or purchases they offer, by threatening to withdraw them. Selfishness becomes a moral creed. Individuals are encouraged at every turn to put their own interests first, and to demand the freedom to make their own choices regardless of the implications for the civic order.

In order to provide an alternative to individualism and authoritarianism, communitarianism sets out the way in which social and political practices are to be reformed in relation to their attributions to the development of sustainable forms of community life. Such life is fundamentally based upon reformed power relations at every level in society so that all those affected by them can participate as equal citizens in determining how the power in question is to be exercised. This means that questions about the collective action are to be taken for the common good are considered through informed community discussions and are not to be left to the political elite, who are rarely answerable to their fellow citizens (Tam, 1998).

Recently, a new rhetoric has also found ground and that is "Good Governance". Different scholars look at good governance differently but in general, good governance means that which ensures people's participation, enhances accountability and transparency for effectiveness, efficiency, equity, and capacity building. Decentralisation has become a mechanism through which public goods and services can be distributed effectively and efficiently. In its heyday, many schools observed that decentralisation could reduce the disparities in income and wealth between urban and rural areas and increase productivity and income. Decentralisation is thus a process, which allows peoples' involvement in administration and development programmes. Decentralisation is an instrument to reduce costs, improve outputs, and more effectively utilize human resources to improve efficiency with which demands are locally met. It remains significant for the realization of people-centred development and therefore, decentralisation is a strategy for enjoying equal rights with the majority population and it is an ability to build the capacity for economic development.

Decentralised Planning

Decentralised planning is defined as that from of planning where the task of formulating, adopting, executing and supervising the plan is placed not only a Central authority but also on different planning authority of appropriate levels. In this method of planning local bodies are given greater freedom to formulate and implement the plan. Planning in India is decentralised. Here planning is done at Central, State, district, block and Panchayat-level. Decentralisation of planning process makes planning more meaningful. Because in this process, local bodies make plans as per their needs. Functions are also performed at appropriate level with greater efficiency.

According to S.N. Jha (1999) "Decentralised planning refers specifically to the involvement of institutions below the state-level, necessitated both by administrative developmental exigencies and the constitutional status of local institutions after the 1992 Amendments." The process of national planning was centralized planning process since 1950s. The bureaucratic plan implementation practice becomes failure due to lack of people's participation in the planning and implementation process. The 73rd Constitutional Amendment provides power, authority and responsibility to Panchayati Raj Institutions to prepare plan and execute those plans at local level by ensuring people's participation.

Decentralisation of planning process would be fruitful and effective only when the levels of planning will have clear idea about their functions. One of the important steps in decentralised planning is to divide clearly and precisely the local planning functions among various area levels where they can be performed most efficiently.

Decentralisation will have no meaning, if adequate power and responsibilities have been distributed to different levels. Without devolution of adequate power at different level the planning authority will not be able to perform their functions properly.

Participatory Planning

Participatory planning refers to the process by which the hitherto passive recipients of development become actors and governmental departments and their agents both acting in coordination to identify felt needs and prioritize them as per the resources that can be mobilized through a social and political acceptable form of negotiation through the intermediate and supervision of elected local government. In order to satisfy the cannons of development planning there has to be infusion of professionalism preferably in a spirit of voluntarism so that people's idea and expert opinion can blend seamlessly. And to ensure realism and definiteness, planning has to be against a budget revealed in advance fairly allocated and eked by local resource mobilization. In such a scenario participatory planning becomes participatory budgeting (S.M. Vijayanand, 2005).

In order to ensure that national and regional objectives of development get harmonized with local-level needs and aspirations a framework is needed for participatory planning without being restrictive. And to channel the enthusiasm and energies of people into a proper development oriented action a process is required. Finally, to make the whole exercise, legally and administratively valid, the existing rules and regulations have to be suitably restructured to enable participation.

Participatory Planning and Decentralisation

Participatory Planning, as an entry point to decentralisation, has several advantages. It includes:

- (i) Participatory planning is relevant to all local governments, developed and under-developed, urban and rural, big and small entities.
- (ii) Participatory planning facilitates the involvement of different sections each having different development interests and expectations; it affords opportunities for activists, volunteers and professionals to contribute to reconciling the different interests into a development agenda, in partnership with elected representatives and government officials.
- (iii) Participatory local level planning throws up local solutions to difficult development problems unfettered by technological, institutional or ideological fixations.
- (iv) It motivates people to back-up their participation with contribution in cash, kind or labour, to stretch out public resources to match the requirements as per local priorities.
- (v) Participatory planning implies local data collection and analysis facilitated by experts—this is a good base for reflection and development action, leading ultimately to empowerment.
- (vi) It facilitates social accountability through enhanced information flow as well as awareness of deeper developmental issues.
- (vii) Participatory planning generates the desire for developmental learning, affording entry to concepts like gender, social justice, environmental sustainability, mainstreaming the challenged, and so on.

Participatory planning is only a beginning. If properly managed, it can lead on to a demand-led improvement of service delivery and further to responsible and responsive local governments.

Participatory Planning and Budgeting Process

West Bengal has succeeded in providing a practical methodology for participatory planning which attempts to balance the need for participation with the requirements of rational planning. Important steps of this methodology are outlined below:

Step 1 — Every year Gram Panchayat (GP) convey annual Gram Sansad (GS) meeting in May at each GP constituencies.

Step 2 — Every GS or elector has power to review previous year plan implantation, why the previous financial year not implemented the all annual plans. Therefore, GP officials discussed about the present condition of the area or GS. Then the elector or GS members create the demand for critical gaps, for next financial year.

Step 3 — All GS meeting resolution are being collected at GP level in the month of July.

Step 4 — In this regard all plans are divided into the five *Upo-Samitis*. Then the *Artho O Parikalpana Upo-Samiti* called a meeting for fund devolution. After that every *Upo-Samiti* presents their plan for budgeting.

Step 5 — All *Upo-Samiti* priorities the own plan and they go through. The Environment and Social Management Framework (ESMF) and Vulnerable Group Development Framework (VGDF) and then approved their draft plan and budget for next year with support of the majority of members in September.

Step 6 — That approved draft plan and budget submitted to General Body to approve and then provide notice of 15 days in the major public places to get opinion for selecting the approved plan. On the other hand those approved plan and budget must be submitted to Panchayat Samiti within first week of November for any recommendation and clarification.

Step 7 — Then GP called half-yearly GS meeting and discussed elaborately for pre-approved final budget and plan and explain the cause of sanctioning those plans in that meeting within November.

Step 8 — In the month of December GP called Gram Sabha meeting to explain the next year plan and budget to mitigate the problems that have been selected by the voter or *Sansad* in each and every *Gram Sansad*. If there is no correction and adjoint plan and budget then those plan and budget will be submitted to General Body.

Step 9 — Before 31st January, GP, called a meeting to approve final plan and budget for the next financial year with the agreement of the majority of members (The quorum of the meeting will be 50 per cent of the GP members).

Step 10 —After final approval of the plan and budget, GP will send that plan and budget to Panchayat Samiti and nearest Bank before 15th February for their intimation.

A Budget is a quantitative expression of a plan for a defined period of time. It may include planned sales volumes and revenues, resources, costs and expenses, assets, liabilities and cash flows. It expresses strategic plans of institutions, organisations, activities or events in measurable terms. A Budget is a quantified financial plan for a forthcoming accounting period.

Budget of the Gram Panchayat: Under Section 48 of the West Bengal Panchayat Act, 1973:

(1) Every Gram Panchayat shall, at such time and in such manner as prescribed, prepare in each year a budget of its estimated receipt and disbursements for the following year.

(2) (a) The budget prepare under sub-section (1) shall be written in vernacular of the district or the locality concerned and copies of the budget shall be pasted in such prominent places within the Gram Panchayat as may be prescribed, inviting objections and suggestions by the members of the Gram Sabha.

(b) Copies of the budget shall be forwarded to the Panchayat Samiti having jurisdiction over the Gram for its views, if any.

(c) The budget with objections, suggestions and views, if any, received from various quarters shall, within such period, as may be prescribed, be placed in the meeting of the Gram Sabha for discussions proposing modification, if any, of the budget.

(d) The Gram Panchayat shall, within such time as may be prescribed and in a meeting specially convened for the purpose and in the presence of at least half of the existing members, consider the objections, suggestions, and views, if any, and the discussions in the meeting of the Gram Sabha, and approve the budget with modifications, if any.

(e) A copy of the budget approved under clause (d) shall be forwarded to the Panchayat Samiti having jurisdiction.

(3) No expenditure shall be incurred unless the budget is approved [under clause (d) of sub-section (2)].
(*Source*: West Bengal Panchayat Act, 1973; Section 48).

Concept of Self-Help Group (SHG)

The concept of Self-Help Groups (SHGs) had its origin in the co-operative philosophy and the co-operators by and large, including the National Federations in the credit sector, could not think of any better than a primary co-operative credit society itself. Today, the Self-Help Group (SHG) movement is increasingly accepted as an innovation in the field of rural credit in many developing countries including India to help the rural poor considered a vehicle to reach the disadvantaged and marginalized section, which in the normal course cannot avail of credit facility from the bank. A Self-Help Group is defined as a "self-governed, peer controlled information group of people with similar socio-economic background and having a desire to collectively perform common purpose. In other way, a Self-Help Group is defined as a group consisting of people who have personal experience of a similar issue or life situation, either directly or through their family and friends. Sharing experiences enable them to give each other a unique quality of mutual support and to pool practical information and ways of coping.

The concept of SHG services the principle, "by the women, of the women and for the women". Self-help groups are voluntary associations of people with common interests formed to achieve collective social and economic goals. Such groups are organized for mutual help and benefit. It is formed democratically without any political affiliation. They may comprise 15-20 women and/or men, although they generally consist exclusively of women members. In India, more than 90 per cent groups are formed by women is done at micro or macro group level. The initial operations of SHGs start with collecting savings from members. These groups inculcate the habit of thrift among the members. By collecting small savings huge amount can be raised. These groups advance loans to the needy members. The total funds owned by the group are thus circulated in the form of loan among the members. The identification, formation, and nurturing of groups is carried out by NGOs, other development agencies or banks with the promoters inculcating habit of thrift among members. Once the groups are trained and strengthened, they are linked to nearby banks, usually within six months of formation. Banks provide collateral-free credit in increasing proportion to the group's accumulated savings. All the initiatives such as selection of borrowers for availing credit, identification of activity, unit cost volume of loan, management of finance and procedures for repayment are undertaken by the poor at the group-level. Briefly, SHGs can be stated "as a plan by the people, of the people for the people". It reflects the real people's participation in the process of development at micro-level.

Objective of Self-Help Groups (SHGs)

SHGs are novel and innovative organizational set-up in India for the women upliftment and welfare. All women in India are given chance to join any one of SHGs for training and development, so as to be prospective entrepreneur and skilled worker. The SHGs are promoted by the Government as if women in India may not be resourceful enough to be entrepreneurs. The formation of SHGs has certain objectives such as to inculcate the habit of saving and banking bait among the rural women; to build-up trust and confidence between the rural women and the bankers; to develop group activity so that various welfare and developmental programmes can be implemented in a better way with the participation of these women groups; and to achieve women and child welfare programme goals by actively involving these women groups in Universal Immunization Programme, Small Family Norm, Universal Elementary Education etc.

Importance of Self-Help Groups (SHGs): Self-Help Groups are necessary to overcome exploitation, create confidence for the economic self-reliance of rural people, particularly among women who are mostly invisible in the social structure. These groups enable them to come together for common objective and gain strength from each other to deal with exploitation, which they are facing in several forms. A group becomes the basis for action and change. It also helps building of relationship for mutual trust between the promoting organization and the rural poor through constant contact and genuine efforts. Self-Help Groups (SHGs) play an important role in differentiating between consumer credit and production credit, analyzing the credit system for its implication and changes in economy, culture and social position of the target groups, providing easy access to credit and facilitating group/organization for effective control, ensuring repayments and continuity through group dynamics; setting visible norms for interest rates, repayment schedules, gestation period, extension, writing of bad debts; and assisting group members in getting access to the formal credit institutions. Thus, Self-Help Groups (SHGs) disburses micro-credit to the rural women for the purpose of making them women entrepreneurs and encouraging them to enter into entrepreneurial activities. Credit needs of the rural and urban poor women are fulfilled totally through the SHGs. SHGs enhance equality of status of women as participation, decision-makers and beneficiaries in the democratic, economic, social and cultural spheres of life.

The rural poor are in-capacitated due to various reasons, such as most of them are socially backward, illiterate, with low motivation and poor economic base. Individually, a poor is not weak in socio-economic term, but also lacks access to the knowledge and information, which are the most important components of today's development process. However, in a group, they are empowered to overcome many of these weaknesses; hence there are needs for SHGs which is specific in terms are as under:

- To mobilize the resources of the individual members for their collective economic development.
- To uplift the living conditions of the poor.
- To create a habit of savings, utilization of local resources.
- To mobilize individual skills for group's interest.
- To create awareness about right.
- To assist the members financially at the time of need.
- Entrepreneurship development.
- To identify problems, analyzing and finding solutions in the groups.
- To act as a media for socio-economic development of village.
- To develop linkage with institution of NGOs.
- To organize training for skill development.

- To help in recovery of loans.
- To gain mutual understanding, develop trust and self-confidence.
- To build-up teamwork.
- To develop leadership qualities.
- To use it as an effective delivery channel for rural credit. (*Source*: NABARD, 2009).

Empowerment

The word 'Empowerment' literary means to give authority or power or to give strength and confidence in all spheres of life in order to discharge all sorts of physical, mental social activity with dignity and at par excellence. Empowerment is a multidimensional process by which individual or group of individual able to realize their original identity and power in life. It provides greater access to knowledge and resources, greater autonomy in decision-making to enable them to have greater ability to plan their lives in significant ways or have a greater control over the circumstances that influence their lives and free them from barriers imposes on them by age-old orthodox beliefs, customs and practices and to become powerful to win over all types of obstacles and freeing themselves in both mind, body and spirit from all types of servitude. Empowerment is a perpetual process. It is neither a commodity nor a by-product of any item, not it can be transferred.

Empowerment cannot be understood separately from an understanding of power. Power, in fact, can be perceived in four forms. Oxaal and Baden (1997) categorize these as:

Power over: This power involves a relationship either/or of domination/subordination. It is based ultimately on socially sanctioned threats of violence and intimidation, and requires a constant vigilance to maintain. It also invites active and passive resistance.

Power to: This power relates to having decision-making authority, power to solve problems, and can be creative and enabling.

Power with: This power involves people organizing with a common purpose or common understanding to achieve collective goals.

Power within: This power refers to self-confidence, self-awareness, and assertiveness. Through this power individuals can recognize through analyzing their experience how power operates in their lives, and gain the confidence to act to influence and change this.

To begin with the first interpretation of power as *power over,* a person has to be empowered because that person is at the wrong end of a power inequality. Hence, the first interpretation gives the rationale to begin a process of empowerment. The second interpretation of *power to* talks of the ultimate stage of empowerment, when a person has achieved the capacity to take action. Here, empowerment and power collapse positively into action. The third interpretation of *power with* reflects on the methods that such a process can initiate and set into motion, i.e. through purposeful collectives. The fourth interpretation of power as *power within* can be interpreted as the sustenance of the process whereby empowerment does not remain limited in intermittent actions, and instead can be conceived as the building of capacities to carry out future action in a sustained manner.

In the context of development (economic/social/political), empowerment cannot be *given* to anyone, nor is it a goal that can be reached by an organization or state. It is a process that takes place wherein inequality moves towards becoming equality. The inequality, which has to alter into equality, is the inequality in participation in the various processes of development. These can range from education, health services, housing, livelihoods, employment, remuneration etc. "Empowerment is a process whereby constraints that impede equal participation are reduced so that the inequality starts moving towards becoming equality." Often with development interventions such as micro-finance, targets are chased and the achievement of those targets is confused with the achieving of empowerment.

Empowerment through Self-Help Groups (SHGs): Self-Help Group (SHG) is as an instrument to change the conditions of women socially and economically. Once socio-economic experiment is achieved it would have implication on the overall development of women. SHGs enable economic, social, political and psychological empowerment of women.

Economic Empowerment: The economic contribution of women has been found to be related to her role and status in the society. Self-Help Groups provide economic benefits to the women by providing income generating activities. Economic independence facilitates in bringing about sexual equality and increase in women's income translates more directly into family well-being.

Social Empowerment: Self-Help Groups improve the equality of status of women as participants, decision-makers and beneficiaries in the social, democratic, economic and cultural spheres of life. SHGs ensure the equality of status of women as participants, decision-makers and beneficiaries in the democratic, economic, social and cultural spheres of life.

Political Empowerment: SHGs as active, articulate and organized citizenry act on a range of issues, holding the Panchayats accountable in terms of the use, production and distribution of public resources for the common public good. SHGs enable women to develop their communication skills to speak at the *Gram Sansad*, *Grama Sabha*, public meetings etc. An SHG functions through its regular meetings, where members perform transactional activities and discuss over different related issues. Social mobilization through SHGs is inevitable for political empowerment.

Psychological Empowerment: Self-Help Groups enhance the equality of women as participants, decision-makers and beneficiaries in the democratic, economic, social and cultural spheres of life. The SHGs inculcate a great confidence in the minds of rural women to success in their day-to-day life.

Different Models of Self-help Group Credit Linkage

Two models of micro-finance involving credit linkage with banks are SHG-Bank Linkage Model and MFI-Bank Linkage Model.

SHG-Bank Linkage Model: This model involves the SHGs financed directly by the banks, *viz.* Commercial Banks (Public Sector and Private Sector), Regional Rural Banks and Cooperative Banks. The SHG-bank linkage programme is now considered by the banking system as a commercial proposition, with advantages of lower transaction costs and higher coverage of rural clientele by the bank branches. SHG-Bank Linkage Programme is a major plank of the strategy for delivering financial services to the poor in a sustainable manner since its inception in the early 1990s and has made rapid strides exhibiting considerable democratic functioning and group dynamism. The SHG-Bank linkage model is the indigenous model of micro-credit evolved in India and has been widely acclaimed as a successful model.

Different Models of Self-help Group-Bank Linkage: On the basis of the modes of formation and nurturing, SHGs are basically categorized into three models, mentioned as follows:

Model I: SHGs Formed and Financed by Banks: In this model, the bank itself acts as a Self-Help Group Promoting Institution (SHGPI). Banks themselves take up the work of forming the groups, nurturing them over a period time, opening their saving accounts and providing loans to them after satisfying itself about their maturity to absorb credit.

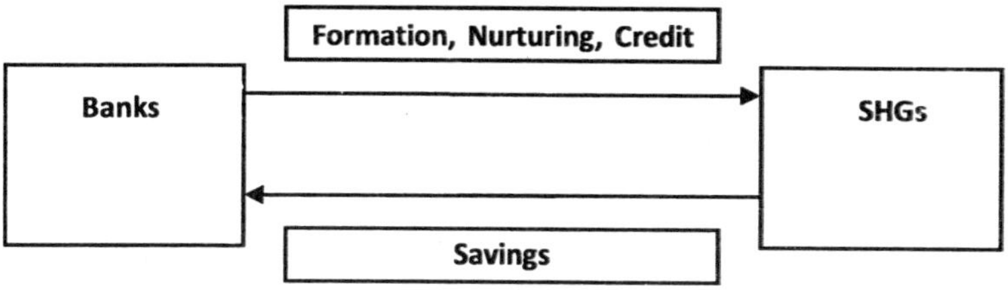

Model I: SHGs Formed and Financed by Banks

Model II: SHGs formed by formal agencies other than banks, but directly financed by banks: In this model, groups are formed by facilitating agencies like NGOs, Government agencies, or other community-based organizations. They facilitate organizing, forming and nurturing of groups and train them in thrift and credit management. Banks give loans directly to these SHGs. A large number of NGOs are actively participating under this model and also the State Governments through their development agencies like the DRDA, DWDA and some of the centrally sponsored social sector missions are involving. Among the three models, this model is popular.

Model III: SHGs financed by banks through NGOs and other agencies as financial intermediaries: In some parts of the country, banks are not in a position to even finance SHGs promoted and nurtured by other agencies due to various reasons. In order to

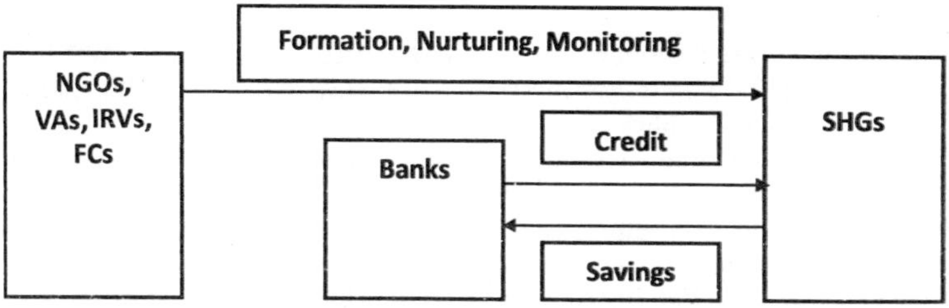

Model II: SHGs Formed by Formal Agencies other than Banks

overcome the constraints of formal banking system, the NGOs are encouraged to approach a suitable bank for bulk loan assistance. This, in turn, is used by the NGO for lending to the SHGs. Thus, the NGOs act as both facilitators and Micro-Finance Intermediaries (MFIs) in such cases. Banks finance these federations who in turn finance their member SHGs.

NABARD provides refinance support to banks under the linkage project. As per operational guidelines of NABARD, bank sanctions savings-linked loans to SHGs (varying from a saving to loan ratio of 1:1 to 1:4).

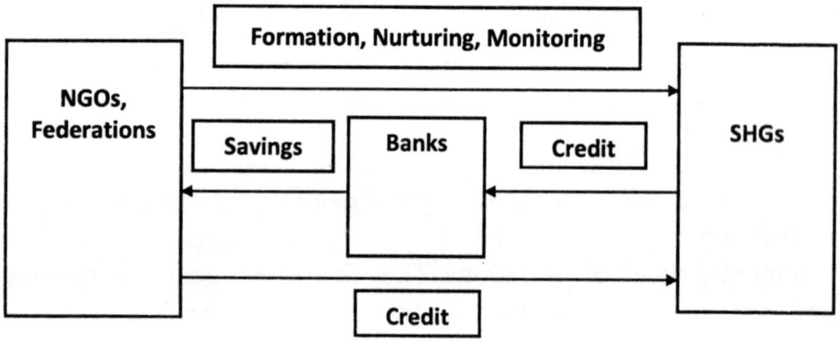

Model III: SHGs Financed by Banks through NGOs

MFI-Bank Linkage Model: This model covers financing of Micro Finance Institutions (MFIs) by banking agencies for lending to SHGs and other small borrowers.

(*Source*: NABARD, 2009)

References

Annual Administrative Report 2008-09, WB: P&RD Department, GoWB.

Altekar, A.S. (1997), *State and Government in Ancient India*, New Delhi: Motilal Banarasi Dass Publications.

Blomkvlst, H. and Swain, A. (2001), Investing Democracy and Social Capital in India, *Economic and Political Weekly*, XXXVI (8).

Breton, A. (1996), Competitive Governments: An Economic Theory of Politics and Public Finance, New York: Cambridge University Press.

Cheema, G.S. and Rondinelli, D.A. (eds.), (1983), *Decentralisation and Development: Policy Implementation in Developing Countries*, Beverly Hills: Sage Publications.

Constitution of India, Directive Principles of State Policy, Article 40.

Conyers, Daina (1983), Decentralisation: The Latest Fashion in Development Administration, *Public Administration and Development.* 3 (1).

Dewey, C. (1972), *Images of the Village Community: A Study in Anglo-Indian Ideology, Modern Asian Studies*, Vol. 6, No. 3, pp. 291-328.

Friedman, H. (1983), Decentralised Government in Asia: Local Policy Alternatives for Decentralised Development. In Cheema and D. Rondinelli (eds.), *Decentralisation and Development*, Beverly Hills: Sage Publications.

Furstenberg, F. and Hughes, M.F. (1995), Social Capital and Successful Development among At-Risk Youth, *Journal of Marriage and Family*, 57 (August).

Ghosh, R. and Pramanik, A.K. (1999), *Panchayat System in India, Historical, Constitutional and Financial Analysis*, New Delhi: Kanishka Publication.

Gruber, J. (2005), *Public Finance and Public Policy*, New York: Worth Publishers.

Haque, S. (1997), Local Governance in Developing Nations: Reexamining the Question of Accountability, *Regional Development Dialogue*, 18 (2).

Harriss, J. (2002), *Depoliticizing Development: The World Bank and Social Capital*, London: Anthem Press.

Heller, P. (1996), Social Capital as a Product of Class Mobilisation and State Intervention: Industrial Workers in Kerala, India, *World Development*, 24(6).

Inman, R. and Daniel, R. (1997), Rethinking Federalism, *Journal of Economic Perspectives*, 11(4).

Islam, Md. N. (2003), Decentralised Governance and Development: A Gandhian Vision, *Gandhi Prasanga*, V (2): 63-8.

Jain, P.C. (1974), *Economics of Public Finance*, New Delhi: Atlantic Publishers and Distributers.

Jha, S.N. (1999), Introduction, in Decentralisation and Local Politics: *Readings in Indian Government and Politics*, Ed. by S.N. Jha and P.C. Mathur; New Delhi: Sage Publications.

Johnson, C. and Start, D. (2001), *Rights, Claims and Capture: Understanding the Politics of Pro-Poor Policy*, ODI Working Paper 145, London: Overseas Development Institute.

Joshi, R.P. and Narwani, G.S. (2002), *Panchayati Raj in India: Emerging Trends Across the States*, Rawat Publications, India.

Ledyard, J.C. (1984), The Pure Theory of Large two Candidate Elections, *Public Choice* 44 (1): 7-41.

Leonard, D. and Marshel, D.R. (eds.), (1982), Institutions of Rural Development for the Poor: Decentralisation and Organisational Linkages, Berkeley: University of California and Institute of International Studies.

Maddick, H. (1963), *Democracy, Decentralisation and Development*, Mumbai: Asia Publishing House.

Maheswari, S.R. (1971), *Local Government in India*, New Delhi: Orient Longman.

Mohapatra, B. (2001), Social Connectedness and Fragility of Social Capital: View from an Orissa Village, *Economic and Political Weekly*, XXXVI (8): 665-72.

Nicholson, N.K. and Russell, C.S. (1981), Public Choice and Rural Development: The Proceedings of a Conference, Washington DC: Resources for the Future.

Oates, W.E. (1972), *Fiscal Federalism*, New York: Harcourt, Brace and Jovanovich.

Oates, W.E. (1999), An Essay on Fiscal Federalism, *Journal of Economic Literature*. 37 (3).

Oppenheimer, J. (1981), Does the Route to Development Pass through Public Choice, In Russel, C.S. and Nicholson, N.K. (eds.) *Public Choice and Rural Development*, Washington DC: Resources for the Future.

Ostrom, V. (1986), The Theory of the Compound Republic, Lincoln, Nebraska: University of Nebraska Press.

Panth, A.S. and Bohra, O.P. (1995), Finance of PRIs, *The Indian Journal of Public Administrations*, Vol. 41, No. 1, January-March 1995, pp. 73-77.

Prud'home, R. (1995), The Dangers of Decentralisation, *The World Bank Research Observer*, 10 (2): 201-20.

Putnam, R.L. and Raffaella, Y.N. (1993), *Making Democracy Work: Civic Tradition in Modern Italy,* Princeton University Press, Princeton, NJ.

Rangarajan, C. (2004), Fiscal Federalism: Some Current Concerns, *Indian Journal of Federal Studies*. 2004 (1).

Rao, C.H. and Linnenmann, H. (eds.) *Economic Reforms and Poverty Alleviation in India*, New Delhi: Sage Publications.

Rao, M.G. (2002), Fiscal Decentralisation in Indian Federalism, In Ehtisham A. and Tanzi, V. (eds.), *Managing Fiscal Decentralisatiom*, London: Routledge.

Rondinelli, Dennis, McCullough, J.S. and Jonald, R.W. (1989), Analyzing Decentralisation Policies in Developing Countries: A Political Economy Framework. *Development and Change*, 20 (1).

Salmon, P. (1987), Decentralisation as an Incentive Scheme, *Oxford Review of Economic Policy*, 36(4).

Schonwalder, G. (1997), New Democratic Spaces at the Grassroots? Popular Participation in Latin American Local Governments, *Development and Changes*, 28(1).

Sharkamsky, I. (1991), *Public Administration, Policy-making in Government Agencies*, London: Purples.

Singh, Raj (1996), *Panchayati Raj Manual: A Socio-Historical-cum-Legal Perspective*, New Delhi: Anmol Publications, p. 10.

Smith, B. (1985), *Decentralisation: The Territorial Dimension of the State*, London: George Allen & Unwin.

Stephen, F.R. (2001), *An Empirical Study of Women in Local Self Governance in Karnataka*, Bangalore: Search Publications.

Tam, Henry (1998), *Communitarianism: A New Agenda for Politics and Citizenship*, London: MacMillan and Co. Ltd.

The Asoka Mehta Committee Report, 1978.

The Balwant Rai Mehta Committee Report, 1957.

The Constitution, Seventy-third Constitutional Amendment Act, 1992.

UNDP (1997), Decentralised Governance Programme: Strengthening Capacity for People-Centred Development, Management Development and Governance Division, Bureau for Development Policy, September 1997.

West Bengal Panchayat Act, 1973.

Woolcock, M. and Narayan, D. (2000), Social Capital: Implications for Development Theory, Research and Policy, *The World Bank Research Observer*, 15(2), 225-49.

World Bank (1997), India Achievement and Challenges in Reducing Poverty. Washington D.C.: World Bank.

World Bank (1997), World Development Report: The State in Changing World, New York: Oxford University Press.

World Bank (2000), *Overview of Rural Decentralisation in India, Volume II: Approaches to Rural Decentralisation in Seven States*, Unpublished Report, World Bank.

World Bank (2000), *Overview of Rural Decentralisation in India, Volume III: Background Papers*, Unpublished Report, World Bank.

World Bank (2000), *World Development Report 2000/1: Attacking Poverty*, Oxford: Oxford University Press.

3
Decentralisation and Self-Help Group Movement in West Bengal

Structure of Panchayati Raj Institutions in West Bengal

Panchayati Raj Insitution Structure of West Bengal

In 1973, the West Bengal Panchayats Act was passed, annulling the previous laws. The four-tier structure was replaced by emerging all Indian patterns of Gram Panchayats, Panchayat Samiti and Zilla Parishad. The new Gram Panchayats were similar to the Anchal Panchayats of 1957 Act and consisted of a group of villages with a population 10 to 12 thousand. Following the Balwant Rai Mehta Committee Report's recommendations, Panchayat Samitis were coterminous with blocks, and Zilla Parishads were coterminous with districts. The Act provided for the direct election of members of all the three-tiers for a five years term. The *Pradhans* of Gram Panchayats were *ex-officio* members of Panchayat Samitis and the *Sabhapatis* of Panchayat Samitis were similarly *ex-officio* members of Zilla Parishads. The Act also provided for nominations of officials without voting rights into the standing committees of Panchayat Samitis and Zilla Parishad and local MLAs and MPs as *ex-officio* members of both block and district tiers. As a framework for decentralisation governance, the 1973 Act was a great improvement on the previous legislation in ensuring organic linkage between various tiers, improving executive efficiency through a system of standing committees, and providing greater clarity regarding the functions. In June 1978 elections were held simultaneously for all tiers of the rural local bodies for the first time. The event heralded a new era for the Panchayati Raj system in West Bengal. Since then, elections to the local bodies have been held at regular five years intervals as stipulated by law, with the most recent elections taking place in 2013.

Gram Panchayat

A Gram Panchayat (GP) normally covers a cluster of villages. This is the lowest tier of Panchayati Raj Institution. On an average each GP covered a group of villages with a population of 10,000 to 12,000 people. The members of GP are directly elected through the vote given by the all adult voters of that respective area or *Sansad*. The Chairman of GP is known as *Pradhan*, Deputy-chairman is called *Upa-pradhan*. The GP members elect these two functionaries from amongst themselves and they can be removed by majority resolutions in the GP. The Act of 1973 provides administrative power to endow the GP with three sets of powers and functions: obligatory, delegated and discretionary. The total elected members would vary between seven and twenty-five depend on the number of voters in the area. There would be a Secretary, a Job Assistant, a Technical Assistant, one or two Assistants and Tax Collectors, Village Chowkidars and a *Gram Sebak* as the officials of the GP.

(*Source*: Prabhat Dutta and Payel Sen, 2009).

Panchayat Samiti

The middle tier of Panchayati Raj Institution is Panchayat Samiti. This tier is converged with development block. This tier replaced the earlier *Anchalik Parishads*. According to the West Bengal Panchayat Act, this consisted of the following representatives:

(a) Maximum of three members elected from each GP area on the basis of adult franchise;
(b) Two persons belonging to SC/ST and two women to be nominated by the State Government;
(c) Pradhans of the GP within the block area; and
(d) Members of Lok Sabha and Vidhan Sabha within the block area (not Minister).

The PS gives emphasis on direct election of members by voters, and at the same time, it provides for co-option and integration with other bodies. The combination enables the PS to emerge as the focal point of people's representation in the block. Panchayat Samiti headed by *Sabhapati* (Chairperson) and a *Sahokari Sabhapati* (Vice-Chairperson). The BDO is now the executive officer of the PS.

(*Source*: Prabhat Dutta and Payel Sen, 2009).

Zilla Parishad

In the three-tier Panchayat System, the Zilla Parishad is the highest tier at the District-Level. According to the West Bengal Gram Panchayat Act of 1973, Zilla Parishad (ZP) had constituted by the following categories of members:

(a) Two persons to be directly elected from each block of the district;
(b) The *Sabhapatis* of all the PSs of the district (*ex-officio*),
(c) All the MPs and MLAs excepting the ministers from the district; and
(d) Two persons from the SC/ST and two women members nominated by the State Government.

The Chairperson of ZP is called *Sabhadhipati* and Deputy-Chairperson is known as the *Sahokari Sabhadhipati*. The members of the ZP elect these two functionaries from amongst the directly elected members only. The DM is the executive officer of the ZP and ADM is its additional executive officer. All district-level officers are statutorily linked to the corresponding standing committees.

(*Source*: Prabhat Dutta and Payel Sen, 2009).

Gram Sansad

Gram Sansad means "a body consisting of persons registered at any time in the electoral rolls pertaining to a constituency of a Gram Panchayat delimited for the purpose of last preceding general election to the Gram Panchayat."

(Section 16A of W.B. Panchayat Act, 1973).

The most vibrant Constitutional Institution at the village-level is Gram Sansad, incorporated by the West Bengal Panchayat (Amendment) Act, 1992. It consists of registered electors of a constituency within the area of a Gram Panchayat. Under the law, the Gram Sansad will take place twice a year, annual meeting in May and half-yearly meeting in November.

Attendance of at least 1/10 (10 per cent) of the total number of members/voters shall form a quorum for the Gram Sansad meeting. If there is no quorum in a meeting, the meeting shall be adjourned to be held at the same place and hour on the seventh day after the date of such meeting. Attendance of at least 1/20 (5%) of the total number of members shall form a quorum for the adjourned meeting.

Source: West Bengal Panchayat (Amendment) Act, 1992.

The Gram Sansad is an institution, which provides an opportunity to participate meaningfully in governance, to all the people willing and capable of participating in the development process. Formation of Self-Help Group (SHG) by help of Swarnajayanti Gram Swarojgar Yojana (SGSY), women participation in the development process is rapidly increasing in GP areas. The voters incorporated in SHGs, mostly under SGSY and majorities are women.

District/Block/Gram Sansads were constituted to provide a forum for accountability of the bodies to the members of the Sansad and through them to the people in general. Adequate information on functioning of the Panchayat body should be made available to the members of the Sansad sufficiently before such meetings so that they may study and appreciate the same, raise appropriate questions and suggest possible ways of improving functioning of those bodies.

The Department of Panchayat and Rural Development, Government of West Bengal has issued an Order *vide* No. 298/PN/O/I/3C-7/03 dated 21.01.2009 directing the PRIs to make proactive disclosure regarding 13 categories of information which should be circulated in the form of a booklet for information of all members. All informations should relate to the previous financial year in respect of the Annual Sansad meeting and the first six months of the year in respect of the half-yearly Sansad meeting. The items of disclosure are—

1. Action taken on the recommendations/proposals made in the previous *Sansad* meeting along with a copy of the resolution of that meeting. Constraints, if any, faced should also be clearly spelt out.
2. The accounts for the relevant period based on Form-27 of the Accounts Rules applicable, with explanatory note, when necessary.

3. Head-wise balance of fund lying unspent at the end of the period and percentage of available fund utilized during the period for all important schemes as well as grants from the State and the Central Finance Commission during the relevant period along with constraints, if any, in utilizing the fund.
4. Own resource mobilized by the body during the relevant period showing total collection against total demand proposing steps for improvement.
5. Availability and utilization of own fund during the period and important items of expenditure from own fund. Visible areas of utilisation and the quantum of fund used for those should be highlighted.
6. Number of meetings of the general body and those held by different *Sthayee/Upa-Samitis* during the relevant period and attendance. For the *Samitis* which held meetings below statutory-level, reasons should be given.
7. Observation of latest audit report both internal and that by the ELA and action taken on those reports, if not already placed before the Sansad. Failure to act on any observation should be explained.
8. Report of the District Council, if any, related to that body and action taken on that report. Failure to act on any issue shall be explained.
9. A brief note on the findings of the latest Self-Evaluation Report, if not already placed before the Sansad. Major areas of strength and weaknesses in functioning of that body should be stated. Actions taken/proposed on areas of weakness should be explained.
10. List of important works completed or on-going during the relevant period.
11. Names of persons to whom individual benefits were extended.
12. Exemplary incidents of people's participation/voluntary contribution may be highlighted for replication for other areas.
13. Number of posts lying vacant and actions taken to fill-up those posts.

Disclosure of information voluntarily is an important element for good governance by the Panchayat. As a practice the Panchayat body compiles report having relevant information about functioning of those bodies and circulates the same in the form of booklets in the Sansad meeting.

(*Source*: Panchayat and Rural Development Department).

Gram Sabha

The Gram Sabha has been regarded as the 'soul' of Panchayati Raj. A Constitutional status was given to the Gram Sabha for the first time in 1993. Gram Sabha have given power to the people to ensure transparency and accountability in the system. All the adult voters of the Gram Panchayat area is the member of Gram Sabha. All State Panchayat Acts have provided for the constitution of the Gram Sabha. Gram Panchayats is the executive committee of Gram Sabha.

Article 243(B) of the Constitution refers to Gram Sabha as "a body consisting of persons registered in the electoral rolls relating to a village comprised with the area of Panchayat at the village-level". Regarding the power of the Gram Sabha, Article 243(A) of the Constitution states that, "A Gram Sabha may exercise such power and perform such functions at the village level as the Legislature of a state, may, by law, provide".

(*Source*: Section 16B of W.B. Panchayat Act, 1973)

The concept of Gram Sabha was introduced by the West Bengal Panchayat (Amendment) Act, 1994. It consists of registered electors of a Gram Panchayat area. It is the duty of a Gram Panchayat to convene a meeting of Gram Sabha in December every year in West Bengal.

In West Bengal Gram Sabha meeting held in the month of December to prepare the next year's plan and budget, beneficiary selection etc. The West Bengal Government provided for a two-tier structure for facilitating direct democracy. Village (Sansad) based bodies are named as Gram Sansads. In every Gram Sansad there is a Gram Unnayan Samiti which is responsible for scheme selection on the basis of local need and priority. Gram Unnayan Samiti makes the scheme list and in the Gram Sansad meeting Sansad-wise scheme is selected. Two meetings of the Gram Sansad guides and advises the Gram Panchayats about schemes for economic development, identifying the beneficiaries for poverty alleviation programmes, giving suggestions regarding budget, audit report, yearly administration report and recording objections regarding failure to implement development schemes. Attendance of at least 1/20 (5%) of the total number of members/voters shall form a quorum for the Gram Sabha meeting. If there is no quorum in a meeting, the meeting shall be adjourned to be held at the same place and hour on the seventh day after the date of such meeting. Quorum for the adjourned meeting is not mandatory. After making the Sansad-wise plans the Gram Panchayat make draft plan as per Upa-Samiti. In the Gram Sabha the final plan is prepared as per priority. And finally after approval of Gram Sabha, the Gram Panchayat makes the final plan and budget and sends those to the upper level for approval.

The West Bengal Panchayat (Amendment) Act, 2010 amend Section 16B of the Principal Act and the following proviso shall be added—"Provided that a Gram Panchayat may, in addition to annual meeting, hold extraordinary meeting of a Gram Sabha at any time if the situation so warrants or if the State Government, by order, so directs and for the purpose of holding such extraordinary meeting, provision of this section shall apply."

[*Source*: The West Bengal Panchayat (Amendment) Act, 2010]

Upa-Samiti

According to 73rd Constitutional Amendment of Panchayat Act, there are five Upa-Samitis (sub-committees) at Gram Panchayat level. Those are:

(i) *Artho O Parikalpana Upa-Samiti* (Finance and Planning Sub-committee),
(ii) *Krishi O Prani Sampada Vikas Upa-Samiti* (Agriculture and Animal Husbandry Development Sub-committee),
(iii) *Shiksha O Janaswastha Upa-Samiti* (Education and Public Health Sub-Committee),
(iv) *Nari Shishu Unnayan O Samaj Kalyan Upa-Samiti* (Women Child Development and Social Welfare Development Sub-Committee), and
(v) *Shilpa O Parikathamo Upa-Samiti* (Industry and Infrastructure Sub-Committee).

Standing committees have wide-ranging powers. They include preparing proposals for execution of a scheme within the budgetary provisions of the Gram Panchayat. The Pradhan shall also not sanction any fund for a scheme, programme or project without considering the views of the members of the Upa-Samiti to whom powers have been delegated by the Gram Panchayat with respect to such scheme programme or project. The Standing Committees have also been given wide powers to call for information, inspect and immovable property of the Gram Panchayat or any work in progress. With effect from 2005-06, each Standing Committee is being given a separate indication of a budget, so that they can plan better within their mandates.

Formation of Upa-Samiti

After *Pradhan* selection of Gram Panchayat, within three months Gram Panchayat has to form *Upa-Samiti*. *Pradhan* and *Upa-Pradhan* (*Ex-Officio*) and directly elected member of Gram Panchayat and *Ex-officio* member of Panchayat Samiti will be member of *Upa-Samiti* but not more than three. BDO will issue a notice after deciding date, place and time before minimum 7 days to call a meeting to select those three members of *Upa-Samiti*. After member selection BDO will also call a meeting in the same way to select "*Sanchalak*". But no member will be selected for *Artho O Parikalpana Upa-Samiti*. Other *Sanchalaks* of rest four *Upa-Samitis* will be *Ex-officio* members of *Artho O Parikalpana*. Leader of opponent party member also will be member of *Artho O Parikalpana Upa-Samiti*. Minimum half of total member of *Nari Shishu Unnayan O Samaj Kalyan Upasamiti* must be women and *Sanchalak* also should be women. If the numbers of Gram Panchayat members is below or equal to 10 then the number of *Upa-Samiti* member should be one. In case of number of GP members 11 to 20 then the *Upa-Samiti* members should be 2 and *Upa-Samiti* members will be 3 when the number of GP member is 21 or more. *Upa-Samiti* will take plans and execute them at Gram Panchayat-level.

Gram Unnayan Samiti

The *Gram Unnayan Samiti* at the level of Gram Sansad was introduced by the West Bengal Panchayats (Amendment) Act, 2003. Gram Sansad will constitute *Gram Unnayan Samiti* and elect the members by simple majority. It will be responsible for ensuring active participation of people at grassroots-level in implementation and equitable distribution of benefits of Rural Development Programmes.

With the objectives of mandatory people's participation, the West Bengal Government established the *Gram Unnayan Samiti*. Its formation, responsibility and duties included in West Bengal Panchayat Rules 70 to 74, framed in 2004. All the voters of Gram Sansad area elect the *Gram Unnayan Samiti*. This *Samiti* is called as working committee of Gram Panchayat. It is mandatory to form *Gram Unnayan Samiti* in each Gram Sansad area. This *Samiti* plays a vital role in executing a small scheme at local-level.

[*Source*: West Bengal Panchayats (Amendment) Act, 2003].

Steps for Gram Unnayan Samiti (GUS) Formation

- Gram Panchayat will call a special Sansad meeting for GUS formation.
- This meeting should be called before 15 days of the meeting mentioning date and time and also should disseminate the information about the meeting by making, leafleting, drums beating etc.
- Gram Panchayat *Pradhan* will be Chairman and in case of his/her absence *Upa-Pradhan* can or in absence of both, Gram Panchayat member of that particular Sansad can chair that meeting.
- Twenty per cent corum is must for that special meeting. If corum is not fulfilled in adjourned meeting then this meeting is again adjourned and this process will go until the *Gram Unnayan Samiti* is formed.
- Gram Panchayat technical assistant or executive assistant or secretary or job assistant should act as presiding officer. And she/he will be responsible for proceeding.
- If Block Development Officer is still needed, then BDO can recruit for an invigilator at block level for that special Gram Sansad meeting.

There are two categories of membership in the GUS, reserve posts and unreserved posts. In reserve post following member can be held—

1. Elected Gram Panchayat member from that particular *Gram* Sansad area.
2. That person who gets second highest votes in last election from that Gram Sansad area.

3. Three representative from three Government registered NGOs or CSOs or other group-wise organizations.
4. Total three SHGs members from three SHGs of that Sansad area (one from each group).
5. One Government employee (Retired or working) of that particular Gram Sansad area.
6. One teacher (Retired or working) who resides of that particular Gram Sansad area.
[*Source*: West Bengal Panchayats (Amendment) Act, 2003].

Ten voters or one per cent of the total voters of Gram Sansad area (which is maximum) will be selected as members in unreserved post.

Gram Unnayan Samiti shall meet three to four times in a month for active performance of the Samiti. In annual Gram Sansad meeting, the Sansad members shall evaluate the *Gram Unnayan Samiti's* work progress and renew their membership.

Gram Unnayan Samiti shall prepare a five year plan and an Annual Action Plan and necessary budget for economic and social development. *Samiti* shall identify the local needs after discussion with local people especially rural poor. Those needs are food security, natural resource and employment, education, health and nutrition, women and child development, infrastructure and service delivery.

Salient Features of West Bengal Panchayat Act, 1973 and 73rd Constitutional Amendment Act, 1992

The West Bengal Panchayat Act, 1973 has following features:

1. "Auditor" means an auditor appointed under section 186 and includes any officer authorised by him to perform all or any of the functions of an auditor under Chapter XVIII.
2. "Block" means an area referred to in section 93.
3. "Block Development Officer" means an officer appointed as such by the State Government.
4. "Case" means a criminal proceeding in respect of an offence triable by a *Nyaya Panchayat*.

4a. "Collector" means an officer appointed as such by the State Government;

4b "Council" means the Darjeeling Gorkha Hill Council constituted under the Darjeeling Gorkha Hill Council Act, 1988;

5. "District Magistrate" includes an Additional District Magistrate, a Deputy Commissioner, an Additional Deputy Commissioner and any other Magistrate appointed by the State Government to discharge all or any of the functions of a District Magistrate under this Act.

6. "Director of Panchayats" means the Director of Panchayats and Rural Development, Government of West Bengal, and includes a Joint Director of Panchayats and Rural Development, a Deputy Director of Panchayats and Rural Development and an Assistant Director of Panchayats and Rural Development.

7. "District Panchayat Officer" means a District Panchayat and Rural Development Officer appointed as such by the State Government.

8. "District Planning Committee" means the District Planning Committee established by the State Government for a district;

9. "Extension Officer, Panchayats" means an officer appointed as such by the State Government.

9a. "General Election" means an election of members held simultaneously for constitution of *Gram Panchayats*, *Panchayat Samitis*, *Mahakuma Parishad*, or *Zilla Parishads* or any two or more of *Gram Panchayats*, *Panchayat Samitis*, *Mahakuma Parishad*, or *Zilla Parishads* in such area as the State Government may by notification specify.

10. "Gram" means an area referred to in section 3.

10a. "Gram Panchayat" means a *Gram Panchayat* constituted under section 4.

11. "Gram Sabha" means a body consisting of persons registered in the electoral rolls pertaining to a Gram declared as such under sub-section (1) of section 3.

11a. "*Gram Sansad*" means a body consisting of persons registered at any time in the electoral rolls pertaining to a constituency of a *Gram Panchayat* delimited for the purpose of last preceding general election to the *Gram Panchayat*;

11b. "Hill areas" has the same meaning as in the Darjeeling Gorkha Hill Council Act, 1988.

12. "*Karmadhyaksha*" means the *Karmadhyaksha* of a *Sthayee Samiti* of a *Panchayat Samiti* elected under section 125 or of a *Sthayee Samiti* of a *Zilla Parishad* elected under section 172, as the case may be—

12a. "*Mahakuma Parishad*" means the *Mahakuma Parishad* for the sub-division of Siliguri in the district of Darjeeling constituted under section 185B.

13. "*Mouza*" means an area defined, surveyed and recorded as such in the revenue record of a district and referred to in clause (g) of Article 243 of the Constitution of India as the lowest unit of area for the purpose of public notification for specifying a village.

13a. "Municipality" means an institution of self-government constituted under Article 243Q of the Constitution of India.

14. "Notification" means a notification published in the Official Gazette.

15. "*Nyaya Panchayat*" means a *Nyaya Panchayat* constituted under section 51.

15a. "Office Bearer" means the *Pradhan*, *Upa-Pradhan*, *Sabhapati*, *Sahakari Sabhapati*, *Sabhadhipati* or *Sahakari Sabhadhipati* or any two or more of them together.

15b. "*Panchayat*" means an institution of 5 [self-government constituted under article 243B of the Constitution of India], and includes *Gram Panchayat*, *Panchayat Samiti*, *Mahakuma Parishad* or *Zilla Parishad*.

16. "*Panchayat Samiti*" means a *Panchayat Samiti* constituted under section 94.

16a. "Population" means the population as ascertained at the last preceding census of which the relevant figures have been published.

17. "*Pradhan* " means a *Pradhan* of a *Gram Panchayat* elected under section 9.

18. "Prescribed" means prescribed by rules made under this Act.

19. "Prescribed Authority" means an authority appointed by the State Government, by notification, for all or any of the purposes of this Act.

20. "Public Street" means any street, road, lane, gully, alley, passage, pathway, bridge, square or court, whether a thorough fare or not, over which the public have a right of way, and includes side drains or gutters and the land up to the boundary

of any abutting property, notwithstanding the projection over such land or any *verandah* or other superstructure.

20a. "Recognised Political Party" means a national party or a State party recognised as such by the Election Commission of India by notification for the time being in force.

21. "*Sabhapati*" means a *Sabhapati* of a *Panchayat Samiti*, elected under section 98.

22. "*Sabhadhipati*" means a *Sabhadhipati* of a *Zilla Parishad* 2 [elected under section 143, and includes the Sabhadhipati of *Mahakuma Parishad*].

23. "*Sahakari Sabhapati*" means a *Sahakari Sabhapati* of a *Panchayat Samiti*, elected under section 98.

24. "*Sahakari Sabhadhipati*" means a *Sahakari Sabhadhipati* of a *Zilla Parishad*, 3 [elected under section 143, and includes the *Sahakari Sabhadhipati* of the *Mahakuma Parishad*].

25. "Scheduled Castes" means such castes, races or tribes or parts of, or groups within, such castes, races or tribes as are deemed to be Scheduled Castes, in relation to the State of West Bengal under Article 341 of the Constitution of India.

26. "Scheduled Tribes" means such tribes or tribal communities or parts of, or groups within, such tribes or tribal communities as are deemed to be Scheduled Tribes in relation to the State of West Bengal under Article 342 of the Constitution of India.

27. "State Planning Board" means the West Bengal State Planning Board established by the State Government. (*Source*: The West Bengal Panchayat Act, 1973).

Constitution of Panchayats

As per 73rd Constitutional Amendment Act, Article 243B, "There shall be constituted, in every State, Panchayats at the village, intermediate and district-levels in accordance with the provisions of this Part". Panchayats at the intermediate level may not be constituted in a State having a population not exceeding twenty lakh.

Composition of Panchayats: As per 73rd Constitutional Amendment Act, Article 243C—

1. "Subject to the provisions of this Part, the Legislature of a State may, by law, make provisions with respect to the composition of Panchayats: Provided that the ratio between

the population of the territorial area of a Panchayat at any level and the number of seats in such Panchayat to be filled by election, shall, so far as practicable, be the same throughout the State.

2. All the seats in a Panchayat shall be filled by persons chosen by direct election from territorial constituencies in the Panchayat area, and for this purpose, each Panchayat area shall be divided into territorial constituencies in such manner that the ratio between the population of each constituency and the number of seats allotted to it, shall, so far as practicable, be the same throughout the Panchayat area.
3. The Legislature of a State may, by law, provide for the representation:
   (a) of the Chairpersons of the Panchayats at the village-level, in the Panchayats at the intermediate-level or, in the case of a State not having Panchayats at the intermediate-level, in the Panchayats at the district level;
   (b) of the Chairpersons of the Panchayats at the intermediate-level, in the Panchayats at the district level;
   (c) of the members of the House of the People and the members of the Legislative Assembly of the State representing constituencies which comprise wholly or partly a Panchayat area at a level other than the village-level, in such Panchayat; and
   (d) of the members of the Council of States and the members of the Legislative Council of the State, where they are registered as electors within:
      (i) a Panchayat area at the intermediate level; and
      (ii) a Panchayat area at the district-level, in Panchayat at the district-level.
4. The Chairperson of a Panchayat and other members of a Panchayat whether or not chosen by direct election from territorial constituencies in the Panchayat area shall have the right to vote in the meeting of the Panchayats.
5. The Chairperson of—
   (a) a Panchayat at the village-level shall be elected in such manner as the Legislature of a State may, by law, provide; and

(b) a Panchayat at the intermediate level or district-level shall be elected by, and from amongst, the elected members thereof.
(*Source*: The West Bengal Panchayat Act, 1973).

Reservation of Seats

As per 73rd Constitutional Amendment Act, 1992, Article 243D:

1. Seats of Panchayats shall be reserved for—(a) the Scheduled Castes, and (b) the Scheduled Tribes in every Panchayat and the number of seats so reserved shall bear, as nearly as may be, the same proportion to the total number of seats to be filled by direct election in that Panchayat as the population of the Scheduled Castes and Scheduled Tribes in that Panchayat area and such seats may be allotted by rotation to different constituencies in a Panchayat.
2. Not less than one-third of the total number of seats reserved under clause (1) shall be reserved for women belonging to the Scheduled Castes or, to the Scheduled Tribes.
3. Not less than one-third (including the number of seats reserved for women belonging to the Scheduled Castes and the Scheduled Tribes) of the total number of seats to be filled by direct election in every Panchayat shall be reserved for women and such seats may be allotted by rotation to different constituencies in a Panchayat.
4. The offices of the Chairpersons in the Panchayats at the village or any other level shall be reserved for the Scheduled Castes, the Scheduled Tribes and women in such manners as the legislature of the state, by law, provide:
   (i) Provided that the number of offices of Chairpersons reserved for the Scheduled Castes and the Scheduled Tribes in the Panchayats at each level in any State shall bear, as nearly as may be, the same proportion to the total number of such offices in the Panchayats at each level as the total population of the Scheduled Castes or of the Scheduled Tribes in the State bears to the population of the state.

(*Source*: The 73rd Constitutional Amendment Act, 1992, Article 243D).

Duration of Panchayats

As per 73rd Constitutional Amendment Act, 1992, Article 243E; "Every Panchayat, unless sooner dissolved under any law for the time being in force, shall continue for five years from the date appointed for its first meeting and no longer". Irregular election of Panchayati Raj Bodies was the general characteristics for some of the states. This provision resists the same.

(*Source*: 73rd Constitutional Amendment Act, 1992, Article 243E).

Powers, authorities and responsibilities of Panchayats: As per provision of the Article 243G of the 73rd Amendment of the Constitution, "the legislature of a State may, by law, endow the Panchayats with such powers and authority as may be necessary to enable them to function as institutions of self-government and such law may contain provisions for the devolution of powers and responsibilities *Upan Panchayats* at the appropriate-level, subject to such conditions as may be specified therein, with respect to—

(a) The preparation of plans for economic development and social justice.
(b) The implementation of schemes for economic development and social justice as may be entrusted to them including those in relation to the matters listed in the Eleventh Schedule."
(*Source*: The 73rd Constitutional Amendment Act, Article 243G).

Constitution of Finance Commission

As per provision of Article: 243-I of the 73rd Amendment to the Constitution.

"The Governor of a State shall, as soon as may be within one year from the commencement of the Constitution (Seventy-third Constitutional Amendment Act, 1992), and thereafter at the expiry of every fifth year, constitute a Finance Commission to review the financial position of the Panchayats and to make position, recommendations to the Governor as to:

(a) The principles which should govern:
    (i) The distribution between the State and the Panchayats of the net proceeds of the taxes, duties, tolls and fees

leviable by the State, which may be divided between them under this Part and the allocation between the Panchayats at all levels of their respective shares of such proceeds;

(ii) The determination of the taxes, duties, tolls and fees which may be assigned to, or appropriated by, the Panchayats;

(iii) The grants-in-aid to the Panchayats from the Consolidated Fund of the State;

(b) The measures needed to improve the financial position of the Panchayats;

(c) Any other matter referred to the Finance Commission by the Governor in the interests of sound finance of the Panchayats. (*Source*: The 73rd Constitutional Amendment Act, 1992, Article: 243-I).

Elections to the Panchayats: As per Article 243K

1. The superintendence, direction and control of the preparation of electoral rolls for, and the conduct of, all elections to the Panchayats shall be vested in a State Election Commission consisting of a State Election Commissioner to be appointed by the Governor.
2. Subject to the appointed of, law made by the Legislature of a State, the conditions of service and tenure of office of the State Election Commissioner shall be such as the Governor may by rule determine: Provided that the State Election Commissioner shall not be removed from his office except in like manner and on the like grounds as a judge of a High Court and the conditions of service of the State Election Commissioner shall not be varied to his disadvantages after his appointment.
3. The Governor of a State shall, when so requested by the State Election Commission, make available to the State Election Commission such staff as may be necessary for the discharge of the function conferred on the State Election Commission by Clause (1).
4. Subject to the provisions of this Constitution the Legislature of a State may, by law, make provisions with respect to all

matters relating to, or connection with, elections to the Panchayats.

(*Source*: The 73rd Constitutional Amendment Act,1992, Article 243K).

Addition of Eleventh Schedule

As provided by Section 243-O, after the Tenth Schedule to the Constitution, the following addition of Schedule shall be added, namely "Eleventh Schedule" (as per Article 243-G) which are as follows:

1. Agriculture including agricultural extension.
2. Land improvement and land conservation.
3. Minor irrigation, water management and watershed development.
4. Animal husbandry, dairying and poultry.
5. Fisheries.
6. Social forestry and farm forestry.
7. Minor forest produce.
8. Small Scale industries including food processing industries.
9. Khadi, Village and Cottage Industries.
10. Rural Housing.
11. Drinking Water.
12. Fuel and Fodder.
13. Roads, culvert, bridge, ferries, waterways, and other means of Communication.
14. Rural Electrification, including distribution of electricity.
15. Non-Conventional Energy Sources.
16. Poverty alleviation programme.
17. Education including primary and secondary schools.
18. Technical training and vocational education.
19. Adult and Non-formal education.
20. Libraries.
21. Cultural activities.
22. Markets and fairs.
23. Health and sanitation including hospital, primary health centres and Dispensaries.
24. Family Welfare.
25. Women and Child Development.

26. Social Welfare including welfare of the handicapped and mentally retarded.
27. Welfare of the weaker sections and in particular, Scheduled Castes and Scheduled Tribes.
28. Public Distribution System.
29. Maintenance of Community Assets.

(*Source*: The 73rd Constitutional Amendment Act, 1992, Article 243-O).

From the Eleventh Schedule it is unambiguously stated that the Constitution of India delegate a large task upon the shoulder of Panchayats in order to establish an active and 'real' Government on local areas.

As this study is on the basis of West Bengal Panchayati Raj Institution, now, discussion has made in some important provision of West Bengal Panchayats.

Duties and Responsibilities of Gram Panchayat

As per West Bengal Panchayat Act, 1973, Section-19, the Obligatory duties of Gram Panchayat are:

(1) A Gram Panchayat shall function as a unit of self-government and, in order to achieve economic development and secure social justice for all, shall, subject to such conditions as may be prescribed or such directions as may be given by the State Government—
   (a) Prepare a development plan for the five-year term of the office of the members and revise and update it as and when necessary with regard to the resources available;
   (b) Prepare an annual plan for each year by the month of October of the preceding year for development of human resources, infrastructure and civic amenities in the area; and
   (c) Implement schemes for economic development and social justice as may be drawn-up by, or entrusted upon it.

(2) Without prejudice to the generality of the provisions of sub-section (1) and subject to such conditions as may be prescribed or such directions as may be given by the State

Government, the duties of a Gram Panchayat shall be to provide within the area under its jurisdiction for—

(i) Sanitation, conservancy and drainage and the prevention of public nuisances;

(ii) Curative and preventive measures in respect of malaria, small pox, cholera or any other epidemic;

(iii) Supply of drinking water and the cleansing and disinfecting the sources of supply and storage of water;

(iv) The maintenance, repair and construction of public streets and the protection thereof;

(v) The removal of encroachments of public streets or public places;

(vi) The protection and repair of buildings or other property vested in it;

(vii) The management and care of public tanks, subject to the provisions of the Bengal Tanks Improvement Act, 1939, common grazing grounds, burning ghats and public graveyards;

(viii) The supply of any local information which the District Magistrate, the *Zilla Parishad,* the *Mahakuma Parishad*, the Council or the Panchayat Samiti within the local limits of whose jurisdiction the Gram Panchayat is situated may require;

(ix) Organizing voluntary labour for community works and works for the upliftment of its area;

(x) The control and administration of the Gram Panchayat Fund established under this Act;

(xi) The imposition, assessment and collection of the taxes, rates or fees leviable under this Act;

(xii) The maintenance and control of *Dafadars*, *Chowkidars* and *Gram Panchayat Karmees* within its jurisdiction and securing due performance by the *Dafadars*, *Chowkidars* and *Gram Panchayat Karmees* of the duties imposed on them under this Act;

(xiii) The Constitution and Administration of the *Nyaya Panchayat* established under this Act; and

(xiv) The performance of such functions as may be transferred to it under section 31 of the Cattle-Trespass Act, 1871.

(3) A Gram Panchayat shall not omit or refuse to act *Upan* any recommendations of a *Gram Sansad* relating to prioritization of any list of beneficiaries or scheme or programme so far as it relates to the area of the *Gram Sansad* unless it decides in a meeting for reasons to be recorded in writing that such recommendations are not acceptable or implementable under the provisions of the Act or any rule, order or direction thereunder; such decision of the Gram Panchayat shall be placed in the next meeting of the *Gram Sansad.*
(*Source*: West Bengal Panchayat Act, 1973, Section-19).

As per Section-20 of West Bengal Panchayat Act, 1973 other duties of Gram Panchayats are as follows:

1. A Gram Panchayat shall also perform such other functions as the State Government may assign to it in respect of—
   - (a) Primary, social, technical, vocational, adult or non-formal education;
   - (b) Rural dispensaries, health centres and maternity and child welfare centres;
   - (c) Management of any public ferry under the Bengal Ferries Act, 1885;
   - (d) Irrigation including minor irrigation, water management and watershed development;
   - (e) Agriculture including agricultural extension and fuel and fodder;
   - (f) Care of the infirm and the destitute;
   - (g) Rehabilitation of displaced persons;
   - (h) Improved breeding of cattle, medical treatment of cattle and prevention of cattle disease;
   - (i) Its acting as a channel through which Government assistance should reach the villages;
   - (j) Bringing waste land under cultivation through land improvement and soil conservation;
   - (k) Promotion of village plantations, social forestry and farm forestry;
   - (l) Arranging for cultivation of land lying fallow;
   - (m) Arranging for co-operative management of land and other resources of the village;
   - (n) Assisting in the implementation of land reform measure in its area;

(o) Implementation of such schemes as may be formulated or performance of such acts as may be entrusted to the Gram Panchayat by the State Government;
(p) Field publicity on matters connected with development works and other welfare measures undertaken by the State Government;
(q) Minor forest produce;
(r) Rural housing programme;
(s) Rural electrification including distribution of electricity;
(t) Non-conventional energy sources; and
(u) Women and Child development.

2. If the State Government is of opinion that a Gram Panchayat has persistently made default in the performance of any of the functions assigned to it under sub-section (7), the State Government may, after recording its reasons, withdraw such function from such Gram Panchayat.
(*Source*: West Bengal Panchayat Act, 1973, Section-20).

Discretionary Duties of Gram Panchayat

Section-21 of West Bengal Panchayat Act, 1973: Subject to such conditions as may be prescribed, a Gram Panchayat may, and shall if the State Government so directs, make provision for—

(a) The maintenance of lighting of public streets;
(b) Planting and maintaining trees on the sides of public streets or in other public places vested in it;
(c) The sinking of wells and excavation of ponds and tanks;
(d) The introduction and promotion of co-operative fanning, co-operative stores, and other co-operative enterprises, trades and callings;
(e) The construction and regulation of markets, the holding and regulation of fairs, *melas* and *haats* (weekly markets) and exhibitions of local produce and products of local handicrafts and home industries;
(f) The allotment of places for storing manure;
(g) Assisting and advising agriculturists in the matter of obtaining State loan and its distribution and repayment;

(h) Filling-up of insanitary depressions and reclaiming of unhealthy localities;

(i) The promotion and encouragement of cottage *Khadi*, village and small-scale including food processing industries;
   (1) Promotion of dairying and poultry;
   (2) Promotion of fishery; and
   (3) Poverty alleviation programme;

(j) The destruction of rabbit or ownerless dogs;

(k) Regulating the production and disposal of foodstuffs and other commodities in the manner prescribed;

(l) The construction and maintenance of rest houses, cattle sheds and cart stands;

(m) The disposal of unclaimed cattle;

(n) The disposal of unclaimed cropses and carcasses;

(o) The establishment and maintenance of libraries and reading rooms;

(p) The organization and maintenance of clubs and other places for recreation or games: (1) cultural activities including sports and games; (2) social welfare including welfare of the handicapped and mentally retarded; (3) welfare of socially and educationally backward classes of citizens and, in particular, of the Scheduled Castes and the Scheduled Tribes; (4) public distribution system; and (5) maintenance of community assets;

(q) The maintenance of records relating to population census, crop census, cattle census and census of unemployed persons and of other statistics as may be prescribed;

(r) The performance in the manner prescribed of any of the functions of the *Zilla Parishad* or the *Mahakuma Parishad* or the Council, as the case may be, with its previous approval, calculated to benefit the people living within the jurisdiction of the *Gram Panchayat*;

(s) Rendering assistance in extinguishing fire and protecting life and property when fire occurs;

(t) Assisting in the prevention of burglary and dacoity; and

(u) Any other local work or service of public utility which is likely to promote the health, comfort, convenience or material prosperity of the public, not otherwise provided for in this Act.

(*Source*: West Bengal Panchayat Act, 1973, Section-21).

Gram Panchayat Meeting

Every Gram Panchayat shall hold a meeting at least once in a month in the office of the Gram Panchayat. Such meeting shall be held on such date and at such hour as the *Gram Panchayat* may fix at the immediately preceding meeting:

1. The *Pradhan* or in his absence the *Upa-Pradhan* shall preside at the meeting of the Gram Panchayat; and in the absence of both or on the refusal of any or both to preside at a meeting, the members present shall elect one of them to be the President of the meeting.
2. One-third of the total number of members subject to a minimum of three members shall form a quorum for a meeting of a Gram Panchayat and no quorum shall be necessary for a adjourned meeting.
3. All questions coming before a Gram Panchayat shall be decided by a majority of votes and in case of equality of votes the person presiding shall have a second or casting vote.

Meetings of Gram Sansad (Section-16A)

In terms of Section-16A of West Bengal Panchayat Act, 1973:

- Every constituency of a Gram Panchayat shall have a *Gram Sansad* consisting of electors of the concerned constituency.
- Every Gram Panchayat shall hold within the local limits of the Gram an annual and a half-yearly meeting for each *Gram Sansad* at such place, on such date and at such hour as may be fixed by the Gram Panchayat.
- The annual meeting of the *Gram Sansad* shall be held ordinarily in the month of May and the half-yearly meeting of the *Gram Sansad* shall be held ordinarily in the month of November every year.
- A Gram Panchayat may, in addition to the annual and the half-yearly meeting, hold extraordinary meeting of a *Gram Sansad* at any time if the situation so warrants or if the State Government, by order, so directs for the purpose of holding such extraordinary meetings.

- Every meeting shall be presided over by the *Pradhan* and, in his absence, by the *Upa-Pradhan* and in the absence of both, the member or one of the members, as the case may be, elected from the constituency comprising the Gram Sabha or, in the absence of such member or members, any other member of the Gram Panchayat shall preside over the meeting.
- One-tenth of the total number of members shall form a quorum for a meeting of a *Gram Sansad.*
- A *Gram Sansad* shall guide and advise the Gram Panchayat in regard to the schemes for economic development and social justice undertaken or proposed to be undertaken in its area and may, without prejudice to the generality of such guidance and advice—
  - (i) Identify, or lay down principles for identification of the schemes which are required to be taken on priority basis for economic development of the village;
  - (ii) Identify, or lay down principles for identification of the beneficiaries for various poverty alleviation programmes;
  - (iii) Mobilize mass participation for community welfare programmes and programmes for adult education, family welfare and child welfare;
  - (iv) Promote solidarity and harmony among all sections of the people irrespective of religion, faith, caste, creed or race; and
  - (v) Record its objection to any action of the *Pradhan* or any other member of the Gram Panchayat for failure to implement any development scheme properly or without active participation of the people of that area.

(*Source*: West Bengal Panchayat Act, 1973, Section 16A).

Gram Sabha Meeting (Section 16-B)

Every Gram shall have a Gram Sabha consisting of all electors pertaining to the area of the Gram Panchayat—

- Every Gram Panchayat shall hold within the local limits of the Gram Panchayat an annual meeting, ordinarily in the month of December every year, of the Gram Sabha after completion of the half-yearly meeting of the *Gram Sansads.*

- The Gram Panchayat shall, at least seven days before the date of holding the meeting give public notice of such meetings by beat of drums as widely as possible, announcing the agenda, place, date and hour of the meeting. A notice of such meeting shall also be hung-up in the office of the Gram Panchayat. Similar publicity shall also be given in the case of an adjourned meeting.
- A meeting of the Gram Sabha shall be presided over by the *Pradhan* of the concerned Gram Panchayat or, in his absence, by the *Upa-Pradhan.*
- The Gram Sabha shall deliberate *Upan*, recommend for, and adopt resolution on, any matter referred to in sub-section (6) of section 16A and section 17A.
- The Gram Panchayat shall, on considering and collating the resolutions of the *Gram Sansads*, place before the Gram Sabha the resolutions of the *Gram Sansads* and the views of the Gram Panchayat together with its report on the actions taken and proposed to be taken on them for deliberation and recommendation by the Gram Sabha.

In pursuance of the provision of 73rd Constitutional Amendment Act, 1992, West Bengal Government lays more emphasis on meeting of Gram Sabha meeting.

(*Source*: West Bengal Panchayat Act, 1973, Section 16B).

Constitution of Upa-Samitis

As per West Bengal Gram Panchayat Administration Rules, 2004, every Gram Panchayat shall, as soon as may be within three months following the first meeting, constitute Five *Upa-Samitis* under sub-section (2) of section 32A of the West Bengal Panchayat Act, 1973.

Sanchalak: Within one week from the date of Constitution of the *Upa-Samiti*, the members of the respective *Upa-Samiti* elect in a meeting one member from themselves as *Sanchalak* of each *Upa-Samiti*. The most important aspects in this regard is that the *Sanchalak* of the *Nari O Shishu Unnayan Upa-Samiti* should be women.

Subjects to be dealt by Upa-Samitis: As per West Bengal Gram Panchayat Administration Rules, 2004.

1. Every *Upa-Samiti* shall prepare schemes and perform the functions of the Gram Panchayat in relation to the subjects

allotted to it within its budgetary provisions. It shall also be responsible for implementation of the works and schemes of the Gram Panchayat and those assigned to it by different departments of the State Government relating to the subjects as specified in the above table: Provided that the financial limits to which an *Upa-Samiti* is competent to execute works and schemes undertaken by the Gram Panchayat, shall be such as may, from time to time, be fixed by the Gram Panchayat or by the State Government.

2. For every item of expenditure exceeding its financial limit, each *Upa-Samiti* shall prepare proposal and place to the Gram Panchayat for approval. It shall be the duty of each *Upa-Samiti* to carry out the decision of the Gram Panchayat on such proposal.
3. An *Upa-Samiti* shall not alter the budgetary allocation of funds made by the Gram Panchayat according to the subjects allotted to it.

   (*Source*: West Bengal Gram Panchayat Administration Rules, 2004).

Decentralised Planning in West Bengal

Administrative decentralisation is not a new concept for West Bengal. Bengal Village Self-Government Act of 1919, which provided for a two-tier structure of Union Boards at the lower-level and District Boards at the higher-level. After Independence, the Act of 1919 was replaced by West Bengal Panchayat Act, 1957, reflecting the Constitutional directive to promote Panchayati Raj Institution. The Act provided for a Gram Panchayat in every village, which will function as the executive of Gram Sabha consisting of all the voters on the electoral role in the village. There were two elected executive posts, one *Adhyaksha* or president and *Upadhyaksha* or Vice-president. The Act of 1957 was prepared before the publication of the Balwant Rai Mehta Committee's report, which provided a shape to the Panchayati Raj. The Community Development Project (CDP) Blocks were not integrated with the Panchayat system in West Bengal. This created problems in the proper implementation of CDP. To incorporate the Panchayat institutions with the CDP framework, the West Bengal Zilla Parishad Act of 1963 decreed that Zilla Parishads were to be set-up in the place of the existing District Boards.

Thereafter, 15 *Zilla Parishads* and 325 *Anchalik Parishads* were formed. These two new institutions, along with the 19,602 Gram Panchayats and 2926 *Anchal Panchayats* formed under the 1957 Act, constituted the basis of a four-tier system of Rural Local Government. (*Source*: West Bengal Human Development Report, 2004).

In the mid-1960s, the State faced by severe economic crisis, particularly for the food distribution, which generated serious social unrest. It also was a period of general political instability with a split in the ruling Congress Party in 1965, the ascension to power of a United Front Government in 1967, its dismissal and return to power in Mid-Term Elections in 1969, President's rule from 1970 and the installation of a new Congress Government in 1972. In these circumstances, elections to the Panchayats—most of which had been formed between 1959 and 1963—could not be held.

The West Bengal Panchayat Act was passed in 1973; the existing structure was replaced by *Gram Panchayat* at village-level, Panchayat Samiti at block or intermediate level and *Zilla Parishad* at the district-level. The new Gram Panchayats were similar to the *Anchal Panchayats* of 1957 Act. As per the Balwant Rai Mehta Committee Report's recommendations, *Panchayat Samitis* were coterminous with blocks, and *Zilla Parishads* were coterminous with districts. As per this Act, election of members of all the three tiers for a five year term become mandatory. The *Pradhans* of Gram Panchayats were *ex-officio* members of Panchayat Samitis and the *Sabhapatis* of Panchayat Samitis were similarly *ex-officio* members of *Zilla Parishads*. The Act also provided for nominations of officials without voting rights into the standing committees of *Zilla Parishad*, and local MLAs and MPs as *ex-officio* members of both block and district-levels.

As per the 1973 Act was improved from the previous legislation by ensuring organic linkage between three-tiers, improving executive efficiency through a system of standing committees, and providing greater clarity regarding the functions. However, elections to these bodies were not held until the Left Front Government came to power in West Bengal in 1977. In June 1978 elections were held simultaneously for all the tiers of the rural local bodies for the first time. Since then, elections to the local bodies are holding at regular five years intervals.

After 1978, the newly elected Panchayats prioritize on execution of land reforms. At first Panchayats took the initiative to find out the *benami* land holdings, ensured the identification of excess land and the declaration of vested land. And ultimately charge handed over to the *bargadars*. By doing this West Bengal Panchayat received success by attaching the poor people with the Panchayati Raj Institutions. In case of rural development projects which were implemented through Panchayats, the beneficiaries of land reform were given priority in the receipt of benefits from those projects. The new leadership after 1978 came out of the tradition of peasant upsurge and struggle for land reform of the past three decades. The occupational engagement of the members showed a very significant picture that 43 per cent of elected members were landless poor. By 1988, 58 per cent of panchayat members were poor peasants or agricultural labourers. These result focused that the power structure shifted from moneylender (before 1978) to the weaker sections of the society.

One of the major objectives of the Panchayati Raj Institutions was involvement in the planning process. A number of reforms were introduced in the planning process from 1983 onwards to ensure the people's participation at the local-level. At the apex the State Planning Board (SPB) and the State Planning Department formed. At the district level there are two-tiers: the District Planning and Coordination Committee (DPCC), more of a deliberative body, and the District Planning Committee (DPC) its executive arm. The DPCs prepare the plan, which approved by the DPCCs. The Block Planning Committee (BPC) is the planning agency at the block level.

The District Planning Committee (DPC) is the nodal institution for decentralised planning structure which is headed by the Chairperson of Zilla Parishad and the District Collector is its member secretary. It has a mixed membership of non-officials and officials. The District Planning Committee was empowered to approve schemes up to ₹ 5 lakh while schemes of higher value and inter-district schemes would require the approval of the State Planning Board (West Bengal Human Development Report, 2004).

The Block Planning Committee headed by the *Sabhapati* of the *Panchayat Samiti*, comprised Chairpersons of all the Standing Committees of the *Samiti* and also of Gram Panchayats as well as the block-level officers of various development departments. The Block Development Officer (BDO) is its member-secretary. This Committee prepared block-level plans and approved block-level schemes that costing less than ₹ 50,000. Schemes involving more expenditure, and inter-block schemes, had to be submitted to the DPC for approval.

(*Source*: West Bengal Human Development Report, 2004).

Functional Decentralisation and Gram Panchayat

In every Gram Panchayat, there must be elected representatives called Gram Panchayat members (Five to Twenty-five). Among the members there are following categories of Office Bearers—

1. *Pradhan* (Head of the Office)-One
2. *Upa-Pradhan*—One
   Every Gram Panchayat shall, at its first meeting at which a quorum is present, elect, in the prescribed manner, one of its members to be *Pradhan* and another to be the *Upa-Pradhan* of the Gram Panchayat.
   (*Source*: W.B. Panchayat Act, 1973, Section 9).
3. *Sanchalak*—Five (One for each *Upa-Samiti*):
   Within one week from the date of constitution of the *Upa-Samiti*, the members referred to in clauses (a) and (b) of sub-section (3) of Section 32A of the Act shall elect in a meeting one member from themselves as *Sanchalak* of each *Upa-Samiti*.
4. Members—As general member.
   (*Source*: The West Bengal Panchayat Act, 1973; Section 32A).

Powers, Functions and Duties of Pradhan and Upa-Pradhan

Under Section 34 of West Bengal Panchayat Act, 1973:

The **Pradhan** shall—

(a) be responsible for the maintenance of the records of the Gram Panchayat;
(b) have general responsibility for the financial and executive administration of the Gram Panchayat;
(c) exercise administrative supervision and control over the work of the staff of the Gram Panchayat and the officers and employees whose service may be placed at the disposal of the Gram Panchayat by the State Government;
(d) for the transaction of business connected with this Act or for the purpose of making any order authorised thereby, exercise such powers, perform such functions and discharge such duties as may be exercised, performed or discharged by the Gram Panchayat under this Act or the rules made thereunder:

Provided that the *Pradhan* shall not exercise such powers, perform such functions or discharge such duties as may be required by the rules made under this Act to be exercised, performed or discharged by the Gram Panchayat at a meeting; and

(e) exercise such other powers, perform such other functions and discharge such other duties as the *Gram Panchayat* may, by general or special resolution, direct or as the State Government may by rules made in this behalf, prescribe.

The **Upa-Pradhan** shall—

(a) exercise such of the powers, perform such of the functions and discharge such of the duties of the *Pradhan* as the *Pradhan* may from time to time, subject to rules made in this behalf by the State Government, delegate to him by order in writing:

Provided that the *Pradhan* may at any time withdraw all or any of the powers, functions and duties so delegated to the *Upa-Pradhan*;

(b) during the absence of the *Pradhan*, exercise all the powers, perform all the functions and discharge all duties of the *Pradhan*;

(c) exercise such other powers, perform such other functions and discharge such other duties as the Gram Panchayat may, by general or special resolution, direct or as the State Government may, by rules made in this behalf, prescribe. (*Source*: West Bengal Panchayat Act, 1973, Section 34).

Duties of the Staff of Gram Panchayat

(i) *Executive Assistant (EA)*: The EA of the Gram Panchayat shall be in charge of the office of the Gram Panchayat. He shall act under the direct supervision of the *Pradhan* (or in his absence, the *Upa-Pradhan*) and shall be responsible to the Gram Panchayat through the *Pradhan* or the *Upa-Pradhan*, as the case may be. Notwithstanding anything contained in any other rules, order or notification, the Executive Assistant shall, subject to the direction and control of the Gram Panchayat and the *Pradhan*—

(a) Remain in executive charge of administrative including establishment functions and financial operation of the Gram Panchayat;

(b) Be the custodian of the Cheque Book and Pass Book for the Bank Account(s) and Post Office Savings Account(s) and the Cheque Book Register and all entries by the Executive Assistant in the Cheque Book Register shall be countersigned and authenticated by the Pradhan;

(c) Prepare the Cheque for encashment out of Gram Panchayat Fund, under the direction of the Pradhan subject to the resolution of the Gram Panchayat, put his signature in the counterfoil of the cheque in token of preparation of the cheque (in case of absence of the counterfoil of the cheque, he shall put his signature on the cover slip of the cheque book against the corresponding cheque number) and place it for the signature of the functionaries referred to in section 45(5) of the Act;

(d) Authenticate all entries in the cash book (to be written by the Secretary) and vouchers in support thereof;

(e) Perform the work relating to the implementation of programmes or schemes as may be prescribed and subject to the decision taken by and control of the *Gram Panchayat*;

(f) Prepare the annual budget of the Gram Panchayat in due time;

(g) Supervise the preparation of demand list in respect of tax and licence fees levied by the Gram Panchayat and take all steps for collection of revenue;

(h) Be responsible for allotting duties to the *Gram Panchayat Karmees*;

(i) Supervise the recording or noting of the resolutions adopted in the *Gram Sansad* and the *Gram Sabha* meeting;

(j) Produce the Cheque Book, Cheque Book Register and Pass Book for the Bank Account(s) and Post Office Savings Account(s) before the Auditors or inspecting officers as and when required; and

(k) Perform such other duties relating to the *Gram Panchayat* and the State Government as the *Pradhan* or the *Upa-Pradhan* or the State Government may direct from time to time.

(ii) *Secretary*: Notwithstanding anything contained in any other rules, order or notification, the Gram Panchayat Secretary shall, subject to the direction and control of the Gram Panchayat and the *Pradhan*, perform the following duties:

(a) Prepare list in respect of tax and license fees levied by Gram Panchayat;

(b) Maintain cash book and books of accounts;

(c) Prepare the monthly, quarterly, half-yearly and annual statement of accounts and placing the same before the Gram Panchayat;

(d) Assist the Executive Assistant towards preparation of Budget of the estimated receipts and disbursement of Gram Panchayat under the direction of Pradhan in due time;

(e) Keep all records of the Gram Panchayat in safe custody and produce the same in the meeting of the Gram Panchayat, Gram Sabha and Gram Sansad, excepting the Cheque Book, Pass Book(s) and the Cheque Book Register;

(f) Oversee payments of wages to labours engaged in various programmes under implementation by the Gram Panchayat;

(g) Record the resolution of the meeting held in the Gram Panchayat, Gram Sabha and Gram Sansad;

(h) Produce all records before the Auditors or inspecting officers as and when required;

(i) Submit to the appropriate authority all grant-in-aid bills in due times;

(j) Perform duties for encashment of cheques and disbursement of fund;

(k) Maintain all registers relating to all categories of Gram Panchayat employees; and

(l) Perform such other duties in respect of the work of the Gram Panchayat and of the State Government as the *Pradhan* or the *Upa-Pradhan* or the State Government may direct.

(iii) *Job Assistant*: Notwithstanding anything contained in any other rules, orders or notifications, the Job Assistant shall, subject to the direction and control of the Gram Panchayat and the *Pradhan*, perform the following duties:

(a) Prepare plans and estimates for work or projects in conformity with the financial and technical guidelines prescribed by the appropriate authority and in accordance with the decisions of the Gram Panchayat;

(b) Prepare measurement sheet, muster roll, token and acquittance roll;

(c) Watch and supervise the process of actual execution of work to ensure the technical standard prescribed for the work;

(d) Collect and compile progress of work, project and programme-wise supported by muster rolls, tokens and measurement sheets;

(e) Submit collected and compiled reports, returns and relevant records in office of the Gram Panchayat;

(f) Submit completion report and utilisation report, project and programme-wise, in respect of the work programme executed by the Gram Panchayat; and

(g) Carry out any other duties as may be assigned from time to time by the *Pradhan* or the *Upa-Pradhan* or the State Government.

(iv) *Nirman Sahayak (NS)*: Notwithstanding anything contained in any other rules, orders or notifications, the *Nirman Sahayak* shall, subject to the direction and control of the Gram Panchayat and the *Pradhan*, perform all the duties of the Job Assistant and any other duty as may be assigned from time-to-time by the *Pradhan* or the *Upa-Pradhan* or the State Government.

(v) *Sahayak*: Notwithstanding anything contained in any other rules, order or notification, the *Sahayak* shall, subject to the direction and control of the Gram Panchayat and the *Pradhan*, perform the following duties:

(a) Assist the Executive Assistant in matters of financial administration if and when required;

(b) Assist the Secretary to facilitate the proper maintenance of accounts and records, including vouchers of financial transactions made in and by the Gram Panchayat and encashment of the cheque;

(c) Assist the Secretary in recording the resolutions of the meetings held in the Gram Panchayat, Gram Sabha and Gram Sansad; and

(d) Any other duty as may be assigned by the *Pradhan* or the *Upa-Pradhan*, or the State Government, from time to time.

(vi) *Gram Panchayat Karmee*: Notwithstanding anything contained in any other rules, order or notification, the *Gram Panchayat Karmee* shall, subject to the direction and control of the Gram Panchayat and the *Pradhan*, perform the following duties:

(a) Discharge the duties pertaining to the functions of the Messenger Peon, Office Peon and Helper, and keeping watch of the Gram Panchayat office at night, if considered necessary by the Gram Panchayat on arrangement of shift duties;

(b) Perform such other duties as may be assigned to him from time to time by the *Pradhan* or the *Upa-Pradhan* or the Executive Assistant.

Inter-tier Demarcation of Functions

There is a lack of delineation of functions among the three-tiers of the PRI. No doubt, 29 items have been included in the 11th Schedule to the Constitution, but it is not clear as to what functions are to be performed by each tier. It varies from State to state.

States which have drawn the list of functions and activities for different levels of Panchayats in a routine manner on the lines of subjects mentioned in the 11th Schedule. These states have also added some other functions.

Most of the states categorised the functions under two heads:

(a) Obligatory or mandatory functions; and

(b) Discretionary functions.

Some states drew their own list.

(*Source*: The West Bengal Panchayat Act, 1973).

The functional transfer of subjects as mentioned in the 11th Schedule has been clarified through a detailed Activity Mapping exercise, which has been completed for 28 subjects (out of 29 subjects) as per Order No(s). 6102/PN/O/ dated 7.11.2005; No. 3969/PN/O/ dated 25.07.2006 and No. 4769/PN/O/dated 29.10.2007. Activity mapping for only one subject, i.e. technical and vocational education is yet to be published.

So far 11 departments of the Government have issued matching orders from their end for the purpose of devolution, namely—

(i) Forest,
(ii) Health and Family Welfare,
(iii) Women and Child Development and Social Welfare,
(iv) Water Investigation and Development,
(v) Micro and Small Scale Enterprises and Textiles,
(vi) Animal Resources Development,
(vii) Mass Education Extension and Library Services,
(viii) Fishery,
(ix) Power,
(x) Food Processing Industries and Horticulture, and
(xi) Panchayat and Rural Development Department.

In addition to those the Land and Land Reforms Department assigned responsibilities to the PRIs from the very beginning of the Panchayat system. The duties and responsibilities of Panchayat functionaries in respect of activities of Land and Land Reforms Department have been laid down in the West Bengal Land and Land Reforms Act, 1955, West Bengal Estate Acquisition Act, 1953 and West Bengal Land Reforms Manual, 1991.

Devolution of Powers and Authority to the Upa-Samitis of Gram Panchayats

Constitution of Upa-Samitis: Under Section 32A of the West Bengal Panchayat Act, 1973:

(1) Subject to such direction as may be issued by the State Government in this behalf, a Gram Panchayat shall as soon as may be within three months following the first meeting referred to in section 9, constitute *Upa-Samitis* as referred

to in sub-section (2) and delegate its powers, functions and duties to such *Upa-Samitis*, in such manner as may be prescribed.

(2) Without prejudice to the generality of any other provisions of this Act, a Gram Panchayat shall constitute in such manner as may be prescribed the following *Upa-Samitis*—

(i) *Artha O Parikalpana Upa-Samiti*,
(ii) *Krishi O Pranisampada Bikas Upa-Samiti*,
(iii) *Shiksha O Janashasthya Upa-Samiti*,
(iv) *Nari, Shishu Unnayan O Samaj Kalyan Upa-Samiti*,
(v) *Shilpa O Parikathama Upa-Samiti*, and

Such other *Upa-Samiti* as the Gram Panchayat may, subject to the approval of the State Government, constitute.

(*Source*: The West Bengal Panchayat Act, 1973; Section 32A).

Subjects to be dealt by Upa-Samitis: In order to ensure better functioning and devolution of power and authority of the Gram Panchayat five *Upa-Samities* are formed (Section: 32A of West Bengal Panchayat Act, 1973) just as there are Sthayee Samities at the upper two-tier.

The *Upa-Samitis* of a Gram Panchayat shall deliberate *Upan* and deal with the subjects specified below:

1. *Artha O Parikalpana Upa-Samiti*: (i) Finance, (ii) Budget, (iii) Accounts, (iv) Audit, (v) Taxation, (vi) Resource Mobilization, (vii) Establishment and Office Management, (viii) Preparation of Gram Panchayat Plans, (ix) Implementation, Monitoring and Evaluation of all Poverty Alleviation including Employment Generation Programmes, (x) Food Security and Public Distribution Programme, (xi) Preparation of Resource Inventory and Database of the Gram Panchayat Planning, (xii) Disaster Control Management, (xiii) Management of *Haat*, Bazar, Ferry Service of Gram Panchayat, and (xiv) Coordination of works assigned to different *Upa-Samitis* and any other work not entrusted with any other *Upa-Samiti*.
2. *Krishi O Pranisampada Bikas Upa-Samiti*: (i) Agriculture and Agro-industries, (ii) Horticulture, (iii) Agri-marketing, (iv) Irrigation including Small Irrigation, (v) Water Resources

Development, (vi) Social Forestry, (vii) Soil Conservation, (viii) Apiculture, (ix) Sericulture, (x) Animal Resources Development, (xi) Fisheries, (xii) Watershed Development, (xiii) Cooperative Movement, (xiv) Provident Fund for Landless Agricultural Labourers etc.

3. *Shiksha O Janashasthya Upa-Samiti*: (i) Literacy campaign, (ii) *Shishu Siksha Karmasuchi*, (iii) *Madhyamik Shiksha Karmasuchi*, (iv) Primary Education, (v) Mass Education, (vi) Rural Library, (vii) Mid-day Meal Programme, (viii) Rural Water Supply, (ix) Rural Dispensaries and Health Clinic, (x) Public Health and Sanitation, (xi) Immunisation and Family Welfare Programmes, (xii) Prevention of Communicable Diseases, etc.
4. *Nari, Shishu Unnayan O Samaj Kalyan Upa-Samiti*: (i) Self-help Groups formed under various programmes including Swarnajayanti Gram Swarozgar Yojana/National Rural Livelihood Mission, (ii) Integrated Child Development Scheme, (iii) National Social Assistance Programme, (iv) Social Welfare and Welfare of Women and Children, and (v) Welfare of Weaker Communities including old and handicapped people.
5. *Shilpa O Parikathama Upa-Samiti*: (i) Cottage and Small Scale Industries, (ii) Rural Artisans, (iii) Infrastructure Development, (iv) Indira Aawas Yojana, (v) Construction of Rural Roads, Culverts and Rural Housing, and (vi) Rural Electrification and Generating Alternative Energy Resources. (*Source*: The West Bengal Panchayat Act, 1973; Section 32A).

Powers of Upa-Samiti

(1) Every *Upa-Samiti* shall prepare schemes and perform the functions of the Gram Panchayat in relation to the subjects allotted to it within its budgetary provisions. It shall also be responsible for implementation of the works and schemes of the Gram Panchayat and those assigned to it by different departments of the State Government relating to the subjects specified above. Provided that the financial limits to which an *Upa-Samiti* is competent to execute works and schemes undertaken by the Gram Panchayat, shall be such as may,

from time to time, be fixed by the Gram Panchayat or by the State Government.

(2) For every item of expenditure exceeding its financial limit, each *Upa-Samiti* shall prepare proposal and place to the Gram Panchayat for approval. It shall be the duty of each *Upa-Samiti* to carry out the decision of the Gram Panchayat on such proposal.

(3) An *Upa-Samiti* shall not alter the budgetary allocation of funds made by the Gram Panchayat according to the subjects allotted to it.

(*Source*: The West Bengal Panchayat Act, 1973; Section 32A).

Functions and Duties of Upa-Samitis

(1) When any scheme is assigned by any department of the State Government or by the Panchayat Samiti or by the Zilla Parishad or executed from its own resources, the Gram Panchayat shall forward the contents of the scheme to the appropriate *Upa-Samiti* for drawing-up a detailed plan for its execution.

(2) While forwarding the scheme, the Gram Panchayat may, issue direction to the *Upa-Samiti* of the manner in which the plan for its execution shall be drawn up.

(3) The *Upa-Samiti* shall cause preparation of plan and estimate of the work by taking assistance of any official of the State Government, the statutory Board, the Corporation or any other official receiving the grant, financial assistance, or the remuneration from the State Government, who shall render all assistance in this regard as may be necessary and proceed to execute the scheme.

(*Source*: The West Bengal Panchayat Act, 1973; Section 32A).

Fiscal Decentralisation and Gram Panchayat in West Bengal

The financial resources of the Panchayats broadly comprise internal revenue mobilized by themselves through the exercise of tax and non-tax powers, and resources received from the State in the form of devolution and grant from both the State and then Union Governments.

Under **Section 45** of the West Bengal Panchayat Act, 1973 (West Bengal Act XLI of 1973):

(1) For every Gram Panchayat there shall be constituted a Gram Panchayat Fund bearing the name of the Gram Panchayat and that shall be placed to the credit thereof—
   (a) Contributions and grants, if any, made by the Central or the State Government;
   (b) Contributions and grants, if any, made by the Zilla Parishad, [*Mahakuma Parishad*, Council] Panchayat Samiti or any other local authority;
   (c) Loans, if any, granted by the Central Government or the State Government;
   (d) All receipts on account of taxes, rates and fees levied by it;
   (e) All receipts in respect of any schools, hospitals, dispensaries-buildings, institutions or works vested in, constructed by or placed under the control and management of the Gram Panchayat;
   (f) All sums received as gift or contribution and all income from any trust or endowment made in favour of the Gram Panchayat;
   (g) Such fines and penalties imposed and realised under the provisions of this Act as may be prescribed; and
   (h) All other sums received by or on behalf of the Gram Panchayat.

(*Source*: The West Bengal Panchayat Act, 1973; Section 45).

Gram Panchayats' Own Source of Revenue (Imposition of Tax and Non-Tax)

(i) Imposition of Tax (on Lands and Buildings) by Gram Panchayats

Articles 243H, 243I and 243X empower the PRIs and municipal bodies to levy and collect the taxes. Under **Section 46** of the West Bengal Panchayat Act, 1973:

(1) Subject to such rules as may be made in this behalf, a Gram Panchayat shall impose yearly—

(a) On lands and buildings within the local limits of its jurisdiction, a tax—
   (i) At the rates of one per centum of the annual value of such lands and buildings when the annual value does not exceed rupees one thousand, and
   (ii) At the rate of two per centum of the annual value of such lands and buildings when the annual value exceeds rupees one thousand, to be paid by the owners and occupiers thereof.

(b) [Clause (b) was omitted by sec. 12 (1) of the West Bengal Panchayat (Amendment) Act, 1992 (West Bengal Act XVII of 1992).]

(2) The following lands and buildings shall be exempted from imposition of tax under sub-section (1), namely—
   (a) Lands and buildings, the annual value of which is not more than two hundred and fifty rupees;
   (b) Lands and buildings belonging to a local authority and used or intended to be used exclusively for a public purpose and not used or intended to be used for purposes of profits;
   (c) Lands and buildings used exclusively for religious, educational or charitable purposes.

(3) The State Government may, by notification, exempt either wholly or in part any other class of properties or classes of properties specified in the notification from the taxes or rates leviable under this section.

(4) *[Sub-section (4) was omitted by sec. 12(2) of the West Bengal Panchayat (Amendment) Act, 1992 (West Bengal Act XVII of 1992).]

(5) Subject to such rules as may be made in this behalf a Gram Panchayat shall levy—
   (a) on all transfers of improvable property situated within the local limits of the Gram, a duty in the shape of an additional stamp duty at the rate of two per centum or, as the case may be, the amount of the consideration for the sale, the value of the property in the case of a gift, the amount secured by the mortgage, the value of the property of the greater value in the case of exchange, or the value of the rent for the first ten years in the case of a lease, as set forth in the instrument;

(b) a duty in the shape of an additional stamp duty at the rate of ten per centum on all payments for admission to any entertainment.

(6) The State Government may make rules for regulating the collection of the duty on transfers of immovable property and duty on entertainment referred to in sub-section (5), the payment thereof to the Gram Panchayat and the deduction of any expenses incurred by the State Government in the collection thereof.

(*Source*: The West Bengal Panchayat Act, 1973; Section 46).

(ii) Imposition of Non-Tax (Levy of the Fees, Rates, Tolls etc.) by Gram Panchayats

Under **Section 47** of the West Bengal Panchayat Act, 1973:

(1) Subject to such maximum rates as the State Government may prescribe, a Gram Panchayat may levy the following fees, rates and tolls, namely—

(i) Fees on registration of vehicles;

(ii) Fees on plaints and petitions and other processes in suits and cases instituted before the *Nyaya Panchayat* concerned;

(iii) A fee for providing sanitary arrangements at such places of worship or pilgrimage, fairs and *melas* within its jurisdiction as may be specified by the State Government by notification.

(iv) A water rate, where arrangement for the supply of water for drinking, irrigation or any other purpose is made by the Gram Panchayat within its jurisdiction;

(v) A lighting rate, where arrangement for lighting of public streets and places is made by the Gram Panchayat within its jurisdiction;

(vi) A conservancy rate, where arrangement for clearing private latrines, urinals and cesspools is made by the Gram Panchayat within its jurisdiction;

(vii) Fees on [registration] for running trade, wholesale or retail, within the jurisdiction of the Gram Panchayat unless such [registration] or such trade is prohibited under any law for the time being in force;

(viii) Tolls on persons, vehicles or animals or any class of them at any toll-bar which is established by the Gram Panchayat on any road or bridge vested in, or under the management of the Gram Panchayat;

(ix) Tolls in respect of any ferry established by or under the management of the Gram Panchayat;

(x) *[Clauses (x) was omitted by sec. 7(1) of the West Bengal Panchayat (Amendment) Act, 2004 (West Bengal Act XVIII of 2004).];

(xi) A general sanitary rate where arrangement for the construction and maintenance of the construction and maintenance of public latrines is made by the Gram Panchayat within its jurisdiction;

(xii) A drainage rate where arrangement for regular clearance of common drains is made by the Gram Panchayat within its jurisdiction;

(xiii) *[Clauses (xiii) was omitted by sec. 7(2) of the West Bengal Panchayat (Amendment) Act, 2004 (West Bengal Act XVIII of 2004).];

(xiv) Fees for use of burning ghat vested in or under the management and control of, the Gram Panchayat;

(xv) Fees on registration for [shallow or deep tubewells] fitted with motor-driven pump sets and for irrigation for commercial purpose, subject to such terms and conditions as may be prescribed. [*Explanation*—In this clause, "commercial purpose" includes any purpose for which irrigation water is supplied to the land of any persons, other the owner of the shallow tubewell, on realisation of water rates, by whatever name called, from the owner of such land.];

(xvi) Fees on the village produces sold in the village market organized by the Gram Panchayat to be determined by means of weight, measurement or by number or any two or more of them;

(xvii) Fees on erection, exhibition, fixing or retaining upon or over any land, building, wall, hoarding, or structure, any advertisement for public display in any manner whatsoever, in any place whether public or private excepting those exhibited by the State Government in the public interest.

(2) The Gram Panchayat shall not undertake registration of a vehicle or levy fee therefor and shall not provide sanitary arrangements at places of worship or pilgrimage, fairs and melas within its jurisdiction or levy fee therefor if such vehicle has already been registered by any other authority under any law for the time being in force or if such provision for sanitary arrangement has already been made by any other local authority.

(3) The scales of tolls, and the fees or rates and the terms and condition of imposition thereof, shall be such a may be provided by bye-laws.

(4) Such bye-laws may provide for exemption from all or any of the tolls, fees or rates in any cases.

(*Source*: The West Bengal Panchayat Act, 1973; Section 47).

Devolution of Fund

Gram Panchayats received fund/resources from the State in the form of devolution and grant from both the State and then Union Governments. Major devolution of funds:

1. *State Finance Commission (SFC)*: Grants under Third State Finance Commission (SFC) will be divided into two segments:

- Fund under first segment (98%) will be termed as *Bangla Gram Bikash Prakalpa*. Fund under *Bangla Gram Bikash Prakalpa* will be allocated to the Zilla Parishads, Panchayat Samitis and Gram Panchayats in the ratio of 12:18:70.
- Fund under second segment (2%) will be allotted among PRIs of all tiers as Incentive Grant in proportion to the "Own Source Revenue" collected by PRI body in excess of the collection of the last year. This incentive grant will henceforth be termed as *Panchayat Sampad Bikash Prakalpa*.

2. *Central Finance Commission (CFC)*: Government of India has accepted the recommendations of the Thirteenth Central Finance Commission (CFC) for devolution of grants-in-aid. The General Basic Grant for the three-tier Panchayati Raj Institutions (PRIs) and the Special Area Basic Grant for the Hill Areas of Darjeeling District will be given in two instalments in the months of July and January of every year up to 2014-15. The State will be eligible for the second

installment depending on the utilization of at least 75 per cent of the available fund under Thirteenth CFC for the entire State.

Scarcity of drinking water is a common problem of most of the districts during summer. Hence, fund for maintenance of the sources for drinking water @ ₹ 1 lakh per Gram Panchayat has been estimated to be required annually and 50 per cent of such requirement has been allotted separately from the available fund of Thirteenth CFC to the Gram Panchayats.

After earmarking the required fund for the above mentioned purposes, the rest amount has been allotted to the Zilla Parishad, Panchayat Samitis and Gram Panchayats in the ratio of 12:18:70. Allocation of fund to the Panchayat Samitis and Gram Panchayats within a district has been made following the criteria laid down in the guideline of Third SFC.

3. *Mahatma Gandhi National Rural Employment Guarantee Scheme (MGNREGS)*: The Indian job guarantee scheme, enacted as Act by legislation on 25 August, 2005. The law was initially called the NREGA but was renamed as the MGNREGA on 2 October, 2009. The scheme provides a legal guarantee for at least one hundred days of employment in every financial year to adult members of any household willing to do public work-related unskilled manual work.

From 1st April, 2013, an unskilled job card holder receives ₹ 151 for a day's labour and on completion of appropriate quantum of work as per the Scheduled of Rates (SOR) as in vogue [Memo. No. 1852(19)/RD/P/NREGA/18S-01/08; 06.03.2013 of P&RD Dept., GoWB].

The Central Government shall meet the cost of the following, namely—

(a) the amount required for payment of wages for unskilled manual work under the Scheme; and
(b) up to three-fourths of the material cost of the Scheme including payment of wages to skilled and semi-skilled workers subject to the provisions.

The State Government shall meet the cost of the following, namely—

(a) the cost of unemployment allowance payable under the Scheme; and
(b) one-fourth of the material cost of the Scheme including

payment of wages to skilled and semi-skilled workers subject to the provisions.

4. *Backward Regions Grant Fund (BRGF)*: The BRGF is designed to redress regional imbalances in development. The fund will provide financial resources for supplementing and converging existing developmental inflows into identified districts, so as to—

(a) Bridge critical gaps in local infrastructure and other development requirements that are not being adequately met through existing inflows;
(b) Strengthen, to this end Panchayat and Municipality-level governance with more appropriate capacity-building, to facilitate participatory planning, decision-making, implementation and monitoring, to reflect local felt needs;
(c) Provide professional support to local bodies for planning, implementation and monitoring their plans; and
(d) Improve the performance and delivery of critical functions assigned to Panchayats, and counter possible efficiency and equity losses on account of inadequate local capacity.

BRGF consists of two funding windows, as follows:

(a) A Capability Building Fund, and
(b) A substantially untied Grant.

Criteria for Distribution of Funds: The substantially untied grants will be distributed among the districts concerned as follows:

(a) Every district will receive a fixed minimum amount of ₹ 10 crore per annum;
(b) Fifty per cent of the balance allocation under the Scheme will be allocated on the basis of the share of the population of the district in the total population of all backward districts; and
(c) The remaining 50 per cent will be distributed on the basis of the share of the district in the total area of all backward districts.

Financial Autonomy: It means Share of *Gram Panchayat*'s Own Fund (Tax and Non-Tax) in Gram Panchayat's total (include all funds) expenditure. The Financial Autonomy Ratio (FAO) shows the extent of reliance on own sources of funds which lead to autonomy. In this case the top ranker is the Gram Panchayat with the highest FAR. Higher autonomy may be appreciated but it could also mean that the flow of Government and other funds are inadequate for the development of a particular Gram Panchayat.

SHG and Decentralised Planning

Making legal provision and providing structural framework were not enough for the poorer section of the community and the women to participate in the process of decentralisation and rural development. In order to have the voice of the vulnerable and the marginalized sections heard, they were organized and their capacities have been increased for being able to voice their demands and influence functioning of the Panchayats in their favour. This has been done by organizing the poor, particularly the women in Self-Help Groups (SHGs). SHG movement, especially of the women, in the State has gained a lot of momentum and a large number of SHGs have been formed out of which majority have been formed by women. Organizing the poor in groups has been strengthened further so that every poor rural family has at least one member included in an SHG within the Eleventh Plan period.

(*Source*: Bandyopadhyay and Mukherjee, 2004).

Special focus has been taken up to improve the understanding of the SHGs regarding the socio-economic situations in their own context as well as services to be made available by the Panchayats for its improvement. They were encouraged to participate in the affairs of the Panchayat as citizen and to avail due services from the Panchayats for their socio-economic advancement for which the State Government would take measures for building up their capacity. The State has lent its support to provide access to credit to all the SHGs within the Eleventh Five Year Plan period. Their achieving minimum- level of income has been crucial for being able to participate freely, which is essential for expansion of democracy.

Legal provision has been made for the representation of SHGs in the *Gram Unnayan Samities* and *Upa-Samities*. Also, the SHGs were being organized further in Sub-Clusters within the *Gram Sansad*, Clusters within the GPs. The Clusters are being federated in bigger bodies known as Federations in each Block for synergy in their functioning. Those are being formed by the women SHGs in general and men are also involved in certain areas. Orders have been issued for representation of the Clusters and the Federations in the *Upa-Samitis* and *Sthayee Samitis* of the GP and the PS respectively, as invited members, so that, they can give their feedback for decision-making in their favour and whatever decision is taken can be communicated to their members for wider knowledge and participation. The task is to form such Sub-Clusters, Clusters and Federations in all *Gram Sansads*, Gram Panchayats and Panchayat Samitis respectively within the Eleventh Five Year Plan period so that every GUS, *Upa-Samiti* and *Sthayee Samiti* has representations of the poor group of women to act as a pressure group. These organizations, apart from playing the most crucial roles of ensuring benefit to their members, will also influence the local Governments to remain pro-poor for maximizing benefit to the most deprived section of the community. The responsibility of the State Government were to build capacities of the Panchayats to utilize the Sub-Clusters, Clusters and Federations as their agents for poverty alleviation and making social changes for uplift of the women will be an important task to be achieved within the said period.

References

Dutta, P. and Sen, P. (2009), *Good Governance and Development: Contexts and Concerns*, Kolkata: Progressive Publishers.

The 73rd Constitutional Amendment Act, 1992.

The Gazette of India; Ministry of Law and Justice, September 7, 2005.

The West Bengal Human Development Report, 2004.

The West Bengal Panchayat Act, 1973.

The West Bengal Panchayat (Amendment) Act, 1992.

The West Bengal Panchayat (Amendment) Act, 1994.

West Bengal Panchayats (Amendment) Act, 2003.

The West Bengal Panchayat Amendment Act, 2010.

4
Analytical Framework and Methodology of the Study

Analytical Framework

This chapter is to explain the analytical framework in the light of the objectives as mentioned in the introductory chapter. It may be recalled that in theory, the promotion of effective decentralisation can only be ensured when necessary factors like knowledge, skill, attitude and participation of major stakeholders of the PRI are being integrated properly. Again, Decentralisation is an interdisciplinary planning system for ensuring sustainable development. It consists of economic development, women empowerment, development of education, housing, infrastructure, child care, health, sanitation, drinking water, environment and other development indicators of sustainable development. Through decentralisation, rural people can get interdisciplinary service from PRIs and SHGs can boost the delivery mechanism.

So, it is very clear that decentralisation, Panchayati Raj Institutions and Self-Help Groups are interlinked with each other as these are the key variables of sustainable development. Their relationship can be conceptualized by a simple Fig. 4.1.

Hence, the research objectives can be analyzed through illustrating the relationship between various variables of the entire system as mentioned in Fig. 4.1. In this context the idea of analytical framework is inspired and partly conceptualized by a framework as

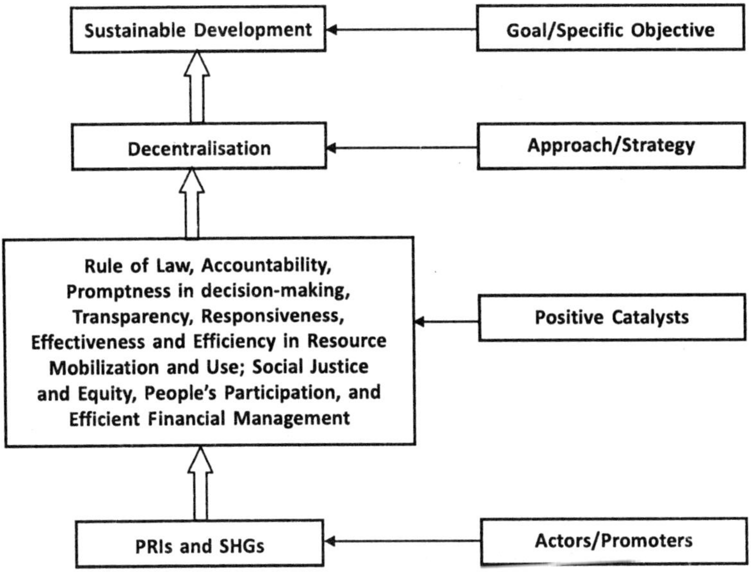

Fig. 4.1: Analytical Framework of the Study

elucidated by Romeo (1999) in the "*Decentralisation-to-Rural Development*" paradigm. To analyze the relationships between different factors, Romeo describes the concept *"Ecology of Governance"* that transcends the activity of the State sector and refers to a balance and network between the state, Civil Society (stated as social capital) and market place.

The framework explains the relationships between different conditions that affect the performance of decentralised governance. Decentralised governance provides a set of institutions that transcends public activity and carry out a network among local community, local institutions [Panchayati Raj Institutions (PRIs)] and different actors (elected or non-elected representatives, officials, SHG Members). It insists on devolution and de-concentration of powers and functions to the people. On the basis of this framework we have developed a modified version for ensuring the research outcome as per the objectives mentioned in the introductory chapter. In the new framework, analysis has been done on every aspect of Gram Panchayats including General Profile Gram Panchayats, Socio-Economic condition of the Gram Panchayat members, role of PRI and SHG, planning and implementation process of micro-level plan and people's participation, financial or fiscal status, role and Status of various committees, knowledge, attitude, perceptions and participation-level of various actors of Gram Panchayat, socio-cultural constrains.

Variables and Measuring Indicators

General Profile of Gram Panchayat

General profile of Gram Panchayat is measured by the basic information related to demography, livelihood structure and infrastructure within a Gram Panchayat. Basic information in this context is measured by the physical data available in the Gram Panchayat register, other secondary sources and perceptions of the Gram Panchayat officials. Indicators which are developed for this analysis are given in Table 4.1:

Table 4.1: Measuring Indicator of Gram Panchayat General Profile

Variables	*Indicators*
General Profile of the Gram Panchayat	Demographic Status, Literacy Status, Infrastructure Details

Socio-economic and Political Status of the Gram Panchayat Members

This is measured through the information gather from the Gram Panchayat members and later all the information are cross checked from Gram Panchayat official data. The data in this context is gathered through interview method. All the GP members are interviewed on a pre-designed schedule. Indicators are developed for these analysis are given in Table 4.2.

Role of Panchayati Raj Institutions (PRIs) and Self-Help Groups (SHGs)

Role of Panchayati Raj Institutions and Self-Help Group is measured by analyzing various secondary literatures, Government Order and rule and information gather from Focused Group Discussion (FGD)

Table 4.2: Measuring Indicators of Socio-economic and Political Status of Panchayat Members

Variable	*Indicators*
Socio-economic and Political Status of the Gram Panchayat Members	Gender Composition, Caste Composition, Literacy Status, Status of SHG Engagement, Occupational Status, Political Representation

of various actors (GP members, Officials, Common People, SHG members) and development professionals. Indicators developed for this analysis are given in Table 4.3.

Table 4.3: Measuring Indicators of PRI and SHG Role

Variable	*Indicators*
Role of PRI	Strengthen Democratic Structure, Improving Civic Services, Management of Natural Resources, Promotion of Livelihood Opportunities, Poverty Alleviation, Ensuring Social Equity, Planning from below for development, Developing Panchayat Private Partnership, Mobilizing Own Source of Revenue, Budget and Financial Management, Social Audit
Role of SHG	Participation in Gram Panchayat Meetings, Ensure Effective Plan Preparation and implementation, Participation in Various Committees of GP, Participation in Training Programme, Play Active Role in Various Panchayat Activities, Motivate other Villagers to participate in the Gram Panchatyat activities.

Planning and Implementation Process of Micro-Level Plan and People's Participation

Planning and implementation process of micro-level plan and people's participation is measured through analyzing the Gram Panchayat Plan Documents at various levels (Sansad Level Plan Resolution, Gram Sabha Plan Resolution, *Upa Samiti*-wise plan documents and Annual Action Plan). Analysis is been done to quantify the percentage of plan finally incorporated in Annual Action Plan and implemented in the field. The entire planning process is also been analyzed in the context of Planning Cycle to study the actual scenario of decentralised planning process. The people's participation is measured through the attendance of Gram Sabha and Gram Sansad meeting. Participation is also measured as per gender and in the basis of SHG engagement. The analysis is done as per the indicators mentioned in Table 4.4.

Table 4.4: Measuring Indicators of Planning and Implementation Process of Micro-Level Plan and People's Participation

Variable	*Indicators*
Planning and Implementation Process of Micro Level Plan and People's Participation	People's Participation in Gram Sabha and Gram Sansad Meeting, Status of Planning and Implementation of Sansad Level Plans, Status of Sector-wise Plan.

Financial/Fiscal Status

Fiscal or Financial Status is measured through analyzing the financial statement of the Gram Panchayats. Data related to own fund, tied and untied fund have been analyzed to find out the amount of fund received, utilized and percentage of fund expended. Major fund sources like GP's own fund, 3rd State Finance Commission, 13th Central Finance Commission, MGNREGA has taken for this analysis. The Financial sustainability of Gram Panchayats is also measured through the Financial Autonomy Ratio (FAR). In this context, the ratio of Own Fund and Development expenditure has been calculated. The indicators which are used to analyze the financial status of the Gram Panchayat are given in Table 4.5.

Table 4.5: Measuring Indicators of Financial/Fiscal Status

Variable	*Indicators*
Financial/Fiscal Status	Status of Own Fund Collection and Per Capita Collection, Expenditure of Own Fund and Per Capita Expenditure, Income Expenditure, Status of Major Schemes like 3rd SFC, 13th CFC, MGNREGA, Financial Autonomy Ratio.

Status and Role of Various Samities/Committees under Gram Panchayat

Various Samitis or Committees were formed under the Gram Panchayat Structure to improve the participation of common villagers in planning and implementation process, improve the women participation and efficient implementation of development schemes. The role of these committees is measured through the perception of SHG, Non-SHG villagers. The perception has been measured in terms of score obtained by individuals on the scale developed for this analysis. The perception score depended on the nature of the response (Yes/No) expressed by the respondents for the different statements given in the scale. Scale was developed by using different indicators as given in Table 4.6.

Table 4.6: Measuring Indicators of Status and Role of Various Samitis/ Committees

Variable	*Indicators*
Role of Various Samitis/Committees	Existence, Structure of the Committee, Effectiveness

Knowledge, Attitude and Perception of Various Actors of Gram Panchayat

The knowledge attitude and perceptions of various actors of Gram Panchayat is measured through level of awareness-level and perceptions of Gram Panchayat members, SHG members and Non-SHG women members. For the present study, data related to awareness in terms of PRI related issues, Administrative, Planning and Implementation process were collected from the respondents through different area scales consisting of different indicators. The awareness on different issues was measured through the nature of response (Yes/ No) expressed by the respondents for different statements given in the scale. The scale was developed by using various indicators under different sections as mentioned in Table 4.7. The perception of Gram Panchayat members were measured through their responses (strongly agree, agree, disagree and strongly disagree) on various statements related to Gram Panchayats. The data in this context presented in the percentage form. The perceptions of SHG members and Non-SHG villagers were measured through their response (Yes/No) on various statements given in the scale. Finally, the perception score was calculated to analyze the perception of the respondents. The indicators used for developing the scale are given in Table 4.7.

Testing of Hypothesis Regarding Changing Status of Decentralisation

To measure the effect of SHG movement on decentralisation process

Table 4.7: Measuring Indicators of Knowledge, Attitude and Perception of Various Actors

Variable	*Indicators*
Awareness level of the GP members on PRI Related Issues	Awareness on Three-tier PRI System, Role of Gram Panchayat, Caste Reservation System, Women Reservation System, *Gram Unnayan Samiti, Gram Sansad, Gram Sabha, Upa-Samiti*, Development Schemes.
Awareness level of the GP members on Administration related Issues of PRIs	Awareness on Planning Process, Budget Making, Various Development Schemes, Prioritization of Schemes, Implementation Process.
Awareness level of SHG Members and Non-SHG Villagers on PRI	Panchayat Vote, Awareness on Three-tier PRI System, Role of Gram Panchayat, Caste Reservation System, Women Reservation System, Development Schemes.
Awareness level of the SHG members and Non-SHG Villagers on Planning and Implementation Process	Awareness on *Gram Unnayan Samiti, Gram Sansad, Gram Sabha, Upa-Samiti*, Planning or Budgeting Process, Implementation Process, Income Expenditure Details.
Perception of Gram Panchayat Members	Perceptions on Significance of decentralisation process, true transfer of power, Gram Panchayat Focus on Decentralisation, Significance of *Gram Unnayan Samiti*, Political Influence, People's Participation, Importance of Gram Sabha, SHG-PRI Linkages, SHG as Parallel Power Structure, Women Empowerment in Political Spare, Sensitivity, SHG's Capacity and Involvement, Role of SHG etc.
Perceptions of SHG Members and Non-SHG Villagers on PRI	Perceptions on Training Programme Organized by Panchayat, Panchayat's Sensitivity and Response, Participation.

some variables have been identified to conduct the association test. The responses on different issues have been measured through the nature of response (Yes/No) expressed by the respondents for different statements. Association test has been done by using these data.

Method of Association Test

H_0—Null Hypothesis (this hypothesis is nullified the hypothesis).
H_1—Alternative Hypothesis.

There are two types of error in testing hypothesis.

Error I: Rejecting a null hypothesis when it is true.
Error II: Accepting a null hypothesis when it is false.

Probability of type I error is known as the level of significance. This is also known as size of the critical region.

Qualitative data test or Chi-square Test (χ^2): χ^2 test of independence.

Table of Observed Frequency

Variable		*A*		
B		A1	A2	Total
	B1	AB11	AB12	AB11+AB12=C
	B2	AB21	AB22	AB21+AB22=D
	Total	**AB11+AB21=E**	**AB12+AB22=F**	**AB11+AB12+AB21+ AB22=GT**

H_0 — Variable A is independent of Variable B.
H_1 — Variable A is dependent on variable B.

Table of Expected Frequency

Variable		*A*		
		A1	*A2*	*Total*
B	B1	C*E/GT=Q	C*F/GT=W	(Q+W)
	B2	D*E/GT=R	D*F/GT=P	(R+P)
	Total	**(Q+R)**	**(W+P)**	**GT**

k=2; l=2

Here, k = number of columns and
l = number of rows

$$\text{Degree of Freedom} = (k-1) \times (l-1) = (2-1) \times (2-1) = 1$$

$$\chi^2_1 = (AB11-Q)^2/Q + (AB12-W)^2/W + (AB21-R)^2/R + (AB22-P)^2/P$$

After calculating Chi-square value, the value should be at 5 per cent or 1 per cent level of significance.

From the table we have to find out the value of χ^2 at 5 per cent or 1 per cent level of significance. These values are denoted in the table as $\chi^2_{.05,1}$ or $\chi^2_{.01,1}$ respectively.

If the null-hypothesis is rejected then the degree of association or odds ratio is needed to calculate or find out.

The estimated odds ratio is—

m = (AB11*AB22)/(AB12*AB21)

Socio-Cultural Constrains

The Focused Group Discussions were conducted with the villagers to identify the major challenges or constrain, hindering the decentralisation process on the three major perspectives, i.e. personal, political and administrative. This exercise had recognized 5 major constrains for each of the perspectives. In the second phase respondents were asked to give score to the predetermined constrains. The highest score was 5 and lowest score was 1. On the basis of this data statistical analysis has been done to provide rank to each constrain within each three perspectives. Here, degree of variability has been measured through calculating the Coefficient of Variation (CV). The Coefficient of Variation (CV) is used to compare the consistency of measurement or reliability. The smaller the Coefficient of Variation (CV), the higher is the consistency or reliability.

Coefficient of Variation = (Standard Deviation/Arithmetic Mean) × 100

The indicators are given in Table 4.8.

Table 4.8: Measuring Indicators of Socio-Cultural Constrains

Variable	*Indicators*
Socio-Cultural Constrains	Personal Constrains, Social Constrains, Administrative Constrains

Research Design

The present study is exploratory in nature. The main purpose of the study is to measure the impact of PRI and SHG on decentralisation process. The general strategy and methodology adopted keeping in view the broad objectives and scope of the study. The preliminary information was collected on pre-tested schedule. Schedule and questionnaire for fieldwork were developed and refined after pilot testing the field. Interaction with various respondents identified, i.e. Gram Panchayat members, Officials, SHG members and Non-SHG villagers. Gram Panchayat visit and wall to wall survey was done to collect information from the primary sources. Later these data were analyzed as per the Analytical framework to fulfil the objectives of the present study.

Sample Design

Sample was selected by the use of Multi-Level Purposive sampling for this study. This study relies mainly on primary data. The data were collected from three different groups of respondents: (i) Elected Members of GP, (ii) SHG Office Bearers, and (iii) Non-SHG Villagers. As for the selection of respondents concerned it was proposed to make a survey of GP members, SHG Members and Non-SHG villagers of selected eight Gram Panchayats. The research had conducted in Birbhum and Burdwan districts of West Bengal. Two blocks from each respective district had been selected on the basis through matrix scoring exercise. Again 2 Gram Panchayats from each block was selected. Two Gram Sansads were selected from each Gram Panchayats for this study. Hence, the total number of Gram Sansad was 16 for this study. However, in respect of respondent all the Gram Panchayat members of selected eight Gram Panchayats were interviewed. Besides these GP members two SHGs were selected randomly from each Gram Sansad. Two office bearers and two general member from each SHG and four non-SHG villagers from each selected Gram Sansad were interviewed. As number of Respondents concerned all the GP elected members, 128 SHG members and 128 non-SHG villagers were interviewed with a view to collecting information on their awareness, perceptions and participation and their views on how Gram Panchayat administration can be strengthened and sustained.

Beside this, Gram Panchayat Officials, Officials from ISGP cell, Block Office, Zilla Parishad, few political leaders were met and information regarding various issues of Gram Panchayat was also collected.

Table 4.9: Detail of Study Sample

District	*Block*	*Gram Panchayat*	*No. of GP Members*	*No. of SHG Members*	*No. of Non-SHG Villagers*
Birbhum	2	4	40	64	64
Burdwan	2	4	50	64	64
Total	**4**	**8**	**90**	**128**	**128**

The sample at SHG and non-SHG villager's-level were selected purposively from each Gram Panchayats. The selection of sample depends on the nature of study. However, this study's main objective is to understand the impact of PRI and SHGs on strengthening rural decentralisation. Also, it attempts to understand present scenario of rural decentralisation, knowledge and perceptions of various actors of PRI, status of people's participation, fiscal status, role and magnitude of SHG involvement etc. In this case, the absolute size of the sample is important than the size of sample in relation to the size of population (Cochran, 1977:75). The absolute size means the respondents' level of education; political affiliation, sex, caste, economic status, and maturity regarding objective evaluation, opinion, responses and reaction, knowledge about local institutions, decentralisation process and its goals, progress and weakness. Therefore, equal number of respondents was selected based on the above mentioned criterion from each Gram Panchayat.

Sources and Types of Data

The data required for this study were drawn both from secondary and primary sources. Secondary data were obtained from various sources like:

- *Various Governmental Departments* like Labour Community Development Block, All Gram Panchayats under Labour Block, ISGPP Cell, MGNREGS Cell, DRDC Cell.

- *Various Publication of Government* like Census Report-2001 and 2011 (Provisional), The West Bengal Panchayat Act, 1973, Annual Performance Assessment of Gram Panchayat 2012, Roadmap for the Panchayats in West Bengal—A Vision Document, Booklets of Blocks and GPs etc.
- Other Sources like websites, books, magazines, journals and newspapers.

This study relies mainly on primary data. The data were collected from different groups of respondents: (1) Gram Panchayat Elected Members, (2) Gram Panchayat and Block-level Officials, and (3) SHG Office bearers and Non-SHG villagers. The respondents were interviewed with a view to collecting information on their socio-economic status, awareness, perceptions and participation and their views on PRI and Decentralisation Process.

Method of Data Collection

Step 1: Development of Research Plan

The detail Research Plan was developed for the field visits and collection of data from the Gram Panchayats, SHG members and Non-SHG villagers.

Step 2: Collection of Secondary Data

Secondary data were collected to generate the detailed information about the Decentralisation Status, Objectives, strategies variables and the analytical indicators, planning process, involvement of other stakeholders like GP members, officials, SHGs and common villagers; financial details, socio-cultural constrains etc.

Step 3: Design the Data Collection Tools

The research tools were developed and pre-tested to collect the information from the various stakeholders on the basis of information gathered through secondary data. Separate sets of questionnaires and schedule were developed for each category of respondents. The entire research tools are given below:

Details of Research Tool and Respondents

Respondent	Research Tool
1. Block Officials	Matrix Scoring
2. Gram Panchayat Members	Interview/FGD
3. Officials of GP	FGD
4. SHG Members	FGD
5. SHG Members	Interview
6. Non-SHG Villagers	Interview and FGD

Step 4: Collection of Primary Data

Primary data were collected to assess the following issues:

- Gram Panchayat Plan and Budget Documents
- Attendance Sheet of Gram Sansad and Gram Sabha Meeting
- Mode of Utilization of Funds
- Role of various stakeholders especially SHGs
- Awareness Level Perception, Attitude and Response of the Respondents
- Socio-cultural Constrains

Primary Data were Collected by using Following Tools

Matrix Scoring

Matrix Scoring was used for selection of the representative Gram Panchayats. The scoring exercise was conducted on the basis of some parameter related to the present study.

Focused Group Discussion

Focus group discussions were conducted among various actors to gather their perceptions and concern about the PMS. The detail FGD plan is given in Table 4.10.

In-depth Interview Method

In-depth interviews with the key actors like Gram Panchayat members, Officials, SHG members and Non-SHG villagers were conducted to

Table 4.10: Focus Group Discussion (FGD) Plan

Respondent	*FGD Issues*	*Expected Outcome*
1. Gram Panchayat Members	1. Role of Gram Panchayat in Decentralised Planning	Information about status of decentralised planning in the respective GP and the perception and attitude of GP members about the decentralisation
	2. Status of peoples participation in in Gram Sabha	Actual Scenario of Gram Sabha Meeting
	3. Planning Process, Budget Allocation and Implementation Process	Information about the actual planning and implementation mechanism adopted by the respective Gram Panchayat
	4. Role of Women/ SHGs in Planning Process	Perceptions and Attitude of Panchayat Members about Women/SHG
2. SHG Members	1. Role of SHGs and Women in the Micro-level Planning Process	Information about the knowledge level of decentralisation among the SHG members
	2. Major Problem/ Constrains Faced by the SHGs and Women in Attending the Meeting	Major constrains hindering the women participation
	3. Initiatives of Gram Panchayat for SHGs	Perceptions and Attitude of SHG about Panchayat
3. Village Common People	1. Role of village people in the Micro-level Planning Process	Information about the knowledge level of decentralisation among the village people
	2. Major problem/ constrains faced by the village people in attending the meeting	Major constrains hindering the active participation of village people
	3. Development Initiatives of Gram Panchayat	Status of Gram Panchayat Activities

generate information about the knowledge, awareness perceptions and constraints faced comments and suggestions for improvement.

Preference Ranking

This tool was used to identify the Key socio-cultural constrains that hindering the effective and efficient participation.

Step 5: Documentation, Analysis of Data and Preparation of Report

The data gathered were documented in a prescribed format and analyzed as per the analytical framework. Score, Percentage, tabulation and graphical analysis have been made for the interpretation of data. Finally, a detailed project report was prepared with the help of analyzed data.

Stage of Study

In order to collect the required data from the sample selected for the study, fieldwork was conducted in eight GPs in Burdwan and Birbhum District. The fieldwork was carried out in two stages: pilot study and the main study.

Pilot Study

A pilot study was considered necessary to understand the nature of the sample. To verify appropriateness of the tools and to get an initial feedback on the problem set for the study. Based on pilot study necessary changes were made and tools were finalized.

Final Study

The main fieldwork was carried out after finalization of tools and methods of the study.

Challenges for Data Collection

Due to shortage of time the study was restricted to eight Gram Panchayats of Birbhum and Burdwan District. Some basic challenges had been faced during the field study. These are:

- Unavailability of Gram Panchyat members in Gram Panchayat Office.
- Shyness and less participation of SHG members and villagers.
- Unnecessary delay in providing data from Gram Panchayats.
- The major challenge of the study is the time as of Gram Panchayat Election. As Gram Panchayat election was held in the study period it was quite difficult to gather information. The members were already stands at their end of term. So, they were lack interested for giving response. Again the unstable political environment of the rural Bengal affected the flow of study.

References

Cochran, W.G. (1977), *Sampling Techniques, (Wiley Series in Probability and Statistics*, John Wiley & Sons.

Panchayat and Rural Development Department (P&RD Department), Government of West Bengal (GoWB); (2008), *Annual Administrative Report 2008-09*, P&RD Department, GoWB, Kolkata, WB.

Panchayat and Rural Development Department (P&RD Department), Government of West Bengal (GoWB), (2010), *Information on West Bengal Panchayats: Their Members and Functionaries,* P&RD Department, GoWB, Kolkata, WB.

Panchayat and Rural Development Department (P&RD Department), Government of West Bengal (GoWB), (2008), *SRD Annual Report 2007-08*, P&RD Department, GoWB, Kolkata, WB.

Panchayat and Rural Development Department (P&RD Department), Government of West Bengal (GoWB), (2009), *Roadmap for Panchayat in West Bengal: A Vision Document*, P&RD Department, GoWB, Kolkata, WB.

Panchayat and Rural Development Department (P&RD Department), Government of West Bengal (GoWB), (2011), *SRD Project Completion Report* 2011 (ARIES Project Code: 107904-101 & 107904-102), Kolkata, WB: P&RD Department, GoWB.

Romeo, L. (1999), Systems Experiments in Support of Decentralisation Reforms: Reflections on Local Development Funds, *Regional Development Dialogue*, 20(2).

The West Bengal Human Development Report, 2004.

5
Profile of the Study Area

West Bengal

West Bengal was created as a Constituent State of India on 15 August, 1947 as the result of partition of the undivided British Indian Province of Bengal into West Bengal. West Bengal is situated at the eastern side of India.

Geographical Features of West Bengal

West Bengal stretches for about 700 kms. From the Himalayas in the north and in south covering the coastline of Bay of Bengal. This State bounded by the State Sikkim on the north, Assam covering its eastern side, on the west Bihar and Jharkhand and south-west covering by the Odisha. West Bengal sharing its borders with three of the SAARC countries, i.e. Nepal, Bhutan and Bangladesh. West Bengal shows the diversified geography. In south there are some rare species of wildlife in the Sundarbans that is also the natural habitat of the famous Royal Bengal Tiger. Between the Himalayan mountain region and the delta region lay the fertile Gangetic plains. Geography of West Bengal is diverse, consisting of high peaks of the Himalayas in the northern extremes to coastal regions down south. West Bengal is the only State in India where the Himalayas are to the north and the sea is to the south. It lies between 85 degrees 50 minutes and 89 degrees 50 minutes east longitude, and 21 degrees 10 minutes and 27 degrees 38 minutes north latitude. The capital of the State is Kolkata, the third largest urban agglomeration and the third largest city in

India. West Bengal is characterized with vast bio-diversity and comprises with six agro-climatic zones. As per Census of India, total geographical area of West Bengal in 2001 was 88,752 sq. km. which accounted for 2.7 per cent of the total geographical area of India (32,87,263 sq. km.). As per Forest Survey of India total forest area of the State was 11.88 thousand sq. km. which accounted for 1.53 per cent of the total forest area. Forest area of the State constituted 13.38 per cent of its total geographical area against 82.31 per cent in Sikkim and 23.41 per cent in India as a whole. Total forest area is classified

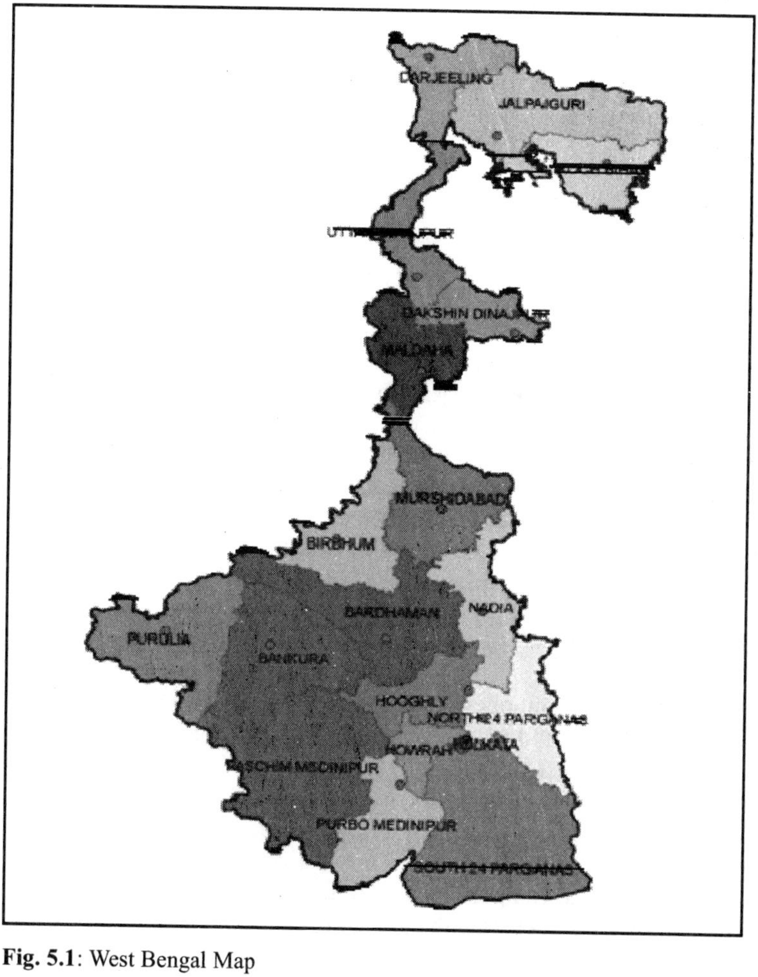

Fig. 5.1: West Bengal Map

into dense forest, open forest, mangrove and scrub. Dense forest accounted for 50.89 per cent of the total forest area of West Bengal against 50.41 per cent in India as a whole. Wastelands of the State accounted for 4.95 per cent of its total geographical area against 17.45 per cent for India as a whole. West Bengal stands third in the country in terms of mineral production. Coal constitutes 99 per cent of the minerals extracted in West Bengal which is the third largest State for coal production, accounting for about 10 per cent of India's total coal production in value terms in 2006. Fireclay, China clay, limestone, copper, iron, wolfram, manganese and dolomite are mined in small quantities. The data on annual rainfall in sub-Himalayan and Gangetic West Bengal show that there is the declining trend in the same during the period from 1991 to 2005 and there is wide fluctuation in annual rainfall during this period.

Climate

West Bengal's climate is in-between tropical savanna in the southern portions and humid sub-tropical in the north. In West Bengal there is a prominent seasonal disparity in the matter of rainfall. The annual rainfalls of the State are ranged from 53 inches to 89 inches. In the sub-Himalayan region, rainfall is considerably greater. The temperatures of Kolkata vary from 38°C in May to 12°C in January.

The year may broadly be divided into three marked seasons—the hot and dry season (March to June), with dry humid days and thunderstorms very common; the hot but wet season (mid-June to September), which is actually rainy season; and the cold (cool) season (October to February), when days are dry and clear and stable atmospheric conditions prevail.

Flora and Fauna

Forests occupy about one-eighth of the total land, and the region as a whole has a rich and varied plant life. In the sub-Himalayan plains the principal forest trees include *Sal* (a timber tree), *Sissoo* (which yields a valuable wood), and *Sisum* (Indian rosewood); in the southern part of this State characterized with dense coastal mangrove forest called Sundarbans. The Sundarban is noted for a reserve project conserving Royal Bengal Tigers. The forests of the northern districts are inhabited by tigers, panthers, elephants, bison, and rhinoceroses, as well as by other animals of the Indian plain, large and small. Reptiles and birds comprise the same species as are common throughout the Indian subcontinent.

There are five national parks in the State which are Sundarban National Park, Buxa Tiger Reserve, Garumara National Park, Neora Valley National Park and Singalila National Park.

Rivers

The main Rivers of this State are Teesta, Brahamaputra, Jaldhaka, Torsha, Sankosh, Raidak, Mahananda, Mahanadi, Balason, Machi, Tangan, Punarbhava, Atrai, Ganga, Bhagirathi, Mayurakshi, Brahmani, Dwaraka, Bakreswar, Kopai, Ajay, Damodar, Hooghly, Rupanarayan, Kansabati or Kasai and Subarnarekha. Except all these there are so many small rivers also found.

The Human Resource

The majority of the people of West Bengal are "Bengali". Some of the original inhabitants of Bihar are scattered throughout the State. Gurkha, Sherpas and ethnic Tibetans can be found mainly in Darjeeling district and also scattered throughout the State.

Hinduism is the main religion of the State. There are so many sub-strata of Scheduled Castes and Scheduled Tribes are found across the State. The Scheduled Tribes are mainly classified into three distinct categories. Santal, Munda, Orang, Birhore, Bhumij, Lodha, Mahali Kora, Ho and others who seem to have migrated from other states are distributed throughout the State including the tea estates of Darjeeling and Jalpaiguri District. Secondly, tribes like Rabha, Garo, Mech, Hajong and Chakma who have came from Assam, Tripura and Bangladesh are mainly found in Duars and foothill areas (Jalpaiguri and Cooch Behar District). The third category includes tribes like Bhutan and Sikkim and ultimately settled in Darjeeling District. Muslims, Buddhists, Christians, Jainas, and Sikhs constitute minority communities throughout the State.

Bengali is the main language of the State. Apart from Bengali other languages are also included like Hindi, Santhali (a tribal dialect), Urdu (primarily the language of Muslims), and Nepali (for North Bengal). Except local languages English language is generally used for administration and communication. English is also widely used as a language for business and academic purposes throughout the State.

Festivals of West Bengal

Besides the other festivals, Durga Puja is the main festival for the Hindu. New clothes are an integral part of Puja for every Bengali. Besides Durga Puja; Saraswati Puja, Lakshmi Puja, Kali Puja and Janmashtami are some other important festivals that are given special attention in Bengal. Yet Bengali festivals celebrated but other religious festivals like Idd, Muharrum, X-Mas are also celebrated with great respect in all over West Bengal.

Economy

West Bengal is mainly agriculture-based State. Large and small industries are also set-up, mostly found on the bank of Hooghly River and surroundings areas. Despite its small size, West Bengal accounts for about one-sixth of India's net domestic product. The art and craft of West Bengal is known world over. Decent with the touch of minute observation, Bengali art and craft are unique. The leather products of Bengal are very famous all over the country.

Agriculture

In West Bengal agriculture has a dominating role in the State economy. Nearly 76 per cent of total population are directly dependent on agriculture. Rice is the main crop in almost every district except Darjeeling. Jute, the second leading cash crop is especially prominent in the districts along the Bangladesh border and south of the Ganga River. Pulses, oilseeds, wheat and potatoes are produced as winter crops throughout the southern districts like Paschim Medinipore, Burdwan, Hooghly, Birbhum, Nadia, and Murshidabad Districts. Darjeeling and Jalpaiguri districts are famous for production of high-quality tea. Darjeeling also produces oranges, apples, pineapple, ginger, and cardamom. The fruits like guava, mango, jackfruit, and bananas are widely produced in the southern and central region of the State.

Industry

The industrial development in West Bengal basically is based in the bank of River Hooghly which was started before the Independence.

Another industrial belt is Durgapur, Asansol and Burnpur region famous for Iron and Steel manufacturing, and Haldia, the terminus of the oil pipeline from Assam and the site of eastern India's largest oil refinery. Other important industries are shipbuilding, automobile manufacture, chemical and fertilizer, software and hardware of computer in Kolkata.

Cultural life

The State West Bengal is known as culture enriched State in the country. Bengalis' have always fostered in literature, art, music, and drama. Bengali literature "*Charchapada*" and the "*Sri Krishnakirtan*" are the famous old literatures. After the early 19th century, due to the contact of the Western culture, Bengalis' culture blended with Western culture. The modern period of culture has emerged out in almost every region of the State. Bengal got the noble prize-winning poet Rabindranath Tagore (1861–1941), whose contribution still encouraging all the generations in India. Another two Nobel laureates in West Bengal are Professor Amartya Sen for his valuable contribution in welfare economics and Mother Teresa for her community service symbolizes the Bengal's rich cultural aspects. The Theatre, *Yatras*, traditional open-air performances are very popular both in the countryside and in urban areas. The "*Kavi Gan*"(Duel of Poet) and "*Kathakata*"(religious recital) are popular throughout the West Bengal.

The important side of West Bengal's culture is the modern film industry. Bengali films have produced several national and international awards. Rittiwik Ghatak, Tapan Sinha, Mrinal Sen, Aparna Sen, Rituparno Ghosh and Oscar winning directors Satyajit Ray, all are famous in very much intelligent film direction in this State.

Traditional music is another important part of Bengali culture. Rabindra Sangeet, songs written and composed by Rabindranath Tagore, which are very famous in all-over the world. Shantiniketan (Visva-Bharati) founded by Rabindranath Tagore, is a world-famous centre for the study of Art, Craft, Music, Agriculture, international cultural relations, social studies and rural reconstruction. Except Rabindra Sangeet, there also Nazrulgeeti, Folk songs, Modern songs are also very popular in the State.

Government

The 'Governor' is the chief executive authority of the State. Governor exercises the executive roles by the subordinate officers. The President of India appointed the Governor. The Constitution provides for an elected Council of Ministers. Chief Minister headed the Elected Council of Ministers. The Council of Ministers is collectively responsible to the legislature. The State Legislature consists of a single house, i.e. the Legislative Assembly (Vidhan Sabha).

The Constitution provides for a High Court, to which the Chief Justice and other judges are appointed by the President of India. District and Sessions Judges are appointed by the Governor in West Bengal.

The State is divided administratively into 19 districts. All districts except Kolkata are administered by a District Magistrate. Each district is divided into a number of sub-divisions. Sub-division Officer is the Principal Officer of Sub-division. Each of the sub-division comprises some Community Development Blocks headed by Block Development Officer. Each Community Development Block consists of some villages.

For democratic decentralisation, Panchayati Raj Institutions are regarded as a very strong body in West Bengal. An elected local

Table 5.1: Socio-economic Profile of West Bengal and India

Sl. No.	*Item*	*West Bengal*	*India*
1.	Total population (Census 2001) (in millions)	80.18	1028.61
2.	Decadal Growth (Census 2001) (%)	17.77	21.54
3.	Crude Birth Rate (SRS 2008)	17.5	22.8
4.	Crude Death Rate (SRS 2008)	6.2	7.4
5.	Total Fertility Rate (SRS 2008)	1.9	2.6
6.	Infant Mortality Rate (SRS 2008)	35	53
7.	Maternal Mortality Ratio (SRS 2004-2006)	141	254
8.	Sex Ratio (Census 2001)	934	933
9.	Population Below Poverty line (%)	27.02	26.10
10.	Scheduled Caste Population (in millions)	18.45	166.64
11.	Scheduled Tribe Population (in millions)	4.41	84.33
12.	Female Literacy Rate (Census 2001) (%)	59.6	53.7

Source: Census 2001.

authority established under the West Bengal Panchayat Act, 1956. In West Bengal three-tier Panchayat system is successfully running. These are:

(a) Zilla Parishad (District, Level Panchayat),
(b) Panchayat Samiti (Block Level Panchayat), and
(c) Gram Panchayat (Village Level Panchayat).

The District

To fulfil the study objectives two districts have been selected from the West Bengal. One is Burdwan and another is Birbhum. District Burdwan is regarded as the relatively advanced district where Birbhum is regarded as relatively backward district. According to the Human Development Index of West Bengal, 2004 Burdwan is ranking in 5th position and Birbhum is in 14th position.

Table 5.2: Human Development Indices District-wise in West Bengal

Districts	*Health Index*	*Income Index*	*Education Index*	*HDI*	*HDI Rank*
Darjeeling	0.73	0.49	0.72	0.65	4
Jalpaiguri	0.61	0.38	0.6	0.53	10
Koch Behar	0.5	0.41	0.65	0.52	11
Dinajpur	0.62	0.39	0.53	0.51	13
Malda	0.49	0.36	0.48	0.44	17
Murshidabad	0.57	0.29	0.52	0.46	15
Birbhum	0.53	0.27	0.61	0.47	**14**
Bardhaman	0.74	0.47	0.71	0.64	5
Nadia	0.65	0.41	0.66	0.57	9
North 24 Parganas	0.72	0.49	0.76	0.66	3
Hooghly	0.77	0.46	0.67	0.63	6
Bankura	0.67	0.26	0.62	0.52	11
Purulia	0.61	0.18	0.55	0.45	**16**
Medinipur	0.68	0.45	0.74	0.62	7
Haora	0.77	0.53	0.75	0.68	2
Kolkata	0.82	0.73	0.8	0.78	1
South 24 Parganas	0.71	0.4	0.68	0.6	8
West Bengal	**0.7**	**0.43**	**0.69**	**0.61**	

Source: West Bengal Human Development Report, 2004.

Geographical Feature of the Study Districts

The District Burdwan is situated in between 23°53' N 22°56' N latitude and in between 80°25' E and 86°48'E longitude. The area of this district is 7024 sq. km. Burdwan is the District Headquarter of this district. The District Birbhum and part of District Murshidabad covered its north side; the District Nadia and Hooghly situated its eastern side and in southern side Bankura District is situated and Purulia District and Santal Pargana covered its western side. The annual rainfall of this district varies between 1100 mm to 1600 mm. The maximum temperature recorded in this district is 45°C and minimum temperature is 5°C.

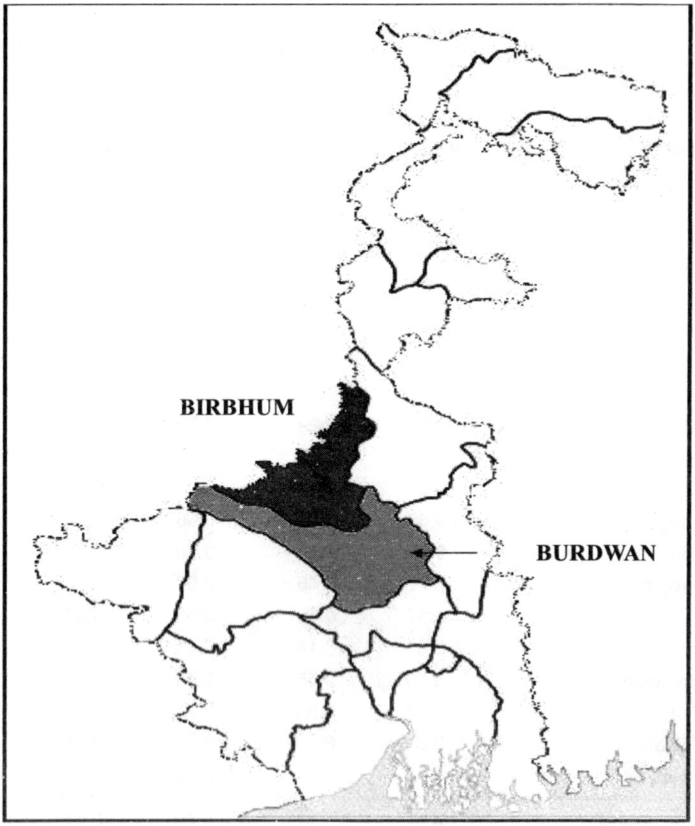

Fig. 5.2: Position of Birbhum District and Burdwan District in West Bengal

The district Birbhum situated between 23°32'30" and 24°35'00" of north latitude and between 87°05'25" and 88°01'40" west longitude. The area of this District is 4545 sq. km. Suri is District town of this district. The District Murshidabad covers the north and east side of this district. Jharkhand or Santal Pargana covered its western side. The District Burdwan is situated in the south side of this district. The yearly rainfall of this district is 1605 mm (year 2006). The highest temperature of this district is 45°C and the lowest temperature 5°C.

Demographic Features

The Burdwan district is quite large district of West Bengal. Total population of this district is 68,95,514. Out of the total population 52.04 per cent are male and 47.96 per cent are female population. The density of population is 982 per sq. km. There are 63.06 per cent people live in rural areas. 8.76 per cent of total population is under 0-4 years and 58.88 per cent of total population is regarded as the productive population. The gender composition or sex ratio is an important indicator for policy implication over gender budgeting. The sex-ratio in State of West Bengal is 934 whereas in Burdwan this ratio is 920 against State's average. In Burdwan 26.98 per cent of total population is belonging to Scheduled Castes as per Census 2001 and 6.40 per cent of total population is Scheduled Tribes (Census, 2001). Santal is the dominating tribe in this District.

The area of Birbhum district is 4545 sq. km. with a population of 30,15,422 (Census, 2001). The growth rate is 17.99 per cent (1991-2001, *Source*: Director of Census Operation, West Bengal). As per Census 2001, the density of population per sq. km. has been recorded to 663 in Birbhum. Predominantly, Birbhum District is rural in nature. The population of 0-6 years provides an important impetus for planning for children. There is 16.18 per cent of total population at the age group of 0-6 years. 56.08 per cent of total population is falling under productive population group (14 plus to 60 years). The gender composition of sex-ratio is an important indicator for policy implication over gender budgeting. The sex-ratio in State of West Bengal is 934 whereas, in Birbhum this ratio is 930 against state's average. In Birbhum there are 29.51 per cent of total population is belonging from scheduled castes. As per Census 2001, 4.82 per cent of total Scheduled Castes population is living in Birbhum. 6.73 per cent of total population is Scheduled Tribes (Census, 2001). Santal is the dominating tribe with 87.03 per cent. In Birbhum, roughly about 28 per cent of the population is living under the Below Poverty Line (BPL). There are 64.49 per cent of population belonging to Hindus, 35 per cent to Muslims, 0.24 per cent to Christianity, 0.01 per cent to Sikh and Buddhism, Jains and other religion from about 0.05 per cent and 0.063 per cent respectively.

Socio-Economic Feature

The economy of Burdwan District depends on both agriculture and industry. Yet coal mines are available in this district but this district is also agriculturally advanced. There was 454.94 thousand hectares cropped area in the year 2005-06. 69.9 per cent cultivated area is irrigated and yield rate of rice is 3081 kg. per hec. 63 per cent people live in rural area in Burdwan District. Burdwan District is regarded as relatively advance district. With the advance agriculture industrial sector is also strengthening this district's economy.

Agriculture is an important source of income of Birbhum district. Agriculture contributes near about 33 per cent of DDP in Birbhum. Birbhum registered 11.5 per cent growth rate in agriculture. In 2005-06 there was 319.96 thousand hectares cropped area in Birbhum district. 91.21 per cent cultivated land have irrigation facilities and yield rate of rice was 3029 kg. per hec. in 2005-06. In Birbhum, more than 91 per cent of people are living in rural areas. As per HDI Birbhum is ranking 14th among the districts in West Bengal. Low per capita income, poor HDI ranking, inadequate transport and communication network, inadequate basic public goods, low rainfall and prone to recurrent drought, low cropping intensity, vast fallow land, low literacy, high infant mortality are the special feature which have a great impact in preparation of developmental plans. The National Rural Health Mission (NRHM) has been introduced by Government of India on 12th April, 2005 with the objectives of reduction of mortality and morbidity rate, universal access to public health service, prevention and control of communicable diseases, stabilization of population, promotion of healthy life style.

The Block

Two Development Blocks have been selected from each district on the basis of highest and lowest SHG concentration. Labpur

Development Block and Suri-II Development Block selected from the Birbhum district and from the Burdwan district Kalna-II Development Block and Mantreswar Development Block have been taken for this study.

The Gram Panchayat

Two Gram Panchayats have been selected from each selected Development Block on basis of highest and lowest SHG concentration. From Burdwan district, Baidyapur Gram Panchayat and Kalayanpur Gram Panchayat have been selected from Kanksa Kalna-II Development Block and Montreswar and Majhergram Gram Panchayats have been selected from the Montreswar Development Block. From the Birbhum District, Hatia Gram Panchayat and Jamna Gram Panchayat have been selected from the Labour Development Block and Purandarpur Gram Panchayat and Koma Gram Panchayat have been taken from the Rajnagar Development Block.

References

Director of Census Operations, 2001, Census of India, 2001.
Director of Census Operations, 2011, Census of India, 2011.
District Statistical Hand Book, Birbhum, 2006, West Bengal.
District Statistical Hand Book, Burdwan, 2006, West Bengal.
The West Bengal Human Development Report, 2004.

6
Results and Discussion

Micro-Level Planning and People's Participation

The term planning implies the working out of sub-components in some degree of elaborate detail. Broader-brush enunciations of objectives may qualify as metaphorical roadmaps. Planning literally just means the creation of a plan; it can be as simple as making a list. It has acquired a technical meaning, however, to cover the area of Government legislation and regulations related to the use of resources. This section of the report evaluates the planning and implementation status of the Gram Panchayats. This section tries to find out information regarding the conduct of meeting by various Gram Panchayat bodies and the status of participation. It also focuses on various documents related to the planning and budgeting process of Gram Panchayats.

Participatory Planning Process of West Bengal

West Bengal has a practical methodology for participatory planning which attempts to balance the need for participation with the requirements of rational planning. Important steps of this methodology are outlined below:

Step 1 — At first, local area plans are prepared by *Gram Unnayan Samiti* and those plans are submitted in the *Gram Sansad* meeting for approval.

Step 2 — Every year Gram Panchayat (GP) convey annual *Gram*

Sansad (GS) meeting in May at each GP constituencies.

Step 3 — Every GS or elector has power to review previous year plan implantation, why the previous financial year have not implemented all the annual plan. Therefore, GP officials discussed about the present condition of the area or GS. Then the elector or GS members create the demand for critical gaps, for next financial year.

Step 4 — All GS meeting resolutions are being collected at GP level in the month of July.

Step 5 — In this regard all plans are divided into the five *Upa-Samitis*. Then the *Artho O Parikalpana Upa-Samiti* called a meeting for fund devolution. After that every *Upa-Samiti* presents its plan for budgeting.

Step 6 — All *Upa-Samiti* priorities of the own plan and they go through The Environment and Social Management Framework (ESMF) and Vulnerable Group Development Framework (VGDF) and then approved their draft plan and budget for next year with support of the majority members on September.

Step 7 — That approved draft plan and budget is submitted to General Body for approval and then provide a notice for 15 days in the major public places to get opinion for selecting the approved plan. On the other hand those approved plan and budget must be submitted to Panchayat Samiti within first week of November for any recommendation and clarification.

Step 8 — Then GP called half-yearly GS meeting and discuss elaborately about pre-approved final budget and plan and explain the cause of sanctioning those plans in that meeting within November.

Step 9 — In the month of December GP called Gram Sabha meeting for explaining the next year plan and budget to mitigate the problems that have been selected by the voter or sansad in each and every *Gram Sansad*. If there is no correction and adjoin plan and budget then those plan and budget will be submitted to General Body.

Step 10— Before 31st January, GP called a meeting to approve final plan and budget for the next financial year with consent of the majority of the members (The quorum of the meeting will be 50 per cent of the GP members).

Step 11—After Final approval of the plan and budget GP will send that plan and budget to Panchayat Samiti and nearest Bank up to 15th February for their intimation.

After getting the final plan from Panchayats, the *Panchayat Samiti* and *Zilla Parishad* started preparing their annual plans. The plan proposal were consolidated at the district level and integrated with the Municipal plans. The task force constituted by the District Planning Committee (DPC) for the purpose has evolved broad strategy for district-level development. The district plan is nothing but only the synthesis of the village plans. At present the rules favour the implementation of planned activities by the Zilla Parishad. The DPC forwards the integrated development plan for rural and urban areas of the district to the State. The State Planning Board is the State-level coordinating agency for planning.

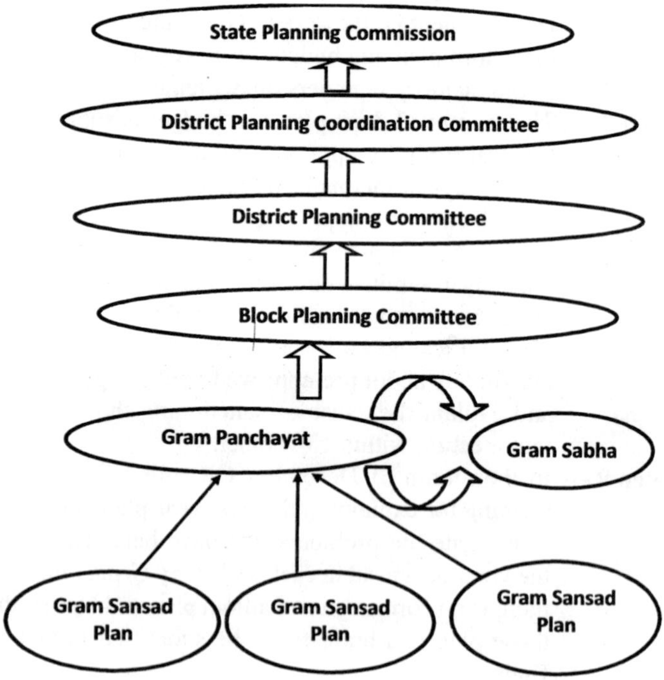

Fig. 6.1: Participatory Planning Process of West Bengal

General Body Meetings and Upa-Samiti-wise Meeting of Gram Panchayats

The General Body (GB) meeting is a vital mechanism available to Gram Panchayat for discussing the overall planning and budgeting process and the whole workflow of the Gram Panchayat. So, holding requisite number of general body meeting is pivotal to the efficient performance of the Gram Panchayat. The meeting is considered to be valid if the proceedings of the meeting have been captured with date in GB meeting register, the signature of the participants and signature of the *Pradhan* is present in the register.

Similarly, every Gram Panchayats have five *Upa-Samities* which are the planning and execution spearheads of the Gram Panchayat through which various projects pertaining to various sectors are planned and executed. The *Upa-Samities* hold regular meetings to discuss about planning and status of various projects, hence these meetings are extremely crucial for the overall functioning of the Gram Panchayats as a development institute as well as to ensure the functional decentralisation at grassroots-level. Table 6.1 indicates the number of general body meetings and *Upa-Samiti* meetings held at sampled Gram Panchayats in the financial years 2011-12 and 2012-13.

Table 6.1 reveals that in Birbhum district the highest number of General Body meetings held at Hatia Gram Panchayat with 15 GB meetings (2011-12 FY) and 18 GB meetings (2012-13 FY). In Burdwan district highest number of general body meetings held at Baidyapur Gram Panchayat with 24 (2011-12 FY) and 25 (2012-13 FY). Similar kind of picture has been found in *Upa-Samiti*-wise meeting also where maximum number of meetings held at Hatia GP of Birbhum and Baidyapur GP of Burdwan District.

Table 6.1 clearly indicates that the average number of General Body meetings of Birbhum district was 11.5 (2011-12 FY) and 13.75 (2012-13 FY). While in Burdwan district the average number of General Body meetings was 17.75 (2011-12 FY) and 18.85 (2012-13 FY). In Birbhum district the average number of *Artha-O-Parikalpana Upa-Samiti* meetings was 11.5 and 13.75 while in Burdwan district it was 17.75 and 18.75 for 2011-12 and 2012-13 financial years respectively. The similar trend is fund in other *Upa-Samitis* also.

Hence, the average number of General Body meeting and *Upa-Samiti* meetings held by Burdwan district were more than the Birbhum

Table 6.1: Number of General Body Meetings and *Upa-Samiti*-wise Meetings of *Gram Panchayats* in the Financial Years 2011-12 and 2012-13

District	*Gram Panchayats*	*Financial Year*	*General Body Meeting*	*Artha O Parikalpana Upa-Samiti Meeting*	*Krishi O Pranisampada Bikasha Upa-Samiti Meeting*	*Siksha C Janasvasthya Upa-Samiti Meeting*	*Nari, Shishu Unnayan O Samaj Kalyan Upa-Samiti Meeting*	*Shilpa O Parikathama Upa-Samiti Meeting*
Birbhum	Jamna	2011-12	14	13	10	9	11	11
		2012-13	17	16	11	11	12	12
	Hatia	2011-12	15	17	10	9	9	9
		2012-13	18	25	11	12	11	11
	Koma	2011-12	8	7	2	2	1	1
		2012-13	10	8	2	2	1	2
	Purandarpur	2011-12	9	8	5	4	4	4
		2012-13	10	10	5	5	5	5
District Average		**2011-12**	**11.5**	**11.25**	**6.75**	**6**	**6.25**	**6.25**
		2012-13	**13.75**	**14.75**	**7.25**	**7.5**	**7.25**	**7.5**
Burdwan	Baidyapur	2011-12	24	23	11	8	7	8
		2012-13	25	22	12	8	8	8
	Kalyanpur	2011-12	16	13	8	10	6	10
		2012-13	17	14	9	13	6	10
	Majhergran	2011-12	15	12	11	8	9	11
		2012-13	16	13	12	8	11	11
	Monteswar	2011-12	16	14	8	11	11	6
		2012-13	17	15	9	12	12	8
District Average		**2011-12**	**17.75**	**15.5**	**9.5**	**9.25**	**8.25**	**8.75**
		2012-13	**18.75**	**16**	**10.5**	**10.25**	**9.25**	**9.25**

Source: Gram Panchayat Meeting Register.

district. It indicates that the Gram Panchayats of Burdwan district is more efficient in terms of holding the GB meetings and *Upa-Samiti* meetings than the Gram Panchayats of Birbhum district. It also indicates the better status of both functional and administrative decentralisation of Gram Panchayats of Burdwan district than the Birbhum district.

Half-Yearly and Annual Meetings of Gram Sansad

The *Gram Sansads* are centres of decentralisation of power because in *Gram Sansad* meetings local people can express their opinion regarding various requisite development initiatives. Hence, percentage of *Gram Sansad* meeting held indicates that the Panchayats are working towards achieving decentralisation of power. The half-yearly meeting is usually held in November and annual meeting held in May.

In the present study it has found that Hatia and Jamna GP of Birbhum district and Baidyapur of Burdwan district were not able to organize both half-yearly and annual Gram Sansad meeting in 2011-12 financial year due to political unrest. Likewise due to lack of fund, poor planning and lack of accountability, various projects/schemes could not be implemented which created widespread public grievance resulting in public unrest in meetings deeming meetings ineligible to get counted.

Gram Sabha Meeting

In Gram Sabha meeting the whole electoral community of a Gram Panchayat area meets once a year to discuss all kinds of issues. The Gram Sabha meeting acts as a platform for information exchange and hence is an effective mechanism to enhance transparency and participatory process in the Gram Panchayat governance system. All the sampled Gram Panchayats of the present study were successfully organized Gram Sabha in the two respective financial years.

Constitution of Gram Unnayan Samiti

The *Gram Unnayan Samiti* is a local level institution through which *Gram Sansad* promotes development at the grassroots level. So, the existence of a *Gram Unnayan Samiti* showcases the level of decentralisation in a *Gram Sansad*. Hence, formation of GUS is very important factor to ensure the decentralised planning. The present study reveals that in Birbhum district only 2 GP (50%), i.e. Hatia and Purandarpur Gram Panchayts were able to form GUS at all *Gram Sansads* and in Burdwan district except Kalayanpur other 3 sampled GP (75%) were able to form GUS at all *Gram Sansads*. However, the effectiveness of these GUS in both the districts is a big question. In spite of being formation majority of the GUS were found to be ineffective and only in registers. So, the purpose and functioning of GUS in effective decentralised planning is now somehow diluted. Another interesting factor revealed from the field study that the Government has allocated a very marginal fund to GUS and due lack of fund GUS could not take developmental initiatives, resulting in lack of good effective developmental work at grassroots level.

People's Participation at Planning Process

People's participation and its relation to development has become an important issue while discussing the decentralisation process. Development agencies have made people's participation the central objective in all aspect of life. The United Nations Economic and Social Council recommended that Government in any country should adopt people's participation as a basic policy measure in national development strategy and should encourage the widest possible active participation of all individuals and Non-Governmental Organisations (NGOs), such as trade unions, youth and women organisations in the development process in setting goals, formulating policies and implementing plans (1975). Besides this, the World Bank has also formally supported Government in an effort to promote a more enabling environment for participatory development within the client countries (World Bank, 1994).

People's participation in planning and implementation ensures effectiveness, efficiency and equity in development. Participation provides the ordinary rural people a means of voicing their view and opinion and of showing by their efforts that they are able to take on responsibilities in planning, organizing, implementing, evaluating, and community development programmes. The issue of participation is primarily associated with the grassroots people including poor and weaker sections, not only because they are the most disadvantaged within the society, but also because the rural areas in comparison to urban areas, have been relatively neglected by various development strategies. This philosophy of a 'people based' development 'from below' assumes that participation is not only an end in itself but also a fundamental condition and a tool of decentralised governance and successful development.

People's participation has become the heart of decentralisation process because it is a means of obtaining information about local conditions, needs and attitudes without which development could fail. Again, people involved in planning and implementation thereby portraying people's commitment in its success and they are more likely to identify with it and see it as their project. Their contribution and assistance in the construction and maintenance of the project is also very much required. It is the only mechanism by which the people can articulate, protect and promote their interests.

In present study people's participation means a mutual cooperation of local people in planning and implementation according to their capacity, knowledge experience, representation and contribution. In West Bengal, people's participation has been considered as a mechanism for village development. The West Bengal Government first ensured people's participation for the grassroots development by conducting party based panchayat elections in late 70s. Since, then the Government has been performing a variety of functions for strengthening the rural decentralisation. The Government has identified a local level planning process in multi-level framework from the village to upwards. The village panchayat is empowered to prepare its own plan for the development. They mobilised the grassroots people to participate in planning.

The Government has taken another step forward by making provision for *Gram Sansad* apart from *Gram Sabha*. Every constituency of a GP has a GS consisting of persons whose names are included in the electoral roll of the West Bengal Legislative Assembly. The power and functions of GS are provided by the West Bengal Panchayat Act that GS shall hold an annual meeting (May) and half-yearly meeting (November). Through, the meeting GS may identify the schemes for economic development of village, identify the beneficiaries for various poverty alleviation programmes and constitute one or more beneficiary committee (by the ordinary people) for ensuring active participation of the people in implementation, and maintaining equitable distribution of benefits. GS may mobilize mass people for participation in community welfare programmes.

Importantly, GS may guide and advise the Gram Panchayat in regard to the scheme for economic development and social justice.

People's participation here is seen as a process variable to decentralised governance. Conceptually, the governing process can be seen as the product or an outcome of the interactive process among the people, elected members and officials. The nature of the outcome, can be reasonably assumed, depends on the quality of such interactive process. The level of participation can be measured by assessing the attendance in *Gram Sabha* and *Gram Sansad* meeting. In *Gram Sabha* meeting the prescribe Coram is 5 per cent and the prescribe Coram for *Gram Sansad* meeting is 10 per cent. One-third should be women from the total Coram.

People's Participation in Gram Sansad Meeting

Table 6.2 shows very low-level of people's participation in *Gram Sansad* meeting, which is not desirable in decentralisation process. It has been found that the most of the GS meeting were dissolved for the first time due to lack of Coram. Table 6.2 indicates that the attendance of *Gram Sansad* meeting in Birbhum district is very poor. In some GP, GS meetings could not be organized due to political unrest. The lowest total Coram of Birbhum district is 6.34 per cent in Metegram GS of Koma Gram Panchayat during May, 2011 GS meeting. The lowest and highest average total Coram of Birbhum district was 1.59 and 13.78 per cent, which are not very impressive for decentralisation process. But in Burdwan district people's participation is comparatively higher than Birbhum district. The lowest and highest average total Coram of Burdwan district was 7.00 and 22.25 per cent respectively, which are quite higher than the in the Birbhum district. Table 6.2 shows that in Burdwan district total attendance are fulfilling the Coram, but female attendance is not up to the target that is 33 per cent. It also shows the same picture in Birbhum district like Burdwan district. Female attendance as well as total attendance in both Birbhum and Burdwan district is not satisfactory and also not so hopeful for decentralisation process. It clearly indicates that the minimum criteria mentioned in the *Gram Sansad* meeting norms which is attendance of 10 per cent voter for Coram along with one-third women participation has not been fulfilled in majority of *Gram Sansad* meetings in both of the districts.

Table 6.2: People's Participation in Gram Sansad Meeting

District	Gram Panchayat	Gram Sansad Name	Total Voter	Total Attendance				Female Attendance			
				May, 11	Nov., 11	May, 12	Nov, 12	May, 11	Nov., 11	May, 12	Nov., 12
Birbhum	Jamna	Bogtore	712	0.00	0.00	9.55	13.06	0.00	0.00	30.88	27.96
		Jamna	687	0.00	0.00	7.86	12.66	0.00	0.00	24.07	24.14
	Hatia	Hatia	823	0.00	0.00	13.73	15.31	0.00	0.00	16.81	23.02
		Bhalkuthi	716	0.00	0.00	13.55	14.66	0.00	0.00	22.68	29.52
	Koma	Januri	684	7.82	10.59	8.31	7.65	29.17	41.54	41.18	34.04
		Metegram	703	6.34	9.88	8.35	16.81	39.53	46.27	31.67	42.98
	Purandarpur	Indragacha	754	0.00	6.76	14.35	14.59	0.00	35.29	19.64	23.64
		Behira	627	0.00	6.46	12.24	14.44	0.00	34.04	21.35	20.00
	Birbhum Average			**1.59**	**4.03**	**11.28**	**13.78**	**34.07**	**40.00**	**24.22**	**27.83**
Burdwan	Baidyapur	Ramnagar II	812	0.00	0.00	18.97	15.76	0.00	0.00	38.31	49.22
		Alketai III	789	0.00	0.00	22.18	23.57	0.00	0.00	42.29	28.49
	Kalyanpur	Hijuli I	732	18.03	19.54	21.04	22.81	26.52	29.37	24.03	28.74
		Rahatpur VII	745	0.00	0.00	15.03	16.51	0.00	0.00	25.89	28.46
	Majhergran	Madhyamgram VII	722	48.48	0.00	12.60	19.11	24.29	0.00	27.47	32.61
		Gabrupur XIII	845	20.59	0.00	13.61	40.12	29.89	0.00	26.96	38.94
	Monteswar	Asanpur VI	818	22.37	15.53	17.48	15.89	33.88	21.26	29.37	23.85
		Lohar VIII	707	24.19	22.91	26.03	22.91	25.73	20.99	13.59	12.35
	Burdwan Average			**16.37**	**7.00**	**18.23**	**22.25**	**27.52**	**23.84**	**28.55**	**31.10**

Source: Gram Panchayat Attendance Register.

People's Participation in Gram Sabha Meeting

The main objective of introducing *Gram Sabha* in the grassroots governance is to have decentralised planning and evaluation with people's participation at the grassroots level. The concept of eradication of discrimination and facilitation of people's participation from all walks of social life in the management of affairs of their locality were the foundation for the emergence of comprehensive society called Gram Sabha. In Constitutional term, the Gram Sabha is a body of all adult members of a village who has the right to vote; it has been conceptualized as a forum of village people to ensure the accountability of the elected representatives at the village-level and has been recommended to act as monitor on the working of Gram Panchayats besides facilitating the rural people's participation in the decision-making process. It is an epitome of participatory and direct democracy, and is the only body, which provides valuable inputs to Gram Panchayat to lead local Government effectively. Decentralisation in West Bengal has taken a huge step with the formation of *Gram Sabha* as a constitutionally mandated body, which is supposed to play a central role in promoting participatory democracy not only by working as an institutionalized platform to represent each and every section of the community and their needs but also by functioning as a mechanism to monitor and evaluate the development initiatives implemented by the Gram Panchayat.

To strengthen the Panchayati Raj as well as decentralisation process Gram Sabha is the best means of ensuring people's participation. Through the *Gram Sabha* and *Gram Sansad*, village people can participate actively in the development process and Panchayat become a system of the people, by the people and for the people. It is regarded that *Gram Sabha* is very active in West Bengal. The present scenario of functioning of *Gram Sabha*, however, is a bit critical considering the assumptions. The study reveals very low participation in *Gram Sabhas* compared to the total number of voters of a particular Gram Panchayat. Table 6.3 shows the people's participation at the *Gram Sabha* meeting. Table 6.3 shows that both Birbhum and Burdwan districts are averagely fulfilling the norms of Coram. However, in case of female attendance majority of the sampled Gram Panchayats of both of the district are miles away from the target. The highest attendance of Birbhum and Burdwan district are 9.98

per cent in Purandarpur GP and 9.99 per cent Kalayanpur GP respectively. While the lowest attendance of Birbhum and Burdwan districts are 4.30 per cent in Koma GP and 5.94 per cent in Baidyapur GP respectively. The average total attendances of Birbhum district for two respective years are 5.53 per cent and 7.62 per cent. In Burdwan district average total attendances of two respective years are 7.00 per cent and 8.47 per cent. In case of female attendance, the average female attendance of Birbhum district for two respective years are 21.65 per cent and 27.07 per cent. In Table 6.3 the same trend Burdwan district also shows the similar kind of picture having 24.23 per cent and 29.75 per cent female attendance for two respective years. Hence, the *Gram Sabha* norm for female attendance which is one-third of the total attendance has not been fulfilled in majority of cases.

Table 6.3: People's Participation in Gram Sabha Meeting

District	*Gram Panchayat*	*Total Voter*	*Total Attendance*		*Female Attendance*	
			Dec., 2011	*Dec., 2012*	*Dec., 2011*	*Dec., 2012*
Birbhum	Jamna	7840	6.53	6.38	19.73	37.40
	Hatia	11356	6.05	7.88	18.63	21.68
	Koma	3840	4.30	4.43	20.61	51.18
	Purandarpur	8045	4.40	9.98	30.79	21.54
	District Average		**5.53**	**7.62**	**21.65**	**27.07**
Burdwan	Baidyapur	14873	5.94	7.04	27.49	34.86
	Kalyanpur	9534	8.13	9.99	26.84	29.83
	Majhergran	9507	7.32	9.32	25.14	29.91
	Monteswar	13761	7.12	8.37	18.57	24.91
	District Average		**7.00**	**8.47**	**24.23**	**29.75**

Source: GP Office. *Note*: Figures in Percentage.

An interesting fact has been revealed during the verification process that the majority of the female attending *Gram Sabha* and *Gram Sansad* are engaged with SHGs. However, they have attended the meeting for their own interest. So, incorporation of SHGs in PRI system along with their capacity building have increased the female participation in *Gram Sabha* and *Gram Sansad* as well as empowering them to actively participate in the decentralised planning process.

Another fact has been found that to maintain the record on paper about the Coram or to avoid the show cause from the higher authority regarding low participation the ruling party members and officials of the respective Gram Panchayat are sometimes making fake attendance sheet by putting false signature in the *Gram Sabha* and *Gram Sansad* meeting. One or two persons put lots of signature as per voter list on behalf of original person.

Factor Responsible for the Low Level of Participation

The reasons behind the low level of people's participation are many. Through Focused Group Discussion (FGD) some of factors were revealed during the field study and these are:

- *Lack of Awareness and Interest among the Villagers*: The development schemes of Government are directly benefited the poor and marginalized section. The so-called middle class and upper class people are not getting direct financial and material support and so ignored to participate in any Gram Panchayat meetings. Thus, people are unable to understand about the indirect benefit from the Gram Panchayats. Common people are not aware about the importance of participation in the development process.
- *Busy Schedule of Villagers*: The villagers are engaged with their daily duties and have very busy schedule. The villagers do not have any so-called holiday and most of the villagers are engaged with their daily courses or go outside the villages for earning. Generally, *Gram Sabha* and *Gram Sansad* meeting are held during the official day and in afternoon. So, due to their livelihood purpose villagers could not participate in the *Gram Sabha* and *Gram Sansad* meeting.
- *Lack of Proper Coordination among the Villagers and Gram Panchayat*: Most of the Gram Panchayat diseminates the information about meeting day, date and time by making or distributing leaflet but this is not properly done. Further, it had become easier for the secretary or others who were in the key position of GP to send a report to the BDO office without conducting any meeting. Subsequently, no one inquired about the budget or plan or beneficiary list.

- *Political Biasness*: Further, the *Gram Sansad* and *Gram Sabha* were the main institutions for people's participation but they never held properly due to political influence apparently for the fear that if it was held, people would like to know about many issues regarding budget, expenditure, beneficiary list etc. for which the responses would be difficult on the part of the officials. While *Pradhan* or members were not to be seen in panchayat activities, people also did not bother the members about the activities of GP. They usually approached the senior leaders for help. When political supporters/workers went to their leaders, the leaders were bound to help them. People think that the *Gram Sabha* and *Gram Sansad* meeting is generally a party meeting. It is found that the supporters of the ruling party are only participating the Gram Panchayat meeting. So, only members of the ruling party are taking initiatives to prepare plans or on the other side the party members given scheme getting priority for selection.

  Another thing is that the priority is given on the basis of Political Involvement in case of Government Facilities. The beneficiaries list is prepared by the Panchayat members on the basis of political engagement. Maximum Government facilities are taken by the politically involved party members instead of actual beneficiary. Further, Political party members' attitude towards *Gram Panchayat* is very much political. Ruling party members of the Gram Panchayat think that Gram Panchayat is their own party office.
- *Lack of Promotional Agencies*: Lack of promoting organization is also a reason behind poor people's participation in *Gram Sabha* and *Gram Sansad* Meeting. It might not have been a weaker means to reflect people's preferences in such decision-making, if there was a good representation of the mass organizations such as Village Development Societies, Kishok Samiti and NGOs. Unfortunately, there were no such organisations found in sampled Gram Panchayats. Although incorporation of Self-Help Groups in grassroots governance has changed the participation scenario to some extent especially in case of female participation.

- *Distant Meeting Venue*: *Gram Sabha* meeting is generally held near the Gram Panchayat offices and time is basically in the afternoon. But it is a major problem for distant villager to attend the meeting due to unavailability of communication mode at the time of their return to the home. Yet the male villagers can attend the meeting by cycle but it is impossible for women villagers to attend the meeting.
- *Lack of Transparency*: Actual budget, income-expenditure status and other important issues are not disclosed by the GP Officials and elected members. Sharing of annual audit report in *Gram Sabha* is a mandatory task but, most of the time Gram Panchayats do not placed annual audit report in front of the common people.
- *Lack of Initiatives from Elected Members*: Political as well as bureaucratic unwillingness is another cause of low participation. Elected members as well as the officials of the respective Gram Panchayat are not taking initiatives in people's participation.
- *Political Conflict*: Political conflict between various political parties turned out into political clashes. It creates problem for those who are not interested in politics but interested in development process.

Scenario of Gram Panchayat Planning and Implementation

The most important step towards devolution of power and resources to the panchayat bodies was taken long back in West Bengal. The GOWB has taken a step forward by making provision for *Gram Sansad* (a village meeting) apart from *Gram Sabha* (groups of village meeting). The GP has to place the deliberation, recommendation and suggestion in the annual meeting of the *Gram Sansad*, the supplementary budget of the GP for the preceding year. The GP also has to discuss the report on the work done during the previous year and the work proposed to be done during the following year. Based on the discussion and recommendation Panchayat-level plans are finalized for budgeting and execution. Budgeting is also a crucial part of decentralised planning. Since, many of the components of planning, implementation as well as expenditure by the Panchayats are scheme based, the practice of proper budgetary control has not yet received enough attention, rather observance of only the scheme guidelines and maintaining scheme based fund utilization became the sole criteria. However, when the fund is credited to a Panchayat, any expenditure has to be duly authorized by the competent authority and actual expenditure should be subject to budgetary control. The target is to ensure that each Standing Committee/*Upa-Samiti* will have positive contribution in preparation of budget and will exercise due budgetary control on expenditure related to its domain of activities and appropriate management practices will be followed for proper application of fund.

Hence, assessing the planning and implementation scenario at *Gram Sansad* level is a good way to judge decentralised planning process. In the existing decentralised planning process, *Gram Sabha* incorporates the plans in the Gram Panchayat Annual Action Plans on the basis of priority as recommended by the *Gram Sansad*. Incorporation of the higher percentage of *Gram Sansad* plan in Gram Panchayat Annual Action plan indicates high level of decentralisation. Similarly, higher-level of execution of plan indicates high-level of efficiency at Gram Panchayat-level. Table 6.4 shows the planning and implementation scenario at *Gram Sansad*-level.

Table 6.4 shows that in 2011-12 financial year, average 11.25 number of schemes were taken by each *Sansad* of Birbhum district. Out of those, only 52.22 per cent schemes were included in GP annual action plan. Out of them, 59.22 per cent schemes were executed. In the same year, average 14.38 numbers of schemes were taken by the *Sansads* of Burdwan district. Out of them 59.13 per cent *Sansad* schemes were included in the annual action plan, and 64.71 per cent schemes were executed from the AAP.

In 2012-13 financial year, average 12.00 number of schemes were taken by the each *Sansad* of Birbhum district. Out of those, only 57.29 per cent schemes were included in GP Annual Action Plan (AAP). Out of them, 61.82 per cent schemes were executed. In the same year, average 14.88 numbers of schemes were taken by the sansads of Burdwan district. Out of them 65.55 per cent *Sansad* schemes were included in the Annual Action Plan, and 69.23 per cent schemes were executed from the AAP.

So, Table 6.4 clearly indicates that the Gram Panchayats are incorporating *Gram Sansad* level plans in their Annual Action Plan but the percentage is not up to the mark (<60%). It also reveals that the status of decentralised planning is quite better in Burdwan district than the Birbhum as well as the Gram Panchayats of Burdwan district

Table 6.4: Planning and Implementation of Sansad Level Plan

District	*Gram Panchayat*	*Gram Sansad Name*	*2011-12*			*2012-13*		
			Number of Scheme Taken in Sansad	*Per cent of Scheme taken in AAP*	*Per cent of Scheme Executed*	*Number of Scheme Taken in Sansad*	*Per cent of Scheme taken in AAP*	*Per cent of Scheme Executed*
Birbhum	Jamna	Bogtore	15	33.33	40.00	16.00	56.25	55.56
		Jamna	9	33.33	33.33	6.00	33.33	50.00
	Hatia	Hatia	12	41.67	60.00	18.00	61.11	63.64
		Bhalkuthi	13	61.54	75.00	15.00	60.00	66.67
	Koma	Kaspai IV	8	25.00	50.00	6.00	50.00	66.67
		Ghaita V	11	81.82	55.56	14.00	64.29	55.56
	Purandarpur	Indragacha	8	62.50	60.00	5.00	40.00	100.00
		Behira	14	71.43	70.00	16.00	62.50	60.00
	District Average		**11.25**	**52.22**	**59.57**	**12.00**	**57.29**	**61.82**
Burdwan	Baidyapur	Ramnagar II	16	56.25	44.44	15.00	73.33	72.73
		Alketai III	19	57.89	63.64	24.00	62.50	80.00
	Kalyanpur	Hijuli I	8	25.00	100.00	3.00	66.67	50.00
		Rahatpur VII	14	57.14	75.00	17.00	64.71	63.64
	Majhergran	Madhyamgram VII	21	76.19	68.75	20.00	70.00	64.29
		Gabrupur XIII	17	64.71	72.73	19.00	68.42	69.23
	Monteswar	Asanpur VI	13	61.54	62.50	16.00	56.25	66.67
		Lohar VIII	7	42.86	33.33	5.00	60.00	66.67
	District Average		**14.38**	**59.13**	**64.71**	**14.88**	**65.55**	**69.23**

Source: GP Office. *Note*: Figures in Percentage.

are more efficient that of GPs of Birbhum district in case of plan implementation. Less inclusion of *Gram Sansad* level plan also indicates the strong role of Gram Panchayat members and officials in formulation of Annual Action Plan. Gram Panchayat members and officials play crucial role in decision-making process of scheme selection as well as their execution.

While analysing the Annual Action Plan an interesting fact has been revealed that the majority of the schemes of AAP are under MGNREGA programme as it has comparatively bigger budgetary allocation than the other programmes. As a demand driven programme MGNREGA needs a bunch of schemes that is why maximum *Sansad* schemes under MGNREGA are included in the AAP.

Further, it has also revealed that the GPs of Birbhum district have more number of supplementary plans in AAP than the Burdwan district. This indicates stronger level of grassroots governance in Burdwan district than the Birbhum district.

Scenario of Own Fund

As per the 243H of 73rd Constitutional Amendment Act, 1992, Gram Panchayat is able to generate own fund by collecting taxes, levy, etc. This is also an important feature of financial/fiscal decentralisation process. The collected own fund is expended on execution of locally immediate schemes, mitigate the other expenditures of the panchayat like electricity bill, telephone bill, newspaper etc. It has found that our sampled Gram Panchayat expended their own fund to execute those schemes which are taken under NREGS, 12th FC, and United Fund to adjust the financial and other official constraints for implementing the above schemes.

It appears from Table 6.5 that, average collection of Own Fund is more in Burdwan district than Birbhum district in two financial years. It has also been found that the percentage expenditure of own fund is high in Burdwan district than in the Birbhum district. However, average expenditure of own fund in Burdwan district was very low in 2011-12 financial year. Higher collection of own fund as well as high percentage of expenditure indicates better level of financial decentralisation.

Scheme-wise Income and Expenditure Statement

Gram Panchayat is the main institution of grassroots governance

Table 6.5: The Receipts (including Opening Balance) and Payments, as well as Percentage (%) of Expenditure of Different Gram Panchayats under Own Fund during the FY 2011-12 and 2012-13

District	*Gram Panchayat*	*Financial Year*	*Own Fund During the Period*	*Own Fund Total Receipt*	*Own Fund Payment*	*Own Fund Closing Balance*	*Percentage (%) of Expenditure (Incl. O.B.)*
Birbhum	Jamna	2011-12	159513	159513	59079	100434	37.04
		2012-13	151660	252094	200761	51333	79.64
	Hatia	2011-12	124483	124483	66484	57999	53.41
		2012-13	314782	399442	362432	37010	90.73
	Koma	2011-12	DNF	DNF	DNF	DNF	DNF
		2012-13	305695	321015	205692	115323	64.08
	Purandarpur	2011-12	DNF	DNF	DNF	DNF	DNF
		2012-13	431178	446282	116799	329483	26.17
	District Average	**2011-12**	**283996**	**283996**	**125563**	**158433**	**44.21**
		2012-13	**1203315**	**1418833**	**885684**	**533149**	**62.42**
Burdwan	Baidyapur	2011-12	396944	396944	103739	293205	26.13
		2012-13	1139515	1432720	1039331	393389	72.54
	Kalyanpur	2011-12	615761	615761	83059	532702	13.49
		2012-13	1027920	1560622	873106	687516	55.95
	Majhergram	2011-12	DNF	DNF	DNF	DNF	DNF
		2012-13	303361	316213	239560	76653	75.76
	Monteswar	2011-12	478171	478171	94462	383709	19.75
		2012-13	845376	1229085	839590	389495	68.31
	District Average	**2011-12**	**1490876**	**1490876**	**281260**	**1209616**	**18.87**
		2012-13	**3316172**	**4538640**	**2991587**	**1547053**	**65.91**

Source: Gram Panchayat. DNF=Do Not Found.

system and appointed to plan and implement various developmental activities within a decentralised matrix structure. Gram Panchayats are assigned to implement various schemes or programmes funded by either Central or State Government. Gram Panchayats are given the power to make budget and expenditure under various schemes. So, income and expenditure statement of various schemes/ programmes can give an idea about financial allocation under various programmes as well as the financial conditions of Gram Panchayats. Here we took some of the major programmes for the study purpose.

Third State Finance Commission (SFC)

Grants under Third State Finance Commission (SFC) are divided into two segments:

1. Fund under first segment (98%) is termed as *Bangla Gram Bikasha Prakalpa*. Fund under *Bangla Gram Bikasha Prakalpa* is allocated to the Zilla Parishads, Panchayat Samitis and Gram Panchayats in the ratio of 12:18:70.
2. Fund under second segment (2%) is allotted among PRIs of all tiers as Incentive Grant in proportion to the "Own Source Revenue" collected by PRI body in excess of the collection of the last year. This incentive grant is termed as *Panchayat Sampada Bikasha Prakalpa*.

Table 6.6 reveals the flow of fund and the status of expenditure under 3rd SFC. Table 6.6 clearly indicates that the fund flow and percentage of expenditure are increased in the second financial year in both of the districts. However, the percentage of expenditure under Third SFC was quite low in 2011-12 financial year in both of the districts. The average percentage of expenditure in 2011-12 financial year was 69.94 per cent in Birbhum district and 18.89 per cent in Burdwan district. The reason behind the low expenditure was the political unrest rather the administrative failure. The State election in 2011-12 hampers the development process in both of the district.

In 2012-13 financial year the average expenditure under Third SFC was increased in both of the district. In Birbhum district the average expenditure was 89.35 per cent and in Burdwan district it was 91.23 per cent. So, political as well as administrative stability will improve the level of local governance in both of the districts.

Table 6.6: The Third Receipts (including Opening Balance) and Payments, Percentage of Expenditure of Different Gram Panchayats under 3rd State Finance Commission (SFC) during the FY 2011-12 and 2012-13

District	*Gram Panchayat*	*Financial Year*	*Receipt During the Period*	*3rd SFC Total Receipt (including Opening Balance)*	*3rd SFC Payment*	*3rd SFC Closing Balance*	*Percentage (%) of Expenditure (Incl. O.B.)*
Birbhum	Jamna	2011-12	390127	390127	380795	9332	97.61
		2012-13	448998	458330	451432	6898	98.49
	Hatia	2011-12	1071384	1071384	641354	430030	59.86
		2012-13	881783	1311813	1146909	164904	87.43
	Koma	2011-12		0		0	0.00
		2012-13	468039	513514	369395	144119	71.93
	Purandarpur	2011-12		0		0	0.00
		2012-13	749175	752128	744849	7279	99.03
	District Average	**2011-12**	**1461511**	**1461511**	**1022149**	**439362**	**69.94**
		2012-13	**2547995**	**3035785**	**2712585**	**323200**	**89.35**
Burdwan	Baidyapur	2011-12	327162	327162	37384	289778	11.43
		2012-13	578335	868113	857787	10326	98.81
	Kalyanpur	2011-12		0	0	0	0.00
		2012-13	814699	1508788	1240608	268180	82.23
	Majhergran	2011-12		0		0	0.00
		2012-13	717438	727863	716274	11589	98.41
	Monteswar	2011-12	50274	50274	33911	16363	67.45
		2012-13	557996	574359	541707	32652	94.32
	District Average	**2011-12**	**377436**	**377436**	**71295**	**306141**	**18.89**
		2012-13	**2668468**	**3679123**	**3356376**	**322747**	**91.23**

Source: GP Office.

Thirteenth Central Finance Commission

Government of India has accepted the recommendations of the Thirteenth Central Finance Commission (CFC) for devolution of grants-in-aid to the PRIs. The General Basic Grant for the three-tiers Panchayati Raj Institutions (PRIs) and the Special Area Basic Grant for the Hill Areas are given in two installments in the month of July and January of every year up to 2014-15. The State is eligible for the second installment depending on the utilization of at least 75 per cent of the available fund under Thirteenth CFC for the entire State. After earmarking the required fund for the proposed purposes, the rest amount has been allotted to the Zilla Parishad, Panchayat Samitis and Gram Panchayats in the ratio of 12:18:70. Allocation of fund to the Panchayat Samitis and Gram Panchayats within a district has been made following the criteria laid down in the guideline of Third SFC.

Table 6.7 reveals that in Birbhum district the fund flow has increased while expenditure has decreased in 2012-13 financial year. In Birbhum district average expenditure under 13th CFC fund were 82.96 per cent and 51.11 per cent in 2011-12 and 2012-13 financial years respectively. While in case of Burdwan district both the fund flow and expenditure has increased in successive years. The average expenditure of Burdwan district were 22.01 per cent and 56.56 per cent in 2011-12 and 2012-13 financial years respectively. It has been found that delayed transaction of fund from the Central and State Governemnt to PRIs is one of the major reasons behind low percentage of expenditure under 13th CFC.

Mahatma Gandhi National Rural Employment Guarantee Scheme (MGNREGS)

The Indian job guarantee scheme, enacted as Act by legislation on 25 August, 2005. The law was initially called the NREGA, but was renamed as the MGNREGA on 2 October, 2009. The scheme provides a legal guarantee for at least one hundred days of employment in every financial year to adult members of any household willing to do public work-related unskilled manual work.

It has been found in the study that the maximum expenditure is done by the Panchayats under MGNREGS. Table 6.8 shows the flow

Table 6.7: The Receipts (including Opening Balance) and Payments, Percentage of Expenditure of Different Gram Panchayats under 13th Central Finance Commission (CFC) during the FY 2011-12 and 2012-13

District	*Gram Panchayat*	*Financial Year*	*Receipt During the Period*	*13th CFC Total Receipt (including Opening Balance)*	*13th CFC Payment*	*13th CFC Closing Balance*	*Percentage (%) of Expenditure (Incl. O.B.)*
Birbhum	Jamna	2011-12	216645	216645	185002	31643	85.39
		2012-13	35691	67334	39060	28274	58.01
	Hatia	2011-12	622243	622243	510954	111289	82.11
		2012-13	1331647	1442936	657885	785051	45.59
	Koma	2011-12	DNF	DNF	DNF	DNF	DNF
		2012-13	758138	833456	459716	373740	55.16
	Purandarpur	2011-12	DNF	DNF	DNF	DNF	DNF
		2012-13	1162219	1165915	637179	528736	54.65
	District Average	**2011-12**	**838888**	**838888**	**695956**	**142932**	**82.96**
		2012-13	**3287695**	**3509641**	**1793840**	**1715801**	**51.11**
Burdwan	Baidyapur	2011-12	391062	391062	56469	334593	14.44
		2012-13	920601	1255194	609722	645472	48.58
	Kalyanpur	2011-12	381148	381148	29565	351583	7.76
		2012-13	1239754	1591137	830449	760688	52.19
	Majhergram	2011-12	131272	131272	26475	104797	20.17
		2012-13	979737	1084534	795126	289408	73.31
	Monteswar	2011-12	182806	182806	126524	56282	69.2121703
		2012-13	956114	1012396	560504	451892	55.3641065
	District Average	**2011-12**	**1086288**	**1086288**	**239033**	**847255**	**22.01**
		2012-13	**4096206**	**4943261**	**2795801**	**2147460**	**56.56**

Source: Gram Panchayat Office. DNF= Do not Found.

Table 6.8: The Receipts (including Opening Balance) and Payments, Percentage of Expenditure of different Gram Panchayat under MGNREGS during the FY 2011-12 and 2012-13

District	*Gram Panchayat*	*Financial Year*	*Receipt During the Period*	*MGNREGS Total Receipt*	*MGNREGS Payment*	*MGNREGS Closing Balance*	*Percentage (%) of Expenditure (Incl. O.B.)*
Birbhum	Jamna	2011-12	7574844	7574844	7038213	536631	92.92
		2012-13	10277726	10814357	10787395	26962	99.75
	Hatia	2011-12	7227683	7227683	7113072	114611	98.41
		2012-13	9198232	9312843	9314837	-1994	100.02
	Koma	2011-12	DNF	DNF	DNF	DNF	DNF
		2012-13	16371994	16372384	16370124	2260	99.99
	Purandarpur	2011-12	DNF	DNF	DNF	DNF	DNF
		2012-13	14945795	15195137	15059362	135775	99.11
	District Average	**2011-12**	**14802527**	**14802527**	**14151285**	**651242**	**95.60**
		2012-13	**50793747**	**51694721**	**51531718**	**163003**	**99.68**
Burdwan	Baidyapur	2011-12	3919521	3919521	3844138	75383	98.08
		2012-13	8318366	8393749	8266047	127702	98.48
	Kalyanpur	2011-12	4601583	4601583	4550117	51466	98.88
		2012-13	11844328	11895794	11820093	75701	99.36
	Majhergram	2011-12	5108502	5108502	4313417	795085	84.44
		2012-13	12979381	13774466	13774466	0	100.00
	Monteswar	2011-12	4041018	4041018	3966462	74556	98.16
		2012-13	10111787	10186343	10185860	483	100.00
	District Average	**2011-12**	**17670624**	**17670624**	**16674134**	**996490**	**94.36**
		2012-13	**43253862**	**44250352**	**44046466**	**203886**	**99.54**

Source: Gram Panchayat Office. DNF= Do not Found.

of fund under MGNREGS and the status of expenditure for the financial years 2011-12 and 2012-13.

In the 2011-12 and 2012-13 financial years average expenditure under MGNREGS in Birbhum district was 95.60 per cent and 99.68 per cent whereas in Burdwan district 94.36 per cent and 99.54 per cent. So, in both of the district the average expenditure has increased in the successive years.

It has found that, Burdwan district is relatively advanced district. The scope of work under MGNREGS in Burdwan is lesser than the Birbhum district in various aspects. Infrastructure development of Burdwan district is already in a better position and that is why, the scope for infrastructure development is less in Burdwan than Birbhum district.

Financial Autonomy Ratio (FAO)

Financial Autonomy Ratio (FAO) is one of the important indicators to analyze the status of fiscal decentralisation. It is calculated by the share of Gram Panchayat's Own Fund (Tax and Non-Tax) in Gram Panchayat's total (include all funds) expenditure. The Financial Autonomy Ratio (FAO) shows the extent of reliance on own sources of funds which lead to autonomy. In this case the top ranker is the Gram Panchayat with the highest FAR. Higher FAO means higher financial sustainability of a Gram Panchayat. Higher autonomy may be appreciated but it could also mean that the flow of Government and other funds are inadequate for the development of a particular Gram Panchayat.

Table 6.9 clearly indicates that Financial Autonomy Ratio (FAO) is much higher in Gram Panchayats of Burdwan district than the Birbhum district. In Birbhum district Purandarpur Gram Panchayat has highest FAO in the financial year 2012-13 which is 2.06. However, the average district FAO for two successive financial years of Birbhum was 1.55 and 1.90. In case of Burdwan district Kalayanpur GP (12.66) and Baidyapur GP (9.86) have highest FAO in 2011-12 and 2012-13 financial years respectively. Average FAO of Burdwan district was also much higher in two successive financial years than the Birbhum district, i.e. 10.53 (2011-12) and 7.03 (2012-13). This data indicates that the share of Gram Panchayat Own Fund in total expenditure is comparatively higher in Burdwan district than the Birbhum district.

Table 6.9: Total Own Fund (Tax and Non-Tax) Collection, Total Expenditure (including all funds) and Financial Autonomy Ratio (FAO) of Gram Panchayats

District	*Gram Panchayat*	*Financial Year*	*Total Own Fund*	*Total Expenaiture*	*Financial Autonomy*
Birbhum	Jamna	2011-12	159513	8023439	1.99
		2012-13	252094	15452901	1.63
	Hatia	2011-12	124483	10251169	1.21
		2012-13	399442	17635357	2.27
	Koma	2011-12	DNF	DNF	0.00
		2012-13	321015	20040231	1.60
	Purandarpur	2011-12	DNF	DNF	0.00
		2012-13	446282	21700449	2.06
	District Average	**2011-12**	**283996**	**18274608**	**1.55**
		2012-13	**1418833**	**74828938**	**1.90**
Burdwan	Baidyapur	2011-12	396944	4863379	8.16
		2012-13	1432720	14537922	9.86
	Kalyanpur	2011-12	615761	4863379	12.66
		2012-13	1560622	17287738	9.03
	Majhergram	2011-12	DNF	DNF	0.00
		2012-13	316213	18398596	1.72
	Monteswar	2011-12	478171	4435523	10.78
		2012-13	1229085	14368267	8.55
	District Average	**2011-12**	**1490876**	**14162281**	**10.53**
		2012-13	**4538640**	**64592523**	**7.03**

Source: *Gram Panchayat* Office; DNF= Do not Found.

It means Gram Panchayats of Burdwan district has better financial autonomy than the Birbhum district.

From the above, it may be inferred that decentralised governance has ability to ensure people's participation at the grassroots-level. Evidences were found in both the Districts that the decisions taken either in the *Gram Sabha/Gram Sansad* meeting at the GP-level were implemented since planning has been devolved below the State Planning Board, District Planning Committee (DPC) at the district level and Block Planning Committee (BPC) at the block-level. However, the political involvements are weaking the decentralisation process in West Bengal.

Socio-Economic Features of the Elected Gram Panchayat Members of Sampled Gram Panchayat

Caste and Gender-wise Distribution of Members of Selected Gram Panchayats

India is one of the largest democracies in the World. The experiment of Panchayati Raj Institutions (PRIs) has sought to provide firm and deep roots democracy and broad-base to democratic structure so as to make the common man a real partner in conduct of his own civic and political affairs. The Panchayati Raj Institutions have also been considered as important aspect of socio-economic structures. PRIs are expected to serve the interests and meet the aspirations of various sections of the Indian Rural Society. Democratic decentralisation is not merely devolution of powers. It must also comprise devolution of responsibility. One of the important responsibilities of protecting and safeguarding the interests of the weaker sections of the society, i.e., the Scheduled Castes, the Scheduled Tribes, the Minorities, the poor, women and other disadvantaged or potentially disadvantaged sections of the society. Generally, in earlier Panchayati Raj bodies were dominated by socially and economically dominated classes. But, 73rd Constitutional Amendment Act, 1992, made a provision for reservation of seats for Scheduled Castes and Scheduled Tribes category in proportionate to their total population of the said Panchayat bodies. The Amendment Act has stipulated for a uniform system of reservations for SCs, STs and Women in all PRIs at all levels and uniform system of elections to all tiers throughout the country.

Table 6.10 represents the caste composition of the selected Gram Panchayats. Table 6.10 reveals that in Jamna Gram Panchayat of Birbhum District, out of total male representative there are 40.00 per cent from Scheduled Castes, 20.00 per cent from Scheduled Tribes and 40 per cent from General caste category. On the other hand, out of total female representatives, there are 80 per cent from general caste category and 20 per cent from Scheduled Tribes category. There is no Scheduled Castes and OBC female representative in this Gram Panchayat.

In Hatia Gram Panchayat, out of total male representatives there are 55.56 per cent from general, 22.22 per cent from Scheduled Castes, 22.22 per cent from OBCs category. On the other hand, out of total

Table 6.10: Caste and Gender-wise Distribution of Members of Selected Gram Panchayats

District	Gram Panchayat	Total Member	General		Scheduled Caste		Scheduled Tribe		OBC	
			Male	Female	Male	Female	Male	Female	Male	Female
Birbhum	Jamna	10	40.00	80.00	40.00	0.00	20.00	20.00	0.00	0.00
	Hatia	15	55.56	33.33	22.22	66.67	0.00	0.00	22.22	0.00
	Purandarpur	9	0.00	0.00	80.00	75.00	20.00	25.00	0.00	0.00
	Koma	6	25.00	0.00	50.00	100.00	25.00	0.00	0.00	0.00
	District Average	**40**	**34.78**	**35.29**	**43.48**	**52.94**	**13.04**	**11.76**	**8.70**	**0.00**
Burdwan	Baidyapur	12	50.00	25.00	37.50	0.00	12.50	75.00	0.00	0.00
	Kalyanpur	13	25.00	20.00	37.50	60.00	25.00	0.00	12.50	20.00
	Majhergram	12	62.50	25.00	37.50	25.00	0.00	50.00	0.00	0.00
	Monteswar	13	25.00	80.00	25.00	20.00	0.00	0.00	50.00	0.00
	District Average	**50**	**40.63**	**38.89**	**34.38**	**27.78**	**9.38**	**27.78**	**15.63**	**5.56**

Source: Primary Data collected from GP Office. *Note*: Figures in percentage.

female representatives there are 66.67 per cent are Scheduled Castes and 33.33 per cent are general caste category. There is no Scheduled Tribes and OBC female representative in this Gram Panchayat.

Purandarpur Gram Panchayat and Koma Gram Panchayat of Suri-II Development Block shows that 80.00 per cent and 50.00 per cent male representative from Scheduled Castes category, 20.00 per cent and 25.00 per cent male from Scheduled Tribes category and 00.00 per cent and 25.00 per cent male representative from general caste category respectively.

In case of female representation in the Purandarpur Gram Panchayat, 75.00 per cent female are Scheduled Castes and 25.00 per cent Scheduled Tribes are in category respectively. There is no General Caste and OBC female representative in this Gram Panchayat.

In Burdwan District, Baidyapur Gram Panchayat and Kalyanpur Gram Panchayat of Kalna-II Development Block shows that 50.00 per cent and 25.00 per cent male representative respectively from 37.50 per cent each male representative are from Scheduled Castes category, 12.5 per cent and 25.00 per cent from Scheduled Tribes category and 0.00 per cent and 12.50 per cent male representative are from OBC respectively.

In Baidyapur Gram Panchayat, out of total female representative, there are 25.00 per cent from General Caste and 75.00 per cent from Scheduled Tribes category. But in Kalyanpur Gram Panchayat, out of total female representative 20.00 per cent are from General categories, 60.00 per cent from Scheduled Castes and 20.00 per cent from OBC category.

Majhergram Gram Panchayat and Montreswar Gram Panchayat of Montreswar Development Block show that male general representatives are 62.50 per cent and 25.00 per cent respectively, 37.50 per cent and 25.00 per cent from Scheduled Castes category respectively whereas in case of Montreswar Gram Panchayat 50.00 male representatives are from OBC category. There are no ST male representative in these two Gram Panchayats.

In Majhergram Gram Panchayat, out of total female representative 25.00 are from General Caste, 25.00 per cent are Scheduled Castes and 50.00 are from Scheduled Tribes category. But in Montreswar Gram Panchayat, out of total female representative percentages of General Caste and Scheduled Castes are 80.00 per cent and 20.00 per cent respectively.

The district-wise average percentage of caste composition among the Gram Panchayat members of the selected Gram Panchayat of both Birbhum and Burdwan district has shown almost similar picture. The General Caste and Scheduled Castes people are holding maximum representative than Scheduled Tribes and OBC representation in the local Government. However, in case of female participation cumulative participation of both Scheduled Castes and Scheduled Tribes women are more than the General Caste women in Burdwan district compared to Birbhum district. Although, individually participation of Scheduled Castes women is high in Birbhum district while participation of General caste women is comparatively high in Burdwan district.

Gender Composition of the Selected Gram Panchayats

Gender composition is one major concern of the 73rd Constitutional Amendment Act,1992, which provides reservation of one third seats for the women representation. Table 6.11 tries to assess the gender composition and the scenario of women reservation in selected Gram Panchayats.

Table 6.11: Gender Composition of the Selected Gram Panchayats

District	*Gram Panchayat*	*Total Member*	*No. of Male Member*	*No. of Female Member*	*Male Member (%)*	*Female member (%)*
Birbhum	Jamna	10	5	5	50.00	50.00
	Hatia	15	9	6	60.00	40.00
	Purandarpur	9	5	4	55.56	44.44
	Koma	6	4	2	66.67	33.33
	District Average	**40**	**23**	**17**	**57.50**	**42.50**
Burdwan	Baidyapur	12	8	4	66.67	33.33
	Kalyanpur	13	8	5	61.54	38.46
	Majhergram	12	8	4	66.67	33.33
	Monteswar	13	8	5	61.54	38.46
	District Average	**50**	**32**	**18**	**64.00**	**36.00**

Source: Primary Data collected from GP Office. *Note*: Figures in percentage.

Table 6.11 reveals that the total number of elected member of selected Gram Panchayats in Birbhum district is 40 and in Burdwan district, it is 50. In Jamna Gram Panchayat and Hatia Gram Panchayat of Labpur Development Block, out of total 10 and 14 Gram Panchayat elected members there are 50.00 per cent and 60.00 per cent male representative whereas 50.00 per cent and 40.00 per cent are female representative respectively.

From the Suri-II Development Block of Birbhum District Purandarpur Gram Panchayat and Koma Gram Panchayat were studied where out of total 9 and 6 panchayat members there are 55.56 per cent and 66.67 per cent are male representative and 44.44 and 33.33 per cent are female representative respectively.

In Baidyapur Gram Panchayat of Kalna-II Development Block of Burdwan District, out of total 12 Gram Panchayat members 66.67 per cent are male and 33.33 per cent are female representative. Another Gram Panchayat of this Development Block selected for this study is Kalyanpur Gram Panchayat. Here, out of total 13 elected members, 61.54 per cent are male and 38.46 per cent are female representatives.

Another Development Block Mantreswar of Burdwan District was selected for this study. Majhergram and Montreswar Gram Panchayats have been taken from Mantreswar Development Block. These two Gram Panchayats are consisting with 12 and 13 elected Gram Panchayat members respectively. Out of total members, 66.67 and 61.54 per cent are male representatives and 33.33 per cent and 38.46 per cent are female members respectively.

Table 6.11 also reveals that the percentage male representation in Birbhum and Burdwan District are 57.50 per cent and 64.00 per cent respectively whereas the female representation are 42.50 per cent and 36.00 per cent respectively. So, it is clear that in case of district average, the Birbhum District has higher female representation than the Burdwan district. Although, it is clear from Table 6.11 that percentage of female members of all selected Panchayats are maintaining the prescribed percentage of the Constitution of India.

Educational Distribution of Gram Panchayat Members

Education is the most important instrument for human resource development and has a great significance. It plays an important role in social and economic upliftment of an individual. Education develops the knowledge, skill and attitude level within an individual person, i.e. better the education level implies betterment in knowledge, skill and attitude-level. Thus, education is an important parameter of human resource which is also an indispensable asset for an efficient leader. Formal educational-level makes a difference for performing any task efficiently. Education also brings social prestige which increases the acceptance of people's representation among the common mass. Hence, the educational status of the Gram Panchayat members is a very important indicator to judge the knowledge and attitudinal-level of Gram Panchayat member about various socio-economic and administrative aspects of decentralisation. Table 6.12 presents the distribution of educational status of Gram Panchayat members.

Table 6.12 reveals that most of the male representative's educational status is varying in between secondary to higher secondary level. Out of total male representative of the selected Gram Panchayats of Birbhum district 13.04 per cent studied up to class IV or primary level, 17.39 per cent studied up to upper primary-level, 17.39 per cent up to class X or secondary-level, 34.78 per cent studied up to class XII, 13.04 per cent are graduate and 4.35 per cent are post-graduate. On the other side, in Burdwan district these percentages are 6.25 per cent, 18.75 per cent, 18.75 per cent, 38.38 per cent, 15.63 per cent, 6.25 per cent respectively.

In case of female representative's educational status is varying in between primary-level to secondary-level, i.e. class X. In Birbhum district, 5.88 per cent female representatives are neo-literate, i.e. they can put their signature only. It may better to say that they can only draw their names. As it is found that in case of female educational status in Birbhum district out of total female representatives, 35.29 per cent female representative studied up to class IV or primary-level, 29.41 per cent female representative studied up to class VIII or upper primary level-and 17.65 per cent female representative studied up to class X or secondary-level, 11.67 per cent studied up to class XII or higher secondary-level, but there are no such female representative who is graduate or post-graduate. On the other side, educational status of the female representatives in Burdwan district shows that 16.67 per cent studied up to class IV or primary-level, 27.78 per cent studied up to class VIII or upper primary-level, 27.78 per cent studied up to class X or secondary-level, 22.22 per cent studied up to class XII but in this district 5.56 per cent graduate women are representing the selected Gram Panchayats. Although there is no such female representative who is post-graduate.

Table 6.12: Educational Status of the GP Members

District	*Gram Panchayat*	*Just Literate*		*Up to Class IV*		*Up to Class VIII*		*Up to Class XI*		*Up to Class XII*		*Graduate*		*Post-Graduate*	
		Male	*Female*	*Male*	*Female*	*Male*	*Female*	*Male*	*Female*	*Male*	*Female*	*Male*	*Female*	*Male*	*Female*
Birbhum	Jamna	0.00	20.00	20.00	20.00	20.00	20.00	20.00	20.00	20.00	20.00	20.00	0.00	0.00	0.00
	Hatia	0.00	0.00	0.00	50.00	11.11	33.33	11.11	16.67	44.44	0.00	22.22	0.00	11.11	0.00
	Purandarpur	0.00	0.00	20.00	25.00	20.00	25.00	20.00	25.00	40.00	25.00	0.00	0.00	0.00	0.00
	Koma	0.00	0.00	25.00	50.00	0.00	50.00	25.00	0.00	50.00	0.00	0.00	0.00	0.00	0.00
	District Average	**0.00**	**5.88**	**13.04**	**35.29**	**17.39**	**29.41**	**17.39**	**17.65**	**34.78**	**11.76**	**13.04**	**0.00**	**4.35**	**0.00**
Burdwan	Baidyapur	0.00	0.00	0.00	0.00	12.50	50.00	12.50	25.00	37.50	25.00	25.00	0.00	12.50	0.00
	Kalyanpur	0.00	0.00	12.50	20.00	12.50	40.00	25.00	20.00	37.50	0.00	12.50	20.00	0.00	0.00
	Majhergram	0.00	0.00	12.50	25.00	37.50	25.00	25.00	25.00	25.00	25.00	0.00	0.00	0.00	0.00
	Monteswar	0.00	0.00	0.00	20.00	12.50	0.00	12.50	40.00	37.50	40.00	25.00	0.00	12.50	0.00
	District Average	**0.00**	**0.00**	**6.25**	**16.67**	**18.75**	**27.78**	**18.75**	**27.78**	**34.38**	**22.22**	**15.63**	**5.56**	**6.25**	**0.00**

Source: Primary Data collected from GP Office. *Note:* Figures in percentage.

The data indicates that the educational status of both Birbhum and Burdwan district have slightly different picture especially in case of female education. Most of the representatives' educational status is varying in between primary and higher secondary-level. The per cent of representatives with higher education are very minimal. However, in case of higher education Burdwan district is standing in slightly higher position than the Birbhum district. The data on education also indicates widening gender gap in educational status which leads to poor access to knowledge, skill and attitude among the female members.

Occupational Distribution of the Gram Panchayat Members

Occupational status in rural area is an integral part of village social structure. The main occupation of a person has been considered to be that occupation from which a person earns more than 50 per cent of income. It is also a fact that in rural areas occupational status is not only related to the measurement of individual's financial status, but it also establish individual's image in the society. Table 6.13 reveals the occupational distribution of the Gram Panchayat members.

In Birbhum district, most of the male representatives are cultivators followed by agricultural or daily labourers. Table 6.13 shows 34.78 per cent are engaged in cultivation, 30.43 per cent as labourer, 21.74 per cent are engaged in business, 4.34 per cent in service, 8.79 per cent in other sector like cottage/household industries, carpenter etc. In Burdwan district 28.13 per cent are engaged in cultivation, 34.38 per cent as labourer, 15.63 per cent are businessman, 12.50 and 9.38 per cent are engaged in service and other sector.

Among the female representatives of Birbhum district, 11.67 per cent are engaged in cultivation, 29.41 per cent as labour, 5.88 per cent in business and 47.06 per cent are engaged in unproductive work, i.e. house-wives. But in Burdwan district, out of total female representatives, 5.56 per cent are cultivators, 27.78 per cent are labour, 5.56 per cent are in other services like insurance agent, tutor and 61.11 per cent are housewives engaged in unproductive household works.

Hence, the data reveals that the female representatives are economically unstable comparison to the male members. Majority of the female representation are housewives, i.e. engaged in unproductive domestic activities. Economic independence put forward to the

Table 6.13: Occupational Status of the Gram Panchayat Members

District	Gram Panchayat	Agriculture		Labour		Business		Service		Others		Unproductive Work	
		Male	Female	Male	Female	Male	Female	Male	Female	Male	Female	Male	Female
Birbhum	Jamna	40.00	0.00	20.00	20.00	20.00	0.00	0.00	0.00	20.00	20.00	0.00	60.00
	Hatia	33.33	16.67	22.22	33.33	22.22	16.67	11.11	0.00	11.11	0.00	0.00	33.33
	Purandarpur	40.00	25.00	40.00	25.00	20.00	0.00	0.00	0.00	0.00	0.00	0.00	50.00
	Koma	25.00	0.00	50.00	50.00	25.00	0.00	0.00	0.00	0.00	0.00	0.00	50.00
	District Average	**34.78**	**11.76**	**30.43**	**29.41**	**21.74**	**5.88**	**4.35**	**0.00**	**8.70**	**5.88**	**0.00**	**47.06**
Burdwan	Baidyapur	25.00	0.00	25.00	50.00	12.50	0.00	25.00	0.00	12.50	0.00	0.00	50.00
	Kalyanpur	37.50	0.00	37.50	20.00	12.50	0.00	12.50	0.00	0.00	20.00	0.00	60.00
	Majhergram	25.00	25.00	50.00	25.00	12.50	0.00	0.00	0.00	12.50	0.00	0.00	50.00
	Monteswar	25.00	0.00	25.00	20.00	25.00	0.00	12.50	0.00	12.50	0.00	0.00	80.00
	District **Average**	**28.13**	**5.56**	**34.38**	**27.78**	**15.63**	**0.00**	**12.50**	**0.00**	**9.38**	**5.56**	**0.00**	**61.11**

Source: Primary Data collected from GP Office. *Note*: Figures in percentage.

psychological advancement as well as greater acceptance to the family and society. Economic independence makes women more empower both socially, politically and economically. But it has been found from Table 6.14 that a significant number of female representatives belong to either less stable income group or totally economically dependent group. Because of less stable economic group or economic insufficiency, the female representatives remain dependent to their husband or family in terms of economically and as well as psychologically.

Political Representation of the Gram Panchayat Members

The 73rd Constitutional Amendment Act, 1992, has provided for mandatory election for the local bodies at an interval of five years. Accordingly, elections were to be held to constitute the local bodies. Before 73rd Constitutional Amendment Act, 1992, Asoka Mehta Committee Report, 1978 also favoured open participation of political parties in Panchayati Raj Institutions as this would not only ensure clear orientation to the development programme but also facilitate their linkage with high level of political process. As per the recommendation of Asoka Mehta Committee; West Bengal, immediately accepted the suggestion for political involvement in the year 1978. Since 1978 West Bengal Panchayat General Election has taken place successfully in every consecutive five year with active participation of various national, State and local-level political parties. Table 6.14 reveals the status of political representation in the study area.

Table 6.14 indicates that the Jamna Gram Panchayat of Labpur Development Block is represented by all major political parties. Here, out of total male members, 40.00 per cent are belonging from Left Front, 40.00 per cent from BJP and 20.00 per cent are Independent. But in case of female representative, 60.00 per cent females are from Left Front and 40.00 per are from TMC. In Hatia Gram Panchayat of the same block out of total male member 77.78 per cent are from Left Front and rest of 22.22 per cent from TMC. In case of female 83.33 per cent are belonging to Left Front and remaining 16.67 per cent are from BJP.

In Purandarpur Gram Panchayat of Suri-II Development Block, out of total male members, 80.00 per cent are belonging from Left Front and only 20.00 per cent are Independent. But in case of female

Table 6.14: Political Representation of Gram Panchayat Member.

District	*Gram Panchayat*	*Political Parties*									
		Left Front		*TMC*		*BJP*		*Congress*		*Independent*	
		Male	*Female*	*Male*	*Female*	*Male*	*Female*	*Male*	*Female*	*Male*	*Female*
Birbhum	Jamna	40.00	60.00	0.00	40.00	40.00	0.00	0.00	0.00	20.00	0.00
	Hatia	77.78	83.33	22.22	0.00	0.00	16.67	0.00	0.00	0.00	0.00
	Purandarpur	80.00	100.00	0.00	0.00	0.00	0.00	0.00	0.00	20.00	0.00
	Koma	100.00	100.00	0.00	0.00	0.00	0.00	0.00	0.00	0.00	0.00
	District Average	**73.91**	**82.35**	**8.70**	**11.76**	**8.70**	**5.88**	**0.00**	**0.00**	**8.70**	**0.00**
Burdwan	Baidyapur	100.00	100.00	0.00	0.00	0.00	0.00	0.00	0.00	0.00	0.00
	Kalyanpur	100.00	80.00	0.00	20.00	0.00	0.00	0.00	0.00	0.00	0.00
	Majhergram	87.50	100.00	12.50	0.00	0.00	0.00	0.00	0.00	0.00	0.00
	Monteswar	100.00	80.00	0.00	20.00	0.00	0.00	0.00	0.00	0.00	0.00
	District Average	**96.88**	**88.89**	**3.13**	**11.11**	**0.00**	**0.00**	**0.00**	**0.00**	**0.00**	**0.00**

Source: Primary Data Collected from GP Office. *Note:* Figures in percentage.

representative, all the females are from Left Front. All the representatives (both male and female) of Koma Gram Panchayat of the same block are from Left Front.

In Burdwan district, the representation of other political parties, except Left Front is almost nil. Out of four Gram Panchayats, two Gram Panchayats are fully occupied by Left Front, only in case of Kalyanpur and Monteswar Gram Panchayat, 20.00 per cent female representatives are from TMC.

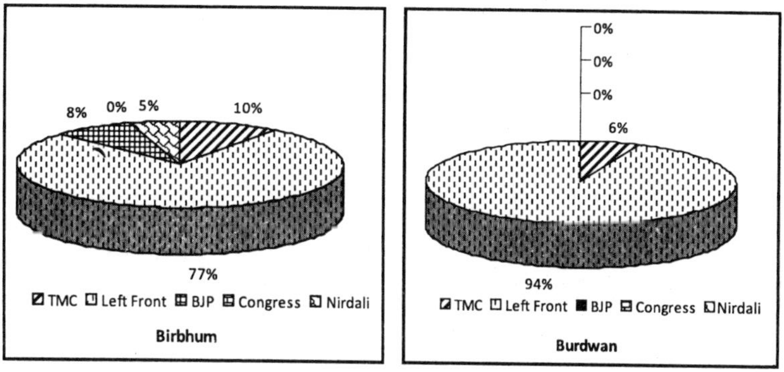

Fig. 6.2: Political Representation of Birbhum and Burdwan Districts

As per overall scenario, in Birbhum district 77.00 per cent seats are occupied by the Left Front, 10.00 per cent are from TMC, 8.00 per cent are from BJP and 5.00 per cent are Independent Candidates. However, in Burdwan district, 94.00 per cent members are from Left Front and only 6.00 per cent are from TMC. In case of political power structure of the Gram Panchayat members, it has found that all selected eight Gram Panchayats are ruled by the Left Front. Another important fact has revealed that no female members from selected Gram Panchayats are elected as Independent Candidate, while in Birbhum district 5.00 per cent male representatives were elected as Independent Candidates. It appears that female members may be only elected under political banner or may not be enough confident to fight independently.

Motivational Source of Gram Panchayat Members

Under the provisions of the West Bengal Panchayat Act, 1973 Panchayat election has been held in the State at an interval of every five years where major political parties took part. In the present context, the Panchayati Raj Institutions has become a political body. So, entering into the Panchayati Raj Institutions equally means entering into the field of political arena. However, appearance into the political spare is not much easy stuff for the rural people. The rural people need some catalytic agents as motivator. The motivators play a key role to inspire the common people to participate in the grassroots level political affairs. Table 6.15 shows various motivators who inspire and motivate Gram Panchayat members to contest in the Panchayat election.

It is appear from Table 6.15 that in Jamna Gram Panchayat of Birbhum district, out of total elected male representatives 20.00 per cent, 40.00 per cent and 40.00 per cent members are motivated by their family members, local political parties and villagers respectively. In case of female representatives, husbands play a vital role to motivate in bringing them into politics. Among the female members of the Gram Panchayat 40.00 per cent have been motivated by their husbands, 20.00 per cent by family members and 40.00 per cent by political members to join politics.

In case of Hatia Gram Panchayat, out of total elected male representatives 44.44 per cent are self-motivated, 22.22 per cent are motivated by family members and same per cent motivated by political parties and 11.11 per cent members are motivated by villagers. In case of female representatives, 33.33 per cent are motivated by husbands, 16.67 per cent by family members and 33.33 per cent by political parties and 16.67 per cent by villagers to join politics.

In case of Purandarpur Gram Panchayat, out of total elected male representatives 40.00 per cent are self-motivated and 60.00 per cent are motivated by political parties. In case of female representatives, 50.00 per cent are motivated by husbands, 25.00 per cent are by family members and same per cent by political parties.

In Koma Gram Panchayat out of total elected male representatives 25.00 per cent each motivated by self, family, political party and villagers respectively. While in case of female representatives, 50.00 per cent motivated by husband and same per cent motivated by the family members.

In Burdwan district, self-motivated male members are 25.00 per cent, 25.00 per cent, 12.50 per cent and 37.50 per cent in Baidyapur Gram Panchayat, Kalyanpur Gram Panchayat, Majhergram Gram Panchayat and Monteswar Gram Panchayat respectively. While

Table 6.15: Motivational Source of Gram Panchayat Members

District	*Gram Panchayat*	*Motivational Sources*									
		Self		*Husband/Wife*		*Family Members*		*Political Parties*		*Villagers*	
		Male	*Female*	*Male*	*Female*	*Male*	*Female*	*Male*	*Female*	*Male*	*Female*
Birbhum	Jamna	0.00	0.00	0.00	40.00	20.00	20.00	40.00	40.00	40.00	0.00
	Hatia	44.44	0.00	0.00	33.33	22.22	16.67	22.22	33.33	11.11	16.67
	Purandarpur	40.00	0.00	0.00	50.00	0.00	25.00	60.00	25.00	0.00	0.00
	Koma	25.00	0.00	0.00	50.00	25.00	50.00	25.00	0.00	25.00	0.00
	District Average	**30.43**	**0.00**	**0.00**	**41.18**	**17.39**	**23.53**	**34.78**	**29.41**	**17.39**	**5.88**
Burdwan	Baidyapur	25.00	0.00	0.00	50.00	12.50	25.00	50.00	25.00	12.50	0.00
	Kalyanpur	25.00	20.00	0.00	20.00	25.00	20.00	37.50	40.00	12.50	0.00
	Majhergram	12.50	0.00	0.00	50.00	25.00	25.00	62.50	25.00	0.00	0.00
	Monteswar	37.50	0.00	0.00	40.00	12.50	40.00	37.50	20.00	12.50	0.00
	District Average	**25.00**	**5.56**	**0.00**	**38.89**	**18.75**	**27.78**	**46.88**	**27.78**	**9.38**	**0.00**

Source: Primary Data collected from GP Office. *Note*: Figures in percentage.

percentage of male representatives motivated by the family members are 12.50 per cent, 25.00 per cent, 25.00 per cent and 12.50 per cent in above mentioned Gram Panchayats respectively. Percentage of male representatives motivated by political party are 50.00 per cent, 37.50 per cent, 62.50 per cent and 37.50 per cent in above mentioned Gram Panchayats respectively. Villagers have motivated 12.50 per cent male members in each of Baidyapur Gram Panchayat, Kalyanpur Gram Panchayat and Monteswar Gram Panchayat respectively.

In case of female representatives only 20.00 per cent females are self-motivated in Kalyanpur Gram Panchayat. While other three Gram Panchayats have no self-motivated female representatives.

The percentage of female representatives motivated by the husbands are 50.00 per cent, 20.00 per cent, 50.00 per cent and 40.00 per cent in Baidyapur Gram Panchayat, Kalyanpur Gram Panchayat, Majhergram Gram Panchayat and Monteswar Gram Panchayat respectively. The percentage of female representatives motivated by family members are 25.00 per cent, 20.00 per cent, 25.00 per cent and 40.00 per cent in above mentioned Gram Panchayats respectively. While percentage of female representatives motivated by political party are 25.00 per cent, 40.00 per cent, 25.00 per cent and 40.00 per cent in above mentioned Gram Panchayats respectively.

Table 6.15 reflects almost same trend in both of the districts. In case of of Birbhum district 30.43 per cent, 17.39 per cent, 34.78 per cent and 17.39 per cent male representatives are motivated by self, family members, political parties and villagers while in case of female members 41.18 per cent motivated by husband, 23.53 per cent by family members, 29.41 per cent by political parties and only 5.88 per cent by villagers to join politics.

In case of Burdwan district 25.00 per cent, 18.75 per cent, 46.88 per cent and 9.38 per cent male representatives are motivated by self, family members, political parties and villagers. However, in case of female members 5.56 per cent are self-motivated, 38.89 per cent are motivated by husband, 27.78 per cent by family members and same per cent motivated by political parties to join politics.

It has been cleared from the above discussion that the political party plays a major role to bring the members (both male and female) into the politics. In case of female members, their husbands play a vital role for that. One more interesting fact is that the frequency of self-motivated female members is almost zero in both of the districts. Similarly, there is no male member motivated by their wives. It clears the fact of male domination in the grassroots politics and as well as in the Gram Panchayats. The actual facts behind the improvement in female representation at Gram Panchayat level is due to provision of 33 per cent women reservation under 73rd Constitutional Amendment Act, 1992. In some case, the husbands, who were earlier the representative of the respective *Sansads*, motivate their wives to contest in the election to restore their power.

Previous Experience of the Gram Panchayat Members

Previous experience plays a significant role in developing better understanding about the functioning and operational system of Panchayat. It provides confidence, maturity and expertise for success in their respective area of operation. So, it is important to discuss the previous experience of the Gram Panchayat members in the study area. Table 6.16 shows the previous experience of the elected Gram Panchayat members.

Table 6.16: Previous Experience of the Gram Panchayat Members

District	*Gram Panchayat*	*Previously Elected Member*		*Previously Associated with Political Parties*	
		Male	*Female*	*Male*	*Female*
Birbhum	Jamna	20.00	0.00	60.00	20.00
	Hatia	22.22	16.67	44.44	16.67
	Purandarpur	20.00	20.00	60.00	20.00
	Koma	25.00	0.00	75.00	0.00
	District Average	**21.74**	**11.76**	**56.52**	**17.65**
Burdwan	Baidyapur	37.50	25.00	75.00	50.00
	Kalyanpur	25.00	20.00	62.50	20.00
	Majhergram	25.00	25.00	75.00	25.00
	Monteswar	25.00	0.00	62.50	20.00
	District Average	**28.13**	**16.67**	**68.75**	**27.78**

Source: Primary Data collected from GP Office. *Note*: Figures in percentage.

It apear in Table 6.16 that in Jamna Gram Panchayat, 20.00 per cent male members are previously elected member, 60.00 per cent male members are previously associated with political party. Out of total female member there are 20.00 per cent are previously associated with political party. But all the female members of this Gram Panchayat participate in election as fresh candidate.

In Hatia Gram Panchayat 22.22 per cent male members are previously elected and 4.44 per cent male are previously associated with political party. In case of female only 16.67 per cent are previously elected and 16.67 per cent female representatives are previous association with the political parties.

In Purandarpur and Koma Gram Panchayat 20.00 per cent and 25.00 per cent male members are previously elected respectively and only 20.00 per cent female members of Purandarpur Gram Panchayat are previously elected. The percentage of male and female political association in these two Gram Panchayats are 60.00 per cent, 75.00 per cent and 20.00 per cent and nil respectively.

In Burdwan district, out of total male members of each selected Gram Panchayat, there 37.50 per cent in Baidyapur Gram Panchayat, 25.00 per cent each in Kalyanpur Gram Panchayat, Majhergram Gram Panchayat and Monteswar Gram Panchayat are elected earlier. In case of female 25.00 per cent, 20.00 per cent and 25.00 per cent are previously elected in Baidyapur Gram Panchayat, in Kalyanpur Gram Panchayat and Majhergram Gram Panchayat respectively. There is no one female members in Monteswar Gram Panchayat who was again elected as Panchayat member from the earlier election.

The percentages of previously elected male and female representatives of Birbhum district are 21.74 per cent and 11.76 per cent respectively and in Burdwan district the percentages are 28.13 per cent and 16.67 per cent respectively. However, male and female representatives associated with political parties in Birbhum district are 56.52 per cent, 17.65 per cent and in Burdwan district are 68.75 per cent and 27.78 per cent respectively. So, it reveals from the discussion that in both of the district, the frequency of previously elected members and political association are high in case of male than the female members.

Awareness Levels of the Elected Gram Panchayat Members

Awareness Level of the GP Members on PRI Related Issues: Awareness levels of Gram Panchayat member is one the most important variable which highly influence the entire decentralised process. It is expected that the elected Gram Panchayat members should have the clear idea about the Panchayat related issues. For better understanding of the study, it is important to know the awareness level on various issues of Panchayat functioning of the elected Gram Panchayat members as well as the related people. The awareness on different issues was measured through the nature of response (Yes/ No) expressed by the respondents for different statements given in the scale. The scale were developed by using various indicators under different sections as mentioned in Table 6.17.

Table 6.17 shows the awareness among the Gram Panchayat members about three-tier system of Panchayati Raj Institution. In Birbhum district, out of total male members of selected four Gram Panchayats, 69.57 per cent male members know this system. But this percentage is much better in Burdwan district; here 84.38 per cent male members are aware about three-tier system.

But in case of female awareness on the same issue, Birbhum district shows very poor percentage in comparison with Burdwan district. In Birbhum district, only 47.06 per cent female members are aware about three-tier systems, whereas, in Burdwan district this percentage is 66.67 per cent.

The role, objectives and functioning of Gram Panchayat is also a crucial indicator to judge the awareness level of GP members as members are directly associating with the Gram Panchayat. But Table 6.17 shows an alarming picture about the awareness among the Gram Panchayat members regarding Gram Panchayat role. In Birbhum district, only 73.91 per cent male members and 47.06 per cent female members know about Gram Panchayat, its objectives, its operation area and method etc., but rest of the members are not aware about this institution. Even their perception is that the G.P. office is ruling party's working office. Same picture is also observed in Burdwan district, but here the condition is better than Birbhum district. Here out of total members, 84.34 per cent male and 55.56 per cent female members are aware about the Gram Panchayat.

The 73rd Constitutional Amendment Act, 1992 has made it mandatory that one-third seats are being reserved for SC, ST and OBC. But Table 6.17 shows the awareness levels among the male representatives are quite high and similar in both of the district while the awareness levels among the women representatives are quite low in both of the districts. The 78.26 per cent and 81.25 per cent male representatives of Birbhum and Burdwan district are aware of caste reservation system while the awareness among the women representatives are only 29.41 per cent and 44.44 per cent respectively.

Table 6.17: Awareness Level of the GP Members on PRI Related Issues

District	Gram Panchayat	Awareness Level									
		Three-Tier PRI System		Role of Gram Panchayats		Caste Reservation System		Women Reservation System		Gram Unnayan Samiti	
		Male	Female	Male	Female	Male	Female	Male	Female	Male	Female
(1)	(2)	(3)	(4)	(5)	(6)	(7)	(8)	(9)	(10)	(11)	(12)
Birbhum	Jamna	80.00	40.00	80.00	60.00	100.00	20.00	80.00	60.00	80.00	20.00
	Hatia	66.67	50.00	77.78	33.33	66.67	33.33	77.78	50.00	55.56	16.67
	Koma	75.00	50.00	75.00	50.00	75.00	50.00	50.00	50.00	50.00	0.00
	Purandarpur	60.00	50.00	60.00	50.00	80.00	25.00	80.00	50.00	60.00	25.00
	District Average	**69.57**	**47.06**	**73.91**	**47.06**	**78.26**	**29.41**	**73.91**	**52.94**	**60.87**	**17.65**
Burdwan	Baidyapur	87.50	75.00	87.50	50.00	87.50	25.00	87.50	50.00	37.50	50.00
	Kalyanpur	87.50	60.00	87.50	60.00	75.00	20.00	75.00	60.00	50.00	20.00
	Majhergran	87.50	75.00	87.50	50.00	75.00	75.00	75.00	50.00	50.00	25.00
	Monteswar	75.00	60.00	75.00	60.00	87.50	60.00	87.50	40.00	75.00	20.00
	District Average	**84.38**	**66.67**	**84.38**	**55.56**	**81.25**	**44.44**	**81.25**	**50.00**	**53.13**	**27.78**

(Contd.)

Table 6.17 (*Contd.*)

District	Gram Panchayat	Awareness Level							
		Gram Sansad		Gram Sabha		Upa-Samiti		Development Schemes	
		Male	Female	Male	Female	Male	Female	Male	Female
(1)	(2)	(13)	(14)	(15)	(16)	(17)	(18)	(19)	(20)
Birbhum	Jamna	100.00	100.00	100.00	80.00	80.00	40.00	100.00	20.00
	Hatia	100.00	66.67	100.00	66.67	77.78	33.33	77.78	33.33
	Koma	100.00	100.00	75.00	50.00	75.00	0.00	75.00	50.00
	Purandarpur	80.00	75.00	80.00	75.00	40.00	50.00	100.00	50.00
	District Average	**95.65**	**82.35**	**91.30**	**70.59**	**69.57**	**35.29**	**78.26**	**35.29**
Burdwan	Baidyapur	100.00	100.00	100.00	75.00	87.50	50.00	87.50	50.00
	Kalyanpur	100.00	100.00	100.00	60.00	75.00	40.00	87.50	40.00
	Majhergran	100.00	100.00	100.00	75.00	62.50	50.00	75.00	75.00
	Monteswar	100.00	100.00	100.00	100.00	62.50	60.00	75.00	40.00
	District Average	**100.00**	**100.00**	**100.00**	**77.78**	**71.88**	**50.00**	**84.34**	**50.00**

Source: Primary Data Collected from GP Office. *Note*: Figures in percentage.

One-third seats are reserved for women in every tire of Panchayati Raj Institutions have been made mandatory by the 73rd Constitutional Amendment Act, 1992. But Table 6.17 shows that till now there is a gap in members' awareness about women reservation. In Birbhum district 73.91 per cent male members and 52.94 per cent female members are aware about women reservation and in Burdwan district these percentages are 81.25 per cent and 50.00 per cent respectively. Rest of members in both the districts are till believe that the political party take decision about nomination for women on respective seats.

Gram Sabha and Gram Sansad have a vital role in Panchayat operation. Through these meetings, grassroots level people can directly participate in planning and implementation process. It is expected that the Gram Panchayat members should know about the detail of *Gram Sabha* and *Gram Sansad*. In Birbhum district, 91.30 per cent male member and 70.59 per cent female members are aware about the Gram Sabha but 95.65 per cent male members and 82.35 per cent female members are aware about the *Gram Sansad* Meeting. However, Burdwan, all the male Gram Panchayat representatives are aware about both *Gram Sabha* and *Gram Sansad*. In case of women representatives, all know about Gram Sansad while 77. 78 per cent are aware of *Gram Sabha*.

Upa-Samiti is also a vital part of Gram Panchayat Structure as well as of administrative decentralisation. Some of members also selected to lead various *Upa-Samitis*. But the awareness about objective and fuctions of *Upa-Samiti* are quite low among the members. In Birbhum district 69.57 per cent male and 35.29 per cent female members are aware of *Upa-Samitis* while in Burdwan district the awareness level among the male and female members are 71.88 per cent and 50.00 per cent respectively. It reveals that only those members who are responsible for leading respective *Upa-samitis* are aware about the fact while others are less aware of *Upa-samitis*.

Rural Development is also a prime focus area of Gram Panchayats. Various Centrally Sponsored and State sponsored development schemes are implemented through the Gram Panchayat. The role of GP member is to plan and implement these programmes efficiently. So, it is expected that the GP member should have proper knowledge about various development schemes. In Birbhum district, 78.26 per cent male members and 35.29 per cent female members are aware about various schemes whereas, in Burdwan district these percentages are 84.38 per cent and 50.00 per cent respectively.

So, it has been observed from the discussion that the awareness-level among the male and female members of Birbhum district is less than the members of Burdwan district. Although, the awareness-level among the female is remarkably low in both of the Birbhum and Burdwan district than the male members. This reveals the male domination picture in the Gram Panchayats. Although after 73rd Constitutional Amendment Act the awareness as well as participation have been inceased among the women representatives in Gram Panchayat.

Awareness Level of the GP Members on Decentralisation-related Issues of PRIs

Decentralisation is the major theme of the present study. So, awareness levels of Gram Panchayat members on various decentralisation issues are very important indicators to assess the level of decentralisation at grassroots level. For analyzing the situation Gram Panchayat members were questioned with some basic issues related to decentralisation.

The first indicator is the awareness about the Panchayat planning process. West Bengal has a unique system of planning at grassroots level which strengthens the decentralised process along with greater people's participation. Here, Table 6.18 shows that in Birbhum district, out of total male members of selected four Gram Panchayats, 60.87 per cent male members know about the planning process. But this percentage is much better in Burdwan district; here 71.88 per cent male members are aware about three-tier system.

But in case of female awareness on the same issue, Birbhum district shows very similar percentage in comparison with Burdwan district. In Birbhum district, only 41.18 per cent female members are aware about Panchayat planning process, whereas, in Burdwan district this percentage is 44.44 per cent.

The formation of budget is also a crucial indicator like planning process to judge the awareness level of GP members. It appears from Table 6.18 that 52.17 per cent male members and 29.41 per cent female members of Birbhum district are aware about the Budget making process. In Burdwan district this picture is showing much better than Birbhum, here 68.75 per cent male members and 38.89 per cent female members know the budget making process.

Prioritization of schemes or sector-wise scheme selection is very important for the development of a particular area. But till now the

Table 6.18: Awareness Level of the GP Members on Administration-related Issues of PRIs

District	*Gram Panchayat*	*Administration-related Issues of PRIs*									
		Planning Process		*Budget Making*		*Various Development Schemes*		*Prioritization of Scheme*		*Implementation Process*	
		Male	*Female*	*Male*	*Female*	*Male*	*Female*	*Male*	*Female*	*Male*	*Female*
Birbhum	Jamna	60.00	20.00	60.00	20.00	80.00	20.00	60.00	0.00	100.00	40.00
	Hatia	66.67	50.00	66.67	33.33	88.89	83.33	55.56	33.33	66.67	66.67
	Koma	50.00	0.00	25.00	0.00	75.00	50.00	75.00	0.00	100.00	50.00
	Purandarpur	60.00	75.00	40.00	50.00	100.00	75.00	60.00	25.00	100.00	75.00
	District Average	**60.87**	**41.18**	**52.17**	**29.41**	**86.96**	**58.82**	**60.87**	**17.65**	**86.96**	**58.82**
Burdwan	Baidyapur	62.50	25.00	62.50	25.00	100.00	75.00	75.00	25.00	100.00	75.00
	Kalyanpur	75.00	40.00	75.00	20.00	100.00	60.00	62.50	40.00	87.50	60.00
	Majhergran	75.00	25.00	62.50	25.00	75.00	75.00	62.50	25.00	75.00	75.00
	Monteswar	75.00	80.00	75.00	80.00	75.00	40.00	75.00	20.00	87.50	60.00
	District Average	**71.88**	**44.44**	**68.75**	**38.89**	**87.50**	**61.11**	**68.75**	**27.78**	**87.50**	**66.67**

Source: Primary Data. *Note*: Figures in Percentage.

percentage of members who can select proper scheme and prioritize them are very low in both Birbhum and Burdwan districts. In Birbhum district 60.87 per cent male Gram Panchayat members and 17.65 per cent female *Gram Panchayat* members are able to select scheme whereas, in Burdwan district 68.75 per cent male members and 27.87 per cent female members are able to do so. Although, 86.96 per cent male members and 58.82 per cent female members in Birbhum district and 87.50 per cent male members and 61.11 per cent female members in Burdwan district are well aware about various developmental schemes.

After planning and getting the sanction of the budget, proper implementation of the selected schemes at the village level is very important characteristics of decentralisation process. In Birbhum district, 86.69 per cent male Gram Panchayat member and 58.82 per cent female Gram Panchayat members know the process of execution of the selected schemes, whereas, 87.50 per cent male Gram Panchayat members and 66.67 per cent female Gram Panchayat members know the process of implementation of the schemes at the village-level in Burdwan district.

So, it has been observed from the discussion that the awareness level among the male and female members of Birbhum district is less than the members of Burdwan district. Although, the awareness level among the female is remarkably low in both of the Birbhum and Burdwan district than the male members. Another factor has been revealed on this issue that at present the planning and budgeting process are becoming more centralised rather than decentralisaed as the level of participation at planning and budgeting process went low. The Gram Panchayat administration is giving an external pressure to develop plans which somehow dilute the actual needs of the villages. The political engagement is also hampering the entire process as it only focuses on fulfilling the political agenda rather than developing the areas.

To sum up, the General Caste and Scheduled Castes people are holding maximum representative in the local Government. However, in case of female participation cumulative participation of both Scheduled Castes and Scheduled Tribes women are more than the General Caste women. The respresentation of female members of all selected Panchayats are maintaining the prescribed percentage of the

Constitution of India. The widening gender gap in educational status leads to poor access to knowledge, skill and attitude among the female members.

Further, in both the Districts there was no significant evidence that awareness and perception determined the increase of people's participation. It was learnt that the level of awareness and perception have been increasing day by day. Therefore, the level of participation also may increase after sometime if favourable environment is created for active participation of people.

Perception of Gram Panchayat Members on Decentralisation Issues

Perception of Gram Panchayat members on various issues regarding PRIs and decentralisation process is also an important indicator to assess the status of grassroots governance as this reflects the opinion, attitude and practice of Gram Panchayat members towards decentralisation. So, in this section an attempt has been made to analyze the perceptions of Gram Panchayat members on various PRI related issues. For this a four point scale has been developed and GP members were asked to give their opinion on various relevant issues.

Perception of the GP Members about the Significance of the Decentralisation of Power at Grassroots Level for Sustainable Development

Table 6.19 indicates that in Birbhum district about 47.50 per cent GP members were strongly agreed and 35.00 per cent agreed with the argument that decentralisation of power at grassroots level is very crucial factor for sustainable development. However, only, 12.5 per cent members were disagreed and 5.00 per cent were strongly disagreed with the fact.

In Burdwan district, 48.00 per cent and 44.00 per cent were found to be strongly agreed and only agreed with the fact that decentralisation is a significant factor for sustainable development. While only 6.00 per cent members disagreed and 2.00 per cent were strongly disagreed with the above mentioned fact.

So, the GP members are very positive about the importance of decentralised governance at grassroots level and this strong argument

Table 6.19: Perception of the GP Members about the Significance of the Decentralisation of Power at Grassroots Level for Sustainable Development

District	*Gram Panchayat*	*Opinion of the GP Members (%)*			
		Strongly Agree	*Agree*	*Disagree*	*Strongly Disagree*
Birbhum	Jamna	50.00	30.00	10.00	10.00
	Hatia	46.67	40.00	13.33	0.00
	Koma	50.00	16.67	16.67	16.67
	Purandarpur	44.44	44.44	11.11	0.00
	District Average	**47.50**	**35.00**	**12.50**	**5.00**
Burdwan	Baidyapur	50.00	41.67	0.00	8.33
	Kalyanpur	35.71	50.00	14.29	0.00
	Majhergran	58.33	41.67	0.00	0.00
	Monteswar	46.15	46.15	7.69	0.00
	District Average	**48.00**	**44.00**	**6.00**	**2.00**

Source: Primary Data. *Note*: Figures in Percentage.

made it very clear that decentralisation is a must factor for sustainable development at grassroots level.

Perception of the GP Members about the Focus of Gram Panchayat on Proper Decentralisation

In case of Gram Panchayats focus on effective decentralisation in Birbhum district about 35.00 per cent GP members were strongly agreed and 52.50 per cent agreed with the argument that Gram Panchayat is giving proper focus on decentralisation of power at grassroots level. However, only, 12.5 per cent members were disagreed with the fact.

In Burdwan district, 44.00 per cent and 50.00 per cent were found strongly agreed and only agreed with the fact that Gram Panchayat is giving proper focus on decentralisation of power at grassroots level. While only 6.00 per cent members were disagreed with the above mentioned fact.

The data clearly indicates that in spite of having high focus of GP members on decentralisation process, the Gram Panchayats have shown less focus on proper decentralisation. The political and

Table 6.20: Perception of the GP Members about the Focus of Gram Panchayat on Proper Decentralisation

District	*Gram Panchayat*	*Opinion of the GP Members (%)*			
		Strongly Agree	*Agree*	*Disagree*	*Strongly Disagree*
Birbhum	Jamna	40.00	50.00	10.00	0.00
	Hatia	33.33	53.33	13.33	0.00
	Koma	33.33	50.00	16.67	0.00
	Purandarpur	33.33	55.56	11.11	0.00
	District Average	**35.00**	**52.50**	**12.50**	**0.00**
Burdwan	Baidyapur	50.00	41.67	8.33	0.00
	Kalyanpur	46.15	53.85	7.69	0.00
	Majhergran	41.67	50.00	0.00	0.00
	Monteswar	38.46	53.85	7.69	0.00
	District Average	**44.00**	**50.00**	**6.00**	**0.00**

Source: Primary Data. *Note*: Figures in Percentage.

bureaucratic prejudice is also a strong factor diluting the entire process.

Perception of the GP Members about the Significance of the Gram Unnayan Samiti on Preparation of Efficient Micro-level Plan

The *Gram Unnayan Samiti* is also an important village level body for analysing local needs and developing plans as per those requirements. The Government of West Bengal has made the *Gram Unnayan Samiti* a mandatory stakeholder in the micro-level planning process at *Gram Śansad*-level. However, the study shows that the GP members are not very convinced with the stake of the *Gram Unnayan Samiti* in micro-level planning.

In Birbhum district only 20.00 per cent GP members strongly agreed and 37.50 per cent members agreed with the fact that the *Gram Unnayan Samiti* (GUS) is very important in preparation of effective micro level plan. However, only, 27.5 per cent members were disagreed and 15.00 per cent strongly disagreed with this fact.

In Burdwan district the picture is quite different. Here, 32.00 per cent and 40.00 per cent were found to be strongly agreed and only agreed with the fact that the *Gram Unnayan Samiti* is very important in preparation of effective micro-level plan. While only 22.00 per

Table 6.21: Perception of the GP Members about the Significance of the Gram Unnayan Samiti in Preparation of Efficient Micro-level Plan

District	*Gram Panchayat*	*Opinion of the GP Members (%)*			
		Strongly Agree	*Agree*	*Disagree*	*Strongly Disagree*
Birbhum	Jamna	20.00	30.00	30.00	20.00
	Hatia	20.00	33.33	33.33	13.33
	Koma	16.67	50.00	16.67	16.67
	Purandarpur	22.22	44.44	22.22	11.11
	District Average	**20.00**	**37.50**	**27.50**	**15.00**
Burdwan	Baidyapur	33.33	33.33	25.00	8.33
	Kalyanpur	30.77	38.46	23.08	7.69
	Majhergran	33.33	41.67	25.00	0.00
	Monteswar	30.77	46.15	15.38	7.69
	District Average	**32.00**	**40.00**	**22.00**	**6.00**

Source: Primary Data. *Note*: Figures in Percentage.

cent members were disagreed and 6.00 per cent strongly disagreed with the above mentioned fact.

So, it is clear that the *Gram Unnayan Samiti* is more effective in Burdwan district than the Birbhum district in preparation of micro-level plans. It has also revealed from the FGD that Burdwan district has shown special focus for effective management of the *Gram Unnayan Samiti* (GUS) than the Birbhum district and which facilitated the GUS for showing efficiency. However, recent political interest has been diluting the role and effectiveness of Gram Unnayan Samiti at grassroots to level and made it only a living structure rather a effective institution.

Perception of the GP Members about the Significance of People's Participation on Effective Micro-level Planning and Implementation

The people's participation has a directly proportionate relation with the effective micro-level planning. It means the improvement of effective people's participation improves the effectiveness of micro-level planning and implementation. In Birbhum district 37.50 per cent GP members strongly agreed and 45.00 per cent members agreed with the fact that people's participation is significant for effective micro-level planning and implementation. However, only, 15.00 per cent members were disagreed and only 2.50 per cent strongly disagreed with this fact.

In Burdwan district the picture is quite similar. Here, 42.00 per cent and 48.00 per cent were found to be strongly agreed and only agreed with the fact that that people's participation is significant for effective micro-level planning and implementation. While only 8.00 per cent members disagreed and 2.00 per cent strongly disagreed with the above mentioned fact.

Table 6.22: Perception of the GP Members about the Significance of People's Participation on Effective Micro-level Planning and Implementation

District	*Gram Panchayat*	*Opinion of the GP Members (%)*			
		Strongly Agree	*Agree*	*Disagree*	*Strongly Disagree*
Birbhum	Jamna	50.00	40.00	10.00	0.00
	Hatia	33.33	40.00	20.00	6.67
	Koma	33.33	50.00	16.67	0.00
	Purandarpur	33.33	55.56	11.11	0.00
	District Average	**37.50**	**45.00**	**15.00**	**2.50**
Burdwan	Baidyapur	41.67	41.67	16.67	0.00
	Kalyanpur	46.15	53.85	7.69	0.00
	Majhergran	41.67	50.00	0.00	0.00
	Monteswar	38.46	46.15	7.69	7.69
	District Average	**42.00**	**48.00**	**8.00**	**2.00**

Source: Primary Data. *Note*: Figures in Percentage.

So, it is clear that members are well aware of the fact that people's participation is very essential for effective decentralisation. However, in practice they have been found to be bound to political parties and the GP officials.

Perception of the GP Members about the Political Influence on Planning and Implementation of Micro-level Plans

The political influence on planning and implementation of micro-level plans is a real fact in West Bengal and this study has no exception. It has been found that the planning and implementation process is highly influenced by the political parties. Table 6.23 also reveals that in Birbhum district 50.00 per cent GP members were strongly agreed and 40.00 per cent members agreed with the fact that the planning and implementation at micro-level is politically influenced. However, only, 7.50 per cent members were disagreed and only 2.00 per cent strongly disagreed with this fact.

In Burdwan district the picture is quite similar. Here, 50.00 per cent and 40.00 per cent were found to be strongly agreed and only agreed with the fact that that the planning and implementation at micro-level is politically influenced. While only 8.00 per cent members disagreed and 2.00 per cent strongly disagreed with the above mentioned fact.

Table 6.23: Perception of the GP Members about the Political Influence on Planning and Implementation of Micro-level Plans

District	*Gram Panchayat*	*Opinion of the GP Members (%)*			
		Strongly Agree	*Agree*	*Disagree*	*Strongly Disagree*
Birbhum	Jamna	70.00	30.00	0.00	0.00
	Hatia	46.67	40.00	13.33	6.67
	Koma	33.33	50.00	16.67	0.00
	Purandarpur	44.44	44.44	0.00	0.00
	District Average	**50.00**	**40.00**	**7.50**	**2.50**
Burdwan	Baidyapur	50.00	41.67	8.33	0.00
	Kalyanpur	53.85	46.15	7.69	0.00
	Majhergran	50.00	41.67	0.00	0.00
	Monteswar	46.15	30.77	15.38	7.69
	District Average	**50.00**	**40.00**	**8.00**	**2.00**

Source: Primary Data. *Note*: Figures in Percentage.

Perception of the GP Members about the Importance of Gram Sabha for Devolution of Power

Regarding the importance of Gram Sabha for devolution of power in Birbhum district 52.50 per cent GP members were strongly agreed and 32.50 per cent members agreed with the fact that the effective Gram Sabha is important for proper devolution of power. However, only, 12.50 per cent members were disagreed and only 2.50 per cent strongly disagreed with this fact.

Table 6.24: Perception of the GP Members about the Importance of Gram Sabha for Devolution of Power

District	*Gram Panchayat*	*Opinion of the GP Members (%)*			
		Strongly Agree	*Agree*	*Disagree*	*Strongly Disagree*
Birbhum	Jamna	60.00	30.00	10.00	0.00
	Hatia	46.67	33.33	20.00	6.67
	Koma	50.00	33.33	0.00	0.00
	Purandarpur	55.56	33.33	11.11	0.00
	District Average	**52.50**	**32.50**	**12.50**	**2.50**
Burdwan	Baidyapur	58.33	41.67	0.00	0.00
	Kalyanpur	61.54	38.46	7.69	0.00
	Majhergran	58.33	33.33	0.00	0.00
	Monteswar	53.85	30.77	7.69	7.69
	District Average	**58.00**	**36.00**	**4.00**	**2.00**

Source: Primary Data. *Note*: Figures in Percentage.

In Burdwan district the picture is quite similar. Here, 58.00 per cent and 36.00 per cent were found to be strongly agreed and only agreed with the fact that the effective Gram Sabha is important for proper devolution of power. While only 4.00 per cent members disagreed and 2.00 per cent strongly disagreed with the above mentioned fact.

So, it clears that the Gram Sabha is a crucial organization for effective implementation of decentralisation process and devolution of power to local people. It is very essential for rural people to argue their right and strengthening the grassroots governance. However, over the year the main agenda of Gram Sabha is being diluting and emerging as a platform for political agenda and conflict.

The above discussion clearly indicates that the GP members are very positive about the importance of decentralised governance at grassroots-level and this strong argument made it very clear that decentralisation is a must factor for sustainable development at grassroots-level. However, the political and bureaucratic prejudice is also a strong factor diluting the entire process. The GP elected members are well aware of the fact that people's participation is very essential for effective decentralisation. However, in practice they have found to be bound to political parties and the GP officials.

Efficacy of SHG and Non-SHG Members in Decentralisation Process

Awareness and perception-level of rural people especially the rural women is one the most important variable which highly influences the grassroots governance as well as entire decentralised process. It is expected that the rural people should have the clear knowledge and perception about the local governance related issues. So, the level of knowledge and perception are the two major variables for judging the efficacy level of SHG members as well as the non-SHG villagers. The awareness and perceptions on different issues related to decentralisation were measured through the nature of response expressed by the respondents for different statements.

Awareness Level of the SHG Members on PRI

Table 6.25 clearly indicates that in Birbhum district, 43.75 per cent sampled SHG members have good knowledge about Panchayat vote, 45.31 per cent and 10.94 per cent SHG members have average and poor knowledge about Panchayat vote respectively. In Burdwan district, 48.44 per cent sampled SHG members have well, 42.19 per cent have average and 9.38 per cent have poor knowledge about Panchayat voting. So, SHG members of each district have similar kind of knowledge level regarding Panchayat vote.

In Birbhum district, 23.44 per cent sampled SHG members have good knowledge about role of PRIs, while 53.13 per cent and 23.44 per cent sampled SHG members have average and poor knowledge about role of PRIs respectively. However, in Burdwan district, 26.56 per cent sampled SHG members have well, 51.56 per cent have average and 21.88 per cent have poor knowledge about role of PRIs. So, SHG members of Burdwan district have better knowledge level than the Birbhum district regarding role of PRIs.

Caste Reservation System is an important issue of decentralised governance. The 73rd Constitutional Amendment Act had a mandatory provision of Caste Reservation. So, it is expected that the villagers have good knowledge about Caste Reservation System. In Birbhum district, 26.56 per cent sampled SHG members have good knowledge about role of Caste Reservation System, while 48.44 per cent and 25.00 per cent sampled SHG members have average and poor knowledge about Caste Reservation System respectively. However,

Table 6.25: Awareness Level of the SHG Members on PRI

District	*Gram Panchayat*	*Knowledge Level*	*Awareness Level of SHG Members on PRI*					
			Panchayat Vote	*Role of PRI*	*Caste Reservation System*	*Women Reservation System*	*Three-tier PRI System*	*Various Schemes under GP*
Birbhum	Jamna	Good	31.25	25.00	31.25	25.00	18.75	31.25
		Average	62.50	50.00	50.00	56.25	56.25	56.25
		Poor	6.25	25.00	18.75	18.75	25.00	12.50
	Hatia	Good	43.75	25.00	31.25	31.25	31.25	31.25
		Average	50.00	43.75	43.75	43.75	43.75	50.00
		Poor	6.25	31.25	25.00	25.00	25.00	18.75
	Koma	Good	50.00	18.75	25.00	18.75	18.75	25.00
		Average	31.25	56.25	43.75	43.75	50.00	43.75
		Poor	18.75	25.00	31.25	37.50	31.25	31.25
	Purandarpur	Good	50.00	25.00	18.75	12.50	18.75	25.00
		Average	37.50	62.50	56.25	56.25	56.25	56.25
		Poor	12.50	12.50	25.00	31.25	25.00	18.75
	District Average	Good	43.75	23.44	26.56	21.88	21.88	28.13
		Average	45.31	53.13	48.44	50.00	51.56	51.56
		Poor	10.94	23.44	25.00	28.13	26.56	20.31

(Contd.)

Table 6.25 (*Contd.*)

District	*Gram Panchayat*	*Knowledge Level*	*Awareness Level of SHG Members on PRI*					
			Panchayat Vote	*Role of PRI*	*Caste Reservation System*	*Women Reservation System*	*Three-tier PRI System*	*Various Schemes under GP*
Burdwan	Baidyapur	Good	62.50	31.25	31.25	25.00	25.00	31.25
		Average	37.50	56.25	43.75	43.75	50.00	43.75
		Poor	0.00	12.50	25.00	31.25	25.00	25.00
	Kalyanpur	Good	50.00	31.25	31.25	31.25	18.75	43.75
		Average	37.50	43.75	50.00	43.75	50.00	37.50
		Poor	12.50	25.00	18.75	25.00	31.25	18.75
	Majhergram	Good	37.50	18.75	18.75	18.75	18.75	25.00
		Average	50.00	50.00	56.25	62.50	56.25	50.00
		Poor	12.50	31.25	25.00	18.75	25.00	12.50
	Monteswar	Good	43.75	25.00	37.50	25.00	31.25	25.00
		Average	43.75	56.25	37.50	56.25	43.75	56.25
		Poor	12.50	18.75	25.00	18.75	25.00	18.75
	District Average	Good	48.44	26.56	29.69	25.00	23.44	31.25
		Average	42.19	51.56	46.88	51.56	50.00	46.88
		Poor	9.38	21.88	23.44	23.44	26.56	18.75

Source: Primary Data. *Note*: Figures in Percentage.

in Burdwan district, 29.69 per cent sampled SHG members have well, 46.88 per cent have average and 23.44 per cent have poor knowledge about Caste Reservation System. So, SHG members of Burdwan and Birbhum district have moderate knowledge level on Caste Reservation System.

Women reservation is another mandatory provision of decentralisation process. It is also expected that women folk of rural areas specially the women engaged with SHGs have better understanding about women reservation system in PRIs. However, the data regarding the knowledge level about women reservation is not satisfactory. In Birbhum district, 21.88 per cent sampled SHG members have good knowledge about women reservation, while 50.00 cent and 28.13 per cent sampled SHG members have average and poor knowledge about women reservation respectively. While, in Burdwan district, 25.00 per cent sampled SHG members have well, 51.56 per cent have average and 26.56 per cent have poor knowledge about women reservation. So, SHG members of Burdwan district have quite better knowledge about women reservation than the Birbhum district.

Regarding PRI structure, in Birbhum district 21.88 per cent sampled SHG members have good knowledge, while 51.56 per cent and 26.56 per cent sampled SHG members have average and poor knowledge about PRI structure respectively. Similarly, in Burdwan district, 23.44 per cent sampled SHG members have well, 50.00 per cent have average and 26.56 per cent have poor knowledge about PRI structure. So, SHG members of both Birbhum and Burdwan districts have similar understanding about PRI structure.

The Government has implemented various schemes and programmes through Gram Panchayat and it is expected that the villagers have good knowledge about these schemes as they are the main stakeholders of these schemes. In recent trend, SHGs are engaged in implementation of these programmes so SHGs should have good knowledge about these programmes. Ground realities also supported this argument. Regarding Schemes under Gram Panchayat, in Birbhum district 28.13 per cent and 51.56 per cent sampled SHG members have good and average level knowledge respectively, while only 20.31 per cent sampled SHG members have poor knowledge about Schemes under Gram Panchayat. Similarly, in Burdwan district, 31.25 per cent sampled SHG members have well, 46.88 per cent have average and 18.75 per cent have poor knowledge about Schemes under Gram Panchayat. So, SHG members of both Birbhum and

Burdwan districts have similar as well as better understanding about Schemes under Gram Panchayat.

Awareness Level of the Non-SHG Villagers on PRI

Table 6.26 clearly indicates that in Birbhum district, 20.31 per cent sampled non-SHG villagers have good knowledge about Panchayat vote, 37.50 per cent and 42.19 per cent sampled non-SHG villagers have average and poor knowledge about Panchayat vote respectively. In Burdwan district, 23.44 per cent sampled non-SHG villagers have well, 37.50 per cent have average and 39.06 per cent have poor knowledge about Panchayat voting. So, non-SHG villagers of each district have almost similar kind of knowledge level regarding Panchayat vote.

In Birbhum district, 12.50 per cent sampled non-SHG villagers have good knowledge about role of PRIs, while 42.19 per cent and 45.31 per cent sampled non-SHG villagers have average and poor knowledge about role of PRIs respectively. However, in Burdwan district, 15.63 per cent sampled non-SHG villagers have well, 43.75 per cent have average and 40.63 per cent have poor knowledge about role of PRIs. So, non-SHG villagers of Burdwan district have better knowledge level than the Birbhum district regarding role of PRIs.

Regarding Caste Reservation System in Birbhum district, 17.19 per cent sampled non-SHG villagers have good knowledge about the role of Caste Reservation, while 35.94 per cent and 46.88 per cent sampled non-SHG villagers have average and poor knowledge about Caste Reservation System respectively. However, in Burdwan district, 14.06 per cent sampled non-SHG villagers have well, 34.38 per cent have average and 51.56 per cent have poor knowledge about Caste Reservation System. So, here non-SHG villagers of Birbhum district have better understanding on Caste Reservation System than the Birbhum.

The data regarding the knowledge level about women reservation are not satisfactory in both of the districts. In Birbhum district, 10.94 per cent sampled non-SHG villagers have good knowledge about women reservation, while 31.25 per cent and 57.81 per cent sampled non-SHG villagers have average and poor knowledge about women reservation respectively. While, in Burdwan district, 14.06 per cent sampled non-SHG villagers have well, 32.18 per cent have average and 53.13 per cent have poor knowledge about women reservation.

Table 6.26: Awareness Level of the Non-SHG Villagers on PRI

District	Gram Panchayat	Knowledge Level	Awareness Level of SHG/Non SHG Villagers on PRI					
			Panchayat Vote	Role of PRI	Caste Reservation System	Women Reservation System	Three-tier PRI System	Various Schemes under GP
Birbhum	Jamna	Good	18.75	12.50	18.75	12.50	12.50	25.00
		Average	43.75	43.75	37.50	37.50	43.75	56.25
		Poor	37.50	43.75	43.75	50.00	43.75	18.75
	Hatia	Good	25.00	18.75	18.75	12.50	18.75	31.25
		Average	37.50	37.50	31.25	31.25	37.50	50.00
		Poor	37.50	43.75	50.00	56.25	43.75	18.75
	Koma	Good	18.75	6.25	18.75	6.25	12.50	18.75
		Average	31.25	43.75	37.50	25.00	37.50	37.50
		Poor	50.00	50.00	43.75	68.75	50.00	43.75
	Purandarpur	Good	18.75	12.50	12.50	12.50	6.25	25.00
		Average	37.50	43.75	37.50	31.25	37.50	56.25
		Poor	43.75	43.75	50.00	56.25	56.25	18.75
	District Average	Good	20.31	12.50	17.19	10.94	12.50	25.00
		Average	37.50	42.19	35.94	31.25	39.06	50.00
		Poor	42.19	45.31	46.88	57.81	48.44	25.00

(Contd.)

Table 6.26 (*Contd.*)

District	*Gram Panchayat*	*Knowledge Level*	*Awareness Level of SHG/Non SHG Villagers on PRI*					
			Panchayat Vote	*Role of PRI*	*Caste Reservation System*	*Women Reservation System*	*Three-tier PRI System*	*Various Schemes under GP*
Burdwan	Baidyapur	Good	31.25	18.75	18.75	18.75	12.50	31.25
		Average	37.50	43.75	31.25	31.25	43.75	43.75
		Poor	31.25	37.50	50.00	50.00	43.75	25.00
	Kalyanpur	Good	18.75	12.50	18.75	12.50	6.25	43.75
		Average	31.25	37.50	37.50	31.25	37.50	37.50
		Poor	50.00	50.00	43.75	56.25	56.25	18.75
	Majhergran	Good	25.00	12.50	6.25	12.50	12.50	25.00
		Average	43.75	43.75	37.50	37.50	43.75	50.00
		Poor	31.25	43.75	56.25	50.00	43.75	12.50
	Monteswar	Good	18.75	18.75	12.50	12.50	18.75	25.00
		Average	37.50	50.00	31.25	31.25	37.50	56.25
		Poor	43.75	31.25	56.25	56.25	43.75	18.75
	District Average	Good	23.44	15.63	14.06	14.06	12.50	31.25
		Average	37.50	43.75	34.38	32.81	40.63	46.88
		Poor	39.06	40.63	51.56	53.13	46.88	18.75

Source: Primary Data. *Note*: Figures in Percentage.

So, non-SHG villagers of Burdwan district have quite better understanding about women reservation than the Birbhum district.

Regarding PRI structure, in Birbhum district 12.50 per cent sampled non-SHG villagers have good knowledge, while 39.06 per cent and 48.44 per cent sampled non-SHG villagers have average and poor knowledge about PRI structure respectively. Similarly, in Burdwan district, 12.50 per cent sampled non-SHG villagers have well, 40.63 per cent have average and 46.88 per cent have poor knowledge about PRI structure. So, non-SHG villagers of both Birbhum and Burdwan districts have similar understanding about PRI structure.

Regarding Schemes under Gram Panchayat, in Birbhum district 25.00 per cent and 50.00 per cent sampled non-SHG villagers have good and average level knowledge respectively, while only 25.00 per cent sampled non-SHG villagers have poor knowledge about Schemes under Gram Panchayat. Similarly, in Burdwan district, 31.25 per cent sampled non-SHG villagers have well, 46.88 per cent have average and 18.75 per cent have poor knowledge about Schemes under Gram Panchayat. So, non-SHG villagers of both Birbhum and Burdwan districts have similar as well as better understanding about Schemes under Gram Panchayat.

However, comparing the data of Table 6.26 on knowledge-level of SHG members and non-SHG villagers an interesting trend has emerged. The data clearly indicates that in both of district the knowledge-level of villagers who were engaged in SHGs are quite better than the non-SHG villagers. However, only in case of Government schemes and programmes under Gram Panchayat the awareness-level were found to be similar. The continuous exposure, mobility and capacity building support to SHG members have helped them to improve their knowledge and awareness-level about PRI related issues. Hence, the above discussion clearly indicates that the SHG movement has improved the knowledge and understanding of villagers about PRIs in West Bengal.

Awareness Level of the SHG Members on Planning and Implementation Process

Participatory planning and implementation is one of the major indicators of decentralisation process. In West Bengal the planning process starts at the *sansad*-level. *Sansad*-level people participate in the planning and implementation process through the *Gram Sansad* meeting. Later the villagers participate in Gram Sabha for final compilation of plan and budget. So, it is very necessary to know about awareness level of the villagers on planning and implementation related issues.

Table 6.27 reveals the scenario of awareness level of SHG members on planning and implementation process. The *Gram Unnayan Samiti* is the lowest structure of grassroots governance in West Bengal. Every *Gram Sansad* has its own *Gram Unnayan Samiti* for planning, implementation, monitoring of Government programmes and ensure better service delivery to the rural people. The effective execution of *Gram Unnayan Samiti* depends on the participation of rural people in decision-making process. So, it is expected that the rural people have good understanding about the *Gram Unnayan Samiti* but the scenario is different in field. Table 6.27 reveals the actual scenario of the field. Table 6.27 clearly indicates that in Birbhum district, 20.31 per cent sampled SHG members have good knowledge about *Gram Unnayan Samiti*, 42.19 per cent and 35.94 per cent sampled SHG members have average and poor knowledge about *Gram Unnayan Samiti* respectively. In Burdwan district, 23.44 per cent sampled SHG members have well, 48.44 per cent have average and 28.13 per cent have poor knowledge about *Gram Unnayan Samiti*. So, SHG members of Burdwan district have better understanding than the Birbhum regarding *Gram Unnayan Samiti*.

In Birbhum district, 32.18 per cent sampled SHG members have good knowledge about *Gram Sansad* related issues, while 48.44 per cent and 18.75 per cent sampled SHG members have average and poor knowledge about *Gram Sansad* related issues respectively. However, in Burdwan district, 34.38 per cent sampled SHG members have well, 51.56 per cent have average and 14.04 per cent have poor knowledge about *Gram Sansad* related issues. So, SHG members of Burdwan district have better knowledge-level than the Birbhum district regarding *Gram Sansad* related issues.

In connection to awareness-level on Gram Sabha related issues, in Birbhum district, 23.44 per cent sampled SHG members have good knowledge about Gram Sabha related issues, while 46.88 per cent and 29.69 per cent sampled SHG members have average and poor knowledge about Gram Sabha related issues respectively. However, in Burdwan district, 25.00 per cent sampled SHG members have well, 48.44 per cent have average and 26.56 per cent have poor knowledge

Table 6.27: Awareness Level of the SHG Members on Planning and Implementation Process

District	*Gram Panchayat*	*Knowledge Level*	*Awareness Level on Planning and Implementation Process*					
			Gram Unnayan Samiti	*Gram Sansad*	*Gram Sabha*	*Planning/ Budgeting Process*	*Implementation Process*	*Income and Expenditure Details*
Birbhum	Jamna	Good	18.75	37.50	25.00	18.75	18.75	12.50
		Average	43.75	43.75	43.75	43.75	50.00	43.75
		Poor	37.50	18.75	31.25	37.50	31.25	43.75
	Hatia	Good	25.00	37.50	31.25	18.75	18.75	18.75
		Average	31.25	43.75	43.75	37.50	43.75	43.75
		Poor	37.50	18.75	25.00	43.75	37.50	37.50
	Koma	Good	18.75	31.25	18.75	18.75	25.00	18.75
		Average	43.75	56.25	50.00	43.75	50.00	50.00
		Poor	37.50	12.50	31.25	37.50	25.00	31.25
	Purandarpur	Good	18.75	25.00	18.75	18.75	18.75	12.50
		Average	50.00	50.00	50.00	50.00	56.25	50.00
		Poor	31.25	25.00	31.25	31.25	25.00	37.50
	District Average	**Good**	**20.31**	**32.81**	**23.44**	**18.75**	**20.31**	**15.63**
		Average	**42.19**	**48.44**	**46.88**	**43.75**	**50.00**	**46.88**
		Poor	**35.94**	**18.75**	**29.69**	**37.50**	**29.69**	**37.50**

(Contd.)

Table 6.27 (*Contd.*)

District	Gram Panchayat	Knowledge Level	Awareness Level on Planning and Implementation Process					
			Gram Unnayan Samiti	Gram Sansad	Gram Sabha	Planning/ Budgeting Process	Implemen-tation Process	Income and Expenditure Details
Burdwan	Baidyapur	Good	25.00	43.75	31.25	25.00	25.00	18.75
		Average	43.75	50.00	50.00	43.75	50.00	50.00
		Poor	31.25	6.25	18.75	31.25	25.00	31.25
	Kalyanpur	Good	18.75	25.00	18.75	18.75	25.00	18.75
		Average	50.00	56.25	56.25	50.00	56.25	50.00
		Poor	31.25	18.75	25.00	31.25	18.75	31.25
	Majhergram	Good	25.00	31.25	25.00	25.00	18.75	18.75
		Average	43.75	50.00	43.75	43.75	50.00	43.75
		Poor	31.25	18.75	31.25	31.25	31.25	37.50
	Monteswar	Good	25.00	37.50	25.00	18.75	18.75	12.50
		Average	56.25	50.00	43.75	50.00	56.25	50.00
		Poor	18.75	12.50	31.25	31.25	25.00	37.50
	District Average	**Good**	**23.44**	**34.38**	**25.00**	**21.88**	**21.88**	**17.19**
		Average	**48.44**	**51.56**	**48.44**	**46.88**	**53.13**	**48.44**
		Poor	**28.13**	**14.06**	**26.56**	**31.25**	**25.00**	**34.38**

Source: Primary Data. *Note*: Figures in Percentage.

about Gram Sabha related issues respectively. So, SHG members of Burdwan and Birbhum districts have similar knowledge level on Gram Sabha related issues.

As mentioned earlier that participatory planning and budgeting is one of the major criteria for effective decentralisation process and it needs high level of knowledge and participation among the villagers. However, the data regarding the knowledge level about women reservation is not satisfactory. In Birbhum district, 18.75 per cent sampled SHG members have good knowledge about planning and budgeting process, while 43.75 cent and 35.50 per cent sampled SHG members have average and poor knowledge about planning and budgeting process respectively. While, in Burdwan district, 21.88 per cent sampled SHG members have well, 46.88 per cent have average and 31.25 per cent have poor knowledge about planning and budgeting process. So, SHG members of Burdwan district have quite better knowledge about planning and budgeting process than the Birbhum district.

The knowledge about implementation process is also an important criterion as the villagers are the main stakeholders of the Government programmes. SHGs also become an effective institution in the implementation process of development programmes in West Bengal. Table 6.27 shows, in Birbhum district 20.31 per cent sampled SHG members have good knowledge, while 50.00 per cent and 29.59 per cent sampled SHG members have average and poor knowledge about implementation process respectively. Similarly, in Burdwan district, 21.88 per cent sampled SHG members have well, 53.13 per cent have average and 25.00 per cent have poor knowledge about implementation process. So, SHG members of both Birbhum and Burdwan districts have similar understanding about implementation process.

The knowledge about income and expenditure is important for ensuring the transparency and accountability. Regarding income and expenditure details, in Birbhum district 15.63 per cent and 48.88 per cent sampled SHG members have good and average level knowledge respectively; while 37.50 per cent sampled SHG members have poor knowledge about income and expenditure details. Similarly, in Burdwan district, 17.19 per cent sampled SHG members have well, 48.44 per cent have average and 34.38 per cent have poor knowledge about income and expenditure details. So, SHG members of both Birbhum and Burdwan districts have low understanding about income and expenditure details, which is not very good for transparency and accountability of Gram Panchayats.

Awareness Level of the Non-SHG Villagers on Planning and Implementation Process

Table 6.28 shows that, in Birbhum district, only 9.38 per cent sampled non-SHG villagers have good knowledge about *Gram Unnayan Samiti*, 39.06 per cent and 51.56 per cent non-SHG villagers have average and poor knowledge about *Gram Unnayan Samiti* respectively. Similarly, in Burdwan district, 12.50 per cent sampled non-SHG villagers have well, 50.00 per cent have average and 37.50 per cent have poor knowledge about *Gram Unnayan Samiti*. So, non-SHG villagers of each Burdwan district have better understanding than the Birbhum regarding *Gram Unnayan Samiti*. However, the percentage of villagers with good understanding about *Gram Unnayan Samiti* is very low in both of the district.

In Birbhum district, 18.75 per cent sampled non-SHG villagers have good knowledge about *Gram Sansad* related issues, while 50.00 per cent and 31.25 per cent sampled non-SHG villagers have average and poor knowledge about *Gram Sansad* related issues respectively. However, in Burdwan district, 23.44 per cent sampled non-SHG villagers have well, 56.25 per cent have average and 20.31 per cent have poor knowledge about *Gram Sansad* related issues. So, non-SHG villagers of Burdwan district have better knowledge level than the Birbhum district regarding *Gram Sansad* related issues.

In connection to awareness level on Gram Sabha related issues, in Birbhum district, 14.06 per cent sampled non-SHG villagers have good knowledge about Gram Sabha related issues, while 48.44 per cent and 37.50 per cent sampled non-SHG villagers have average and poor knowledge about Gram Sabha related issues respectively. However, in Burdwan district, 18.75 per cent sampled non-SHG villagers have well, 53.13 per cent have average and 28.13 per cent have poor knowledge about Gram Sabha related issues respectively. So, non-SHG villagers of Burdwan district have better knowledge level on Gram Sabha related issues than the Birbhum district.

In Birbhum district, only 9.38 per cent sampled non-SHG villagers have good knowledge about planning and budgeting process; while 39.06 per cent and 51.56 per cent sampled non-SHG villagers have average and poor knowledge about planning and budgeting process respectively. While, in Burdwan district, 12.50 per cent sampled non-

Table 6.28: Awareness Level of the Non-SHG Villagers on Planning and Implementation Process

District	Gram Panchayat	Knowledge Level	Awareness Level on Planning and Implementation Process					
			Gram Unnayan Samiti	Gram Sansad	Gram Sabha	Planning/ Budgeting Process	Implemen-tation Process	Income and Expenditure Details
Birbhum	Jamna	Good	6.25	25.00	18.75	6.25	12.50	6.25
		Average	37.50	50.00	37.50	37.50	43.75	31.25
		Poor	56.25	25.00	43.75	56.25	43.75	62.50
	Hatia	Good	12.50	18.75	18.75	12.50	12.50	6.25
		Average	31.25	50.00	50.00	37.50	50.00	37.50
		Poor	56.25	31.25	31.25	50.00	37.50	56.25
	Koma	Good	12.50	18.75	6.25	6.25	12.50	12.50
		Average	37.50	56.25	50.00	37.50	43.75	43.75
		Poor	50.00	25.00	43.75	56.25	43.75	43.75
	Purandarpur	Good	6.25	12.50	12.50	12.50	6.25	6.25
		Average	50.00	43.75	56.25	43.75	50.00	31.25
		Poor	43.75	43.75	31.25	43.75	43.75	62.50
	District Average	Good	9.38	18.75	14.06	9.38	10.94	7.81
		Average	39.06	50.00	48.44	39.06	46.88	35.94
		Poor	51.56	31.25	37.50	51.56	42.19	56.25

(Contd.)

Table 6.28 (*Contd.*)

District	Gram Panchayat	Knowledge Level	Awareness Level on Planning and Implementation Process					
			Gram Unnayan Samiti	Gram Sansad	Gram Sabha	Planning/ Budgeting Process	Implemen-tation Process	Income and Expenditure Details
Burdwan	Baidyapur	Good	12.50	31.25	25.00	12.50	18.75	12.50
		Average	43.75	56.25	56.25	50.00	43.75	43.75
		Poor	43.75	12.50	18.75	37.50	37.50	43.75
	Kalyanpur	Good	6.25	18.75	12.50	12.50	12.50	6.25
		Average	56.25	56.25	56.25	50.00	50.00	43.75
		Poor	37.50	25.00	31.25	37.50	37.50	50.00
	Majhergran	Good	12.50	18.75	13.75	12.50	18.75	12.50
		Average	50.00	56.25	50.00	50.00	50.00	31.25
		Poor	37.50	25.00	31.25	31.25	31.25	56.25
	Monteswar	Good	18.75	25.00	18.75	12.50	12.50	12.50
		Average	50.00	56.25	50.00	50.00	56.25	37.50
		Poor	31.25	18.75	31.25	37.50	31.25	50.00
	District Average	Good	12.50	23.44	18.75	12.50	15.63	10.94
		Average	50.00	56.25	53.13	50.00	50.00	39.06
		Poor	37.50	20.31	28.13	35.94	34.38	50.00

Source: Primary Data. *Note*: Figures in Percentage.

SHG villagers have well, 50.00 per cent have average and 35.94 per cent have poor knowledge about planning and budgeting process. So, non-SHG villagers of Burdwan and Birbhum district have low understanding about planning and budgeting process.

Table 6.28 shows, in Birbhum district 10.94 per cent sampled non-SHG villagers have good knowledge, while 46.88 per cent and 42.19 per cent sampled non-SHG villagers have average and poor knowledge about implementation process respectively. Similarly, in Burdwan district, 15.63 per cent sampled non-SHG villagers have well, 50.00 per cent have average and 34.38 per cent have poor knowledge about implementation process. So, non-SHG villagers of both Birbhum and Burdwan districts have low understanding about implementation process.

Regarding income and expenditure details, in Birbhum district only 7.81 per cent and 35.94 per cent sampled non-SHG villagers have good and average level knowledge respectively; while 56.25 per cent sampled non-SHG villagers have poor knowledge about income and expenditure details. Similarly, in Burdwan district, 10.94 per cent sampled non-SHG villagers have well, 39.06 per cent have average and 50.00 per cent have poor knowledge about income and expenditure details. So, non-SHG villagers of both Birbhum and Burdwan districts have low understanding about income and expenditure details of which is not very good for transparency and accountability of Gram Panchayats.

Perception and Attitude of SHG and Non-SHG Members on PRI and Decentralisation

Apart from knowledge-level perception and attitude of villagers is also an important indicator for judging the decentralised governance. However, the knowledge level of villagers has influenced the perception and attitude of villagers towards PRI and decentralisation issues. So, an attempt has been made to analyse the perception and attitude of SHG members and non-SHG villagers towards decentralisation process.

Perception and Attitude of SHG Members on PRI

Table 6.29 shows the perception and attitude level of SHG members

Table 6.29: Perceptions and Attitude of SHG on PRI

District	Gram Panchayat	Perceptions and Attitude of SHG on PRI											
		Visited Gram Panchayat Office		Know the Gram Panchayat Members		Participate in Training Programmes Arranged by the Panchayat		Panchayat's Sensitivity About the SHG Members		Proper Response from Panchayat		Received Other Support from GP	
		Yes	No	Yes	No	Yes	No	Yes	No	Yes	No	Yes	No
Birbhum	Jamna	75.00	25.00	56.25	43.75	62.50	37.50	43.75	56.25	43.75	56.25	62.50	37.50
	Hatia	62.50	37.50	68.75	31.25	56.25	43.75	56.25	43.75	56.25	43.75	68.75	31.25
	Koma	56.25	43.75	50.00	50.00	50.00	50.00	43.75	56.25	50.00	50.00	68.75	31.25
	Purandarpur	93.75	6.25	75.00	25.00	68.75	31.25	31.25	68.75	31.25	68.75	56.25	43.75
	District Average	**71.88**	**28.13**	**62.50**	**37.50**	**59.38**	**40.63**	**43.75**	**56.25**	**45.31**	**54.69**	**64.06**	**35.94**
Burdwan	Baidyapur	87.50	12.50	81.25	18.75	75.00	25.00	43.75	56.25	43.75	56.25	62.50	37.50
	Kalyanpur	81.25	18.75	68.75	31.25	56.25	43.75	62.50	37.50	62.50	37.50	75.00	25.00
	Majhergram	62.50	37.50	56.25	43.75	50.00	50.00	56.25	43.75	62.50	37.50	81.25	18.75
	Montreswar	75.00	25.00	75.00	25.00	81.25	18.75	56.25	43.75	56.25	43.75	68.75	31.25
	District Average	**76.56**	**23.44**	**70.31**	**29.69**	**65.63**	**34.38**	**54.69**	**45.31**	**56.25**	**43.75**	**71.88**	**28.13**

Source: Primary Data. *Note*: Figures in Percentage.

on PRI related issues. Table 6.29 indicates that 71.88 per cent SHG members have visited Gram Panchayat office for at least once in Birbhum district while in Burdwan district it is 76.56 per cent.

Similarly, in Birbhum district 62.50 per cent SHG members know Gram Panchayat members while in Burdwan district 70.31 per cent SHG members know Gram Panchayat members.

Regarding training programme, 59.38 per cent SHG members in Birbhum and 65.63 per cent SHG members in Burdwan have taken trainings from Gram Panchayat.

Table 6.29 shows, 43.75 per cent SHG members in Birbhum and 54.69 per cent SHG members in Burdwan opined that Panchayat is sensitive about the SHGs.

Table 6.29 also reveals 45.3 per cent SHG members in Birbhum and 56.25 per cent SHG members in Burdwan opined that Panchayats give proper response to SHGs.

Similarly, 64.06 per cent SHG members in Birbhum and 71.88 per cent SHG members in Burdwan opined that they got additional support from Gram Panchayat.

So, it is clear from Table 6.29 that SHG members are getting attention from Gram Panchayats and this has changed the perception and attitude of SHG members and they participate more in governance related issues. This trend is good for strengthening the decentralisation process in West Bengal.

Perception and Attitude of Non-SHG Villagers on PRI

Table 6.30 shows the perception and attitude level of non-SHG villagers on PRI related issues. Table 6.30 indicates that 59.38 per cent non-SHG villagers have visited Gram Panchayat office for at least once in Birbhum district while in Burdwan district it is 67.19 per cent.

However, 54.69 per cent non-SHG villagers in both of the district know Gram Panchayat members.

Regarding training programme, only 18.75 per cent non-SHG villagers in Birbhum and 21.88 per cent non-SHG villagers in Burdwan have taken trainings from Gram Panchayat.

Table 6.30 shows, 42.19 per cent non-SHG villagers in Birbhum and 46.88 per cent non-SHG villagers in Burdwan opined that Panchayat is sensitive about them.

Table 6.30: Perceptions and Attitude of Non-SHG Villagers on PRI

District	*Gram Panchayat*	*Perceptions and Attitude of Non-SHG on PRI*											
		Visited Gram Panchayat Office		*Know the Gram Panchayat Members*		*Participate in Training Programmes Arranged by the Panchayat*		*Panchayat's Sensitivity About the SHG Members*		*Proper Response from Panchayat*		*Received Other Support from GP*	
		Yes	*No*	*Yes*	*No*	*Yes*	*No*	*Yes*	*No*	*Yes*	*No*	*Yes*	*No*
Birbhum	Jamna	62.50	37.50	56.25	43.75	18.75	81.25	50.00	50.00	31.25	68.75	62.50	37.50
	Hatia	56.25	31.25	56.25	43.75	12.50	87.50	43.75	56.25	43.75	56.25	68.75	31.25
	Koma	43.75	56.25	37.50	62.50	18.75	81.25	37.50	62.50	37.50	62.50	56.25	43.75
	Purandarpur	75.00	25.00	68.75	31.25	25.00	75.00	37.50	62.50	25.00	75.00	50.00	50.00
	District Average	**59.38**	**37.50**	**54.69**	**45.31**	**18.75**	**81.25**	**42.19**	**57.81**	**34.38**	**65.63**	**59.38**	**40.63**
Burdwan	Baidyapur	75.00	25.00	68.75	31.25	25.00	75.00	37.50	62.50	37.50	62.50	56.25	43.75
	Kalayanpur	62.50	37.50	56.25	43.75	18.75	81.25	56.25	43.75	56.25	43.75	68.75	31.25
	Majhergram	68.75	31.25	37.50	62.50	12.50	87.50	43.75	56.25	43.75	56.25	75.00	25.00
	Montreswar	62.50	37.50	56.25	43.75	31.25	68.75	50.00	50.00	56.25	43.75	62.50	37.50
	District Average	**67.19**	**32.81**	**54.69**	**45.31**	**21.88**	**78.13**	**46.88**	**53.13**	**48.44**	**51.56**	**65.63**	**34.38**

Source: Primary Data. *Note*: Figures in Percentage.

Table 6.30 also reveals 34.38 per cent non-SHG villagers in Birbhum and 48.44 per cent non-SHG villagers in Burdwan opined that Panchayats give proper response to them.

Further, 59.38 per cent non-SHG villagers in Birbhum and 65.63 per cent non-SHG villagers in Burdwan opined that they got additional support from Gram Panchayat.

So, it is clear from Table 6.30 that in Birbhum district are getting comparatively low attention from Gram Panchayats and that's why the common villagers have lack of participation in the decentralisation process.

However, the data of Table 6.30 clearly indicate that Gram Panchayats have given special focus to SHGs than the common villagers. It also becomes obvious that SHGs make rural women folk aware about their social responsibilities and thereby they create an atmosphere of congenial to the decentralised structure. Further, various trainings at GP level are also helping SHG members to develop their capacity and engage themselves into the economic activities as well as increase their income. These increased incomes often lead to control over such incomes and contribute to social and political empowerment.

Perceptions and Attitude of SHG on Decentralisation Process

Table 6.31 shows the perception and attitude level of SHG members on decentralisation process. Table 6.31 indicates that in Birbhum district 65.63 per cent SHG members have applied voting right while in Burdwan district it is 68.75 per cent.

Regarding decision for voting, in Birbhum district 48.44 per cent SHG members and 57.81 per cent SHG members in Burdwan district take own decision for voting purpose.

Interestingly, 34.38 per cent sampled SHG members in Birbhum and 37.50 per cent sampled SHG members were willing to contest in the Gram Panchayat election.

Table 6.31 also shows, 57.18 per cent SHG members in Birbhum and 59.38 per cent SHG members in Burdwan participated in the *Gram Sansad* meeting. Further, 40.54 per cent participant of Birbhum and 47.37 per cent participant of Burdwan district actively participated in the *Gram Sansad* meeting. It has also found that 51.56 per cent SHG members in Birbhum and 54.69 per cent SHG members in Burdwan district motivated others to attend the *Gram Sansad* meeting.

Table 6.31: Perceptions and Attitude of SHG on Decentralisation Process

District	*Gram Panchayat*	*Perceptions and Attitude of SHG on Decentralisation Process*									
		Apply Voting Right		*Take Own Decision for Voting*		*Want to Contest in Next Election*		*Participate in the Gram Sansad Meeting*		*Degree of Participation (Actively/Passively)*	
		Yes	*No*	*Yes*	*No*	*Yes*	*No*	*Yes*	*No*	*Active*	*Passive*
(1)	*(2)*	*(3)*	*(4)*	*(5)*	*(6)*	*(7)*	*(8)*	*(9)*	*(10)*	*(11)*	*(12)*
Birbhum	Jarnna	56.25	43.75	31.25	68.75	43.75	56.25	50.00	50.00	37.50	62.50
	Hatia	68.75	31.25	56.25	43.75	25.00	75.00	62.50	37.50	60.00	40.00
	Koma	62.50	37.50	43.75	56.25	31.25	68.75	56.25	43.75	22.22	77.78
	Purandarpur	75.00	25.00	62.50	37.50	37.50	62.50	62.50	37.50	40.00	60.00
	District Average	**65.63**	**34.38**	**48.44**	**51.56**	**34.38**	**65.63**	**57.81**	**42.19**	**40.54**	**59.46**
Burdwan	Baidyapur	87.50	12.50	81.25	18.75	50.00	50.00	68.75	31.25	54.55	45.45
	Kalyanpur	68.75	31.25	56.25	43.75	43.75	56.25	62.50	37.50	40.00	60.00
	Majhergram	62.50	37.50	50.00	50.00	25.00	75.00	56.25	31.25	44.44	55.56
	Montreswar	56.25	43.75	43.75	56.25	31.25	68.75	50.00	50.00	50.00	50.00
	District Average	**68.75**	**31.25**	**57.81**	**42.19**	**37.50**	**62.50**	**59.38**	**37.50**	**47.37**	**52.63**

(Contd.)

Table 6.31 (*Contd.*)

District	Gram Panchayat	Perceptions and Attitude of SHG on Decentralisation Process							
		Motivate Other to Attend Gram Sansad Meeting		Participate in Gram Sabha Meeting		Degree of Participation (Actively/Passively)		Motivate other to Attend Gram Sabha Meeting	
		Yes	No	Yes	No	Active	Passive	Yes	No
(1)	(2)	(13)	(14)	(15)	(16)	(17)	(18)	(19)	(20)
Birbhum	Jamna	43.75	56.25	31.25	62.50	40.00	60.00	31.25	68.75
	Hatia	56.25	43.75	50.00	56.25	37.50	62.50	37.50	62.50
	Koma	50.00	50.00	43.75	56.25	28.57	71.43	37.50	62.50
	Purandarpur	56.25	43.75	50.00	50.00	25.00	75.00	43.75	56.25
	District Average	**51.56**	**48.44**	**43.75**	**56.25**	**32.14**	**67.86**	**37.50**	**62.50**
Burdwan	Baidyapur	50.00	50.00	56.25	43.75	33.33	66.67	56.25	43.75
	Kalyanpur	56.25	43.75	50.00	50.00	37.50	62.50	43.75	56.25
	Majhergram	68.75	31.25	43.75	56.25	28.57	71.43	31.25	68.75
	Montreswar	43.75	56.25	37.50	62.50	33.33	66.67	31.25	68.75
	District Average	**54.69**	**45.31**	**46.88**	**53.13**	**33.33**	**66.67**	**40.63**	**59.38**

Source: Primary Data. *Note*: Figures in Percentage.

Further, Table 6.31 also reveals that 43.75 per cent SHG members in Birbhum and 46.88 per cent SHG members in Burdwan participated in the Gram Sabha meeting. Again, 32.14 per cent participant of Birbhum and 33.33 per cent participant of Burdwan district actively participated the *Gram Sansad* meeting. It has also found that 37.50 per cent SHG members in Birbhum and 40.63 per cent SHG members in Burdwan district motivated others to attend the *Gram Sansad* meeting.

So, Table 6.31 clearly indicates that the SHG members are participating in political as well as functional decentralisation process. They are taking part in decision-making process at grassroots level.

Perceptions and Attitude of Non-SHG Villagers on Decentralisation Process

Table 6.32 shows the perception and attitude level of non-SHG villagers on decentralisation process. Table 6.32 shows that in Birbhum district 39.06 per cent sampled non-SHG villagers have applied voting right while in Burdwan district it is 53.13 per cent.

Regarding decision for voting, in Birbhum district 39.06 per cent sampled non-SHG villagers and 48.44 per cent non-SHG villagers in Burdwan district take own decision for voting purpose.

Unfortunately, only 12.50 per cent sampled non-SHG villagers in Birbhum and 17.19 per cent sampled non-SHG villagers were willing to contest in the Gram Panchayat election.

Table 6.32 also indicates only 29.69 per cent non-SHG villagers in Birbhum and 34.38 per cent sampled non-SHG villagers in Burdwan participated in the *Gram Sansad* meeting. Further, 26.32 per cent participant of Birbhum and 27.27 per cent participant of Burdwan district actively participated the *Gram Sansad* meeting. It has been also found that only 20.31 per cent non-SHG villagers in Birbhum and 23.44 per cent non-SHG villagers in Burdwan district motivated others to attend the *Gram Sansad* meeting.

Further, Table 6.32 also reveals that only 10.94 per cent non-SHG villagers in Birbhum and 12.50 per cent sampled non-SHG villagers in Burdwan participated in the Gram Sabha meeting. Again, 20.83 per cent participant of Birbhum and 25.83 per cent participant of Burdwan district actively participated the *Gram Sansad* meeting. It has been also found that only 15.63 per cent non-SHG villagers in

Table 6.32: Perceptions and Attitude of Non-SHG Villagers on Decentralisation Process

District	*Gram Panchayat*	*Perceptions and Attitude of Non-SHG on Decentralisation Process*									
		Apply Voting Right		*Take Own Decision for Voting*		*Want to Contest in Next Election*		*Participate in the Gram Sansad Meeting*		*Degree of Participation (Actively/Passively)*	
		Male	*Female*	*Male*	*Female*	*Male*	*Female*	*Male*	*Female*	*Male*	*Female*
(1)	*(2)*	*(3)*	*(4)*	*(5)*	*(6)*	*(7)*	*(8)*	*(9)*	*(10)*	*(11)*	*(12)*
Birbhum	Jamna	31.25	68.75	25.00	75.00	12.50	87.50	18.75	81.25	33.33	66.67
	Hatia	43.75	56.25	43.75	56.25	12.50	87.50	31.25	68.75	20.00	80.00
	Koma	37.50	62.50	50.00	50.00	18.75	81.25	25.00	75.00	25.00	75.00
	Purandarpur	43.75	56.25	37.50	62.50	6.25	93.75	43.75	56.25	28.57	71.43
	District Average	**39.06**	**60.94**	**39.06**	**60.94**	**12.50**	**87.50**	**29.69**	**70.31**	**26.32**	**73.68**
Burdwan	Baidyapur	50.00	50.00	62.50	37.50	18.75	81.25	25.00	75.00	50.00	50.00
	Kalyanpur	56.25	43.75	50.00	50.00	12.50	87.50	43.75	56.25	28.57	71.43
	Majhergram	62.50	37.50	43.75	56.25	12.50	87.50	37.50	62.50	16.67	83.33
	Montreswar	43.75	56.25	37.50	62.50	25.00	75.00	31.25	68.75	20.00	80.00
	District Average	**53.13**	**46.88**	**48.44**	**51.56**	**17.19**	**82.81**	**34.38**	**65.63**	**27.27**	**72.73**

(Contd.)

Table 6.32 (*Contd.*)

District	*Gram Panchayat*	*Perceptions and Attitude of SHG on Decentralisation Process*							
		Motivate Other to Attend Gram Sansad Meeting		*Participate in Gram Sabha Meeting*		*Degree of Participation (Actively/Passively)*		*Motivate other to Attend Gram Sabha Meeting*	
		Yes	*No*	*Yes*	*No*	*Active*	*Passive*	*Yes*	*No*
(1)	*(2)*	*(13)*	*(14)*	*(15)*	*(16)*	*(17)*	*(18)*	*(19)*	*(20)*
Birbhum	Jamna	12.50	87.50	6.25	93.75	0.00	100.0	6.25	93.75
	Hatia	18.75	81.25	12.50	87.50	50.00	50.00	12.50	87.50
	Koma	18.75	81.25	6.25	93.75	0.00	100.0	25.00	75.00
	Purandarpur	31.25	68.75	18.75	81.25	33.33	66.67	18.75	81.25
	District Average	**20.31**	**79.69**	**10.94**	**89.06**	**20.83**	**79.17**	**15.63**	**84.38**
Burdwan	Baidyapur	18.75	81.25	12.50	87.50	25.00	75.00	18.75	81.25
	Kalyanpur	18.75	81.25	18.75	81.25	33.33	66.67	12.50	87.50
	Majhergram	31.25	68.75	12.50	87.50	25.00	75.00	18.75	81.25
	Montreswar	25.00	75.00	6.25	93.75	20.00	80.00	18.75	81.25
	District Average	**23.44**	**76.56**	**12.50**	**87.50**	**25.83**	**74.17**	**17.19**	**82.81**

Source: Primary Data. *Note:* Figures in Percentage.

Birbhum and 17.19 per cent sampled non-SHG villagers in Burdwan district motivated others to attend the *Gram Sansad* meeting.

So, Table 6.32 clearly indicates that the non-SHG villagers have poor participation in the decentralisation process. So, lack of participation and interest hampers the successful implementation of decentralisation process in West Bengal.

Table 6.32 reveals that the villagers engaged in SHGs have better participation and perception towards decentralisation process. SHG movement has also improved the women participation in *Gram Sansad* and *Gram Sabha* meeting. The data also indicates that SHG approach has successfully promoted improved political participation as well as representation among the rural women. SHG formation has developed a participatory political culture in West Bengal. It also reveals that through SHG approach, the rural people especially the women folk become more aware of their demands and rights once they form group and make use of legitimate political channels to realize those demands. The inclusion of SHG members in *Gram Unnayan Samiti*, the executive committee of *Gram Sansad* has been made following the rule framed on the change of the West Bengal Panchayat Act, 1973, however in practice, the committee is found to be less committed to the concern of the SHGs. Gram Panchayats has been found to be more keen, competent and innovative in involving SHG members in implementing Government programmes especially where this kind of involvement has been instructed (NREG, Mid-day Meals, Pulse Polio) rather than incorporating their collective strength and judgment in enriching the decisions and functioning in addressing local issues, local problems and utilizing local resources. An important observation was that where SHGs as well as Gram Panchayats are equally nurtured, both of them can gain efficiency to initiate development action keeping the local context and concern in the focus.

To sum up, in both the Districts, there are so many evidences that SHG movement has increased the awareness and perception of rural women as well as increased the people's participation. It was found that the knowledge levels of villagers who are engaged in SHGs are quite better than the non-SHG villagers. The continuous exposure, mobility and capacity building support to SHG members have helped them to improve their knowledge and awareness and perception level about PRI related issues. The SHGs make rural women folk aware about their social responsibilities and thereby they create an atmosphere of congenial to the decentralised structure. Through

SHGs, the rural people especially the women folk become more aware of their demands and rights once they form group and make use of legitimate political channels to realise those demands. Gram Panchayats has been found to be more keen, competent and innovative in involving SHG members in implementing Government programmes especially where this kind of involvement has been instructed (NREG, Mid-day Meals, Pulse Polio) rather than incorporating their collective strength and judgment in enriching the decisions and functioning in addressing local issues, local problems and utilizing local resources.

Decentralisation and Self-Help Group (SHG) Movement

In recent time local self-governance has given its emphasis on decentralised community engagement, is tourted for being a much more flexible and democratic way to deal with community problems and requirements in a right-based framework. The most important actor in this new approach of local governance has been Self-Help Groups (SHGs) that have carved out new arenas for these different forms of socio-political engagement. Operating in the spaces between formal Governmental structures and the community, these activities emphasize the growing importance of SHGs as a major agent for decentralised governance and sustainable development. In particular, SHGs have enhanced public involvement in decision-making and at the same time increased the quality and legitimacy of decision-making within a right-based framework. It actually, promotes the enjoyment of human rights for all vulnerable and marginalized people, especially the rural women. It is a bottom-up approach which builds on people's existing capabilities and strength. In other way, it is an empowerment approach which prioritises the building and strengthening of a People's Institution. It does this by investing in social capital and human resources, especially those of women, to enable them to participate in decision-making process at the household, community, and macro-level and to lift themselves out of poverty.

There are also several evidence behind the argument that SHG movement has changed the decentralised governance structure:

Firstly, SHG approach is based on a framework of rights and obligations. The U.N. Development Programme issued a "Statement of Common Understanding" in May 2003, explaining that "in a human rights-based approach, human rights determine the relationship between individuals and groups with valid claims (rights-holders) and State and non-state actors with correlative obligations (duty bearers). It works towards strengthening the capacities of rights-holders to make their claims, and of duty bearers to meet their obligations. Further, SHG approach of development is founded on the conviction that each and every woman is holders of rights. A right entails an obligation on the part of Government to respect, promote, protect and fulfil it. In return, SHGs strengthen the understanding of rights, i.e. understanding the location, forms and perpetrators of rights violations; recognizing who is vulnerable and assessing degrees of vulnerability; and recognizing existing power imbalances in society.

Secondly, SHGs encompass the full range of indivisible, interdependent and interrelated rights (i.e., civil, cultural, economic, political and social rights). It has enhanced women involvement, especially of marginalised section, in local governance and has increased the quality and legitimacy of democratic decision-making. Legitimacy, accountability, decentralisation and participatory character of decision-making are hallmarks of good governance. That way good governance is inseparably connected with micro-politics participation that SHGs develop.

Thirdly, "SHGs develop capacities for the knowledge and awareness so that community can make claims and Government can meet their obligations. The notion of capability is essentially one of freedom—the range of options a person has in deciding what kind of a life to lead. Poverty of a life, in this view, lies not merely in the impoverished State in which the person actually lives, but also the lack of real opportunity—given by social constraints as well as personal circumstances—to choose other types of living" (Dreze and Sen, 1995). The Self-Help Group movements have done a substantial work in developing the capability of the poor.

Fourth, SHG is an empowerment approach which prioritizes the building and strengthening of a People's institution. SHGs create a sense of ownership of development processes through strategies of empowerment among the rural women. It highly emphasized on large scale social, economic and political empowerment of women who are the actual stakeholders.

Fifth, critical feature of SHG approach is that it focuses on raising accountability and transparency in the development process.

Sixth, important feature of SHG approach is that it is increases the degree of community participation in grassroots governance.

Fortunately, the participation has been found to be active, free and meaningful.

Finally, SHG gives specific attention to issues of discrimination, quality, equity and vulnerability.

In West Bengal, the active involvement of grassroots women in local governance through Self-Help Groups (SHGs), in turn builds ownership over local developments as well as the leadership capabilities of women. SHGs advocate for effective functioning of the decentralisation process in West Bengal, by enabling women and marginalized communities to engage in the participatory planning and local self-governance. In the recent past SHGs have come out from its actual shape and play a key role in the grassroots governance. The Self-Help Groups became an interface between the development process and the number of Governments and elected institutions at the grassroots level, particularly the Panchayati Raj Institutions. The efficacy of these Self-Help Groups (SHGs) has been considerably enhanced through a symbiotic relationship with the Panchayati Raj Institutions. The key to this is to integrate these existing groups with the democratically elected and empowered Panchayats when the required devolution of power, functions and authority to them took place. In West Bengal, establishment of a system through which the SHGs and the PRIs interface efficiently, has been experienced and successful because both these institutions have the same mandate and objectives, i.e. ushering people-centred development and through it to empower the disempowered. In the present context SHGs became an important agent of decentralisation as it has been incorporated into the grassroots governance system and as well as the development process.

In West Bengal, Panchayati Raj Institutions (PRIs) have been given a pivotal role in poverty alleviation and Self-Help Groups are being perceived as the building blocks of development process. SHGs are being incorporated in the grassroots governance structure to improve the knowledge, perception and participation of rural women as well as to strengthen the rural decentralisation process. Here, an attempt has been made to analyse the values generated and added by the SHG movement to strengthening rural decentralisation. The data generated from the survey and FGD reveal that SHG movement has been successful to bring some transformation in socio-political and economic sphere of rural women which in-turn strengthen the rural decentralisation. Some of transformations are being briefly discussed below:

- *Knowledge and Perception*: Awareness and perception level of rural people especially the rural women is one the most important variable which highly influences the grassroots governance as well as entire decentralised process. It is expected that the rural people should have the clear knowledge and perception about the local governance related issues. Table 6.31 of this chapter clearly indicates that SHG movement has improved the knowledge and awareness-level of rural women as the level of awareness observed is higher in case of women engaged with SHGs than the non-SHG women. The awareness level among the women is also improved after forming the SHGs. This is because SHG members are more oriented and exposed to the PRI system.
- *Socio-Economic Empowerment*: SHG movement has done a lot in the sphere of socio-economic empowerment of rural women. Improving the access to resources, increased mobility and decision-making power, capacity-building, increased livelihood opportunity and entrepreneurial mind set have ensured socio-economic empowerment of rural women. In FGD respondents opined that their social status and decision-making power regarding financial and family matter have increased after formation of group. Group formation also leads to participation in social work like pulse polio, school meeting, mid-day meal cooking etc. Thus, it becomes obvious that groups gradually make rural women folk aware about their social responsibilities and thereby they create an atmosphere of congenial to the maintenance of rule of law. The SHG respondents also believe that access to Natural Resources will be better enabled with SHGs as a constituent substructure of local self-governance.
- *Political Participation*: Political empowerment of rural women has been a crucial objective of Self-Help Group approach in West Bengal. SHG approach has successfully promoted improved political participation as well as representation among the rural women. Tables 6.31 and 6.32 clearly indicates the political representation is quite high among the SHG members than the non-SHG villagers in both of the district. SHG formation has developed a participatory political culture in West Bengal. It also reveals that through SHG approach, the rural people especially the women folk become more aware of their demands and rights once they

form group and make use of legitimate political channels to realize those demands.

- *Participation in Grassroots Governance*: People's participation has become the heart of decentralisation process because it is a means of obtaining information about local conditions, needs and attitudes without which development could fail. In present study, people's participation means a mutual cooperation of local people in planning and implementation according to their capacity, knowledge experience, representation and contribution. In West Bengal, people's participation has been considered as a mechanism for village development. The Government has identified a local-level planning process in multi-level framework from the village to upwards. The Gram Panchayat is empowered to prepare its own plan for the development. The Gram Panchayat mobilised the grassroots people to participate in planning. To strengthen the grassroots governance as well as decentralisation process *Gram Sabha* and *Gram Sansad* are the best means of ensuring people's participation. Through the *Gram Sabha* and *Gram Sansad*, village people can participate actively in the development process and Panchayat become a system of the people, by the people and for the people. SHG movement has increased the number of women participation as well as the mode of participation which is well recognized in Tables 6.31 and 6.32. The data clears that participation of women in *Gram Sabha* and *Gram Sansad* meeting has increased after SHG movement. This also reveals that Self-Help Group formation ultimately instills participatory character within the group members in the decision-making process.
- *Administrative Participation*: It is evident that the Government has taken various positive steps to build linkages and synergy between PRIs and SHGs. Extending capacity-building support to SHGs and engaging them in various development programmes have been the key strategy for the Government in West Bengal. Government encouraging representation of SHGs in *Upa-Samitis* and making representation mandatory in *Gram Unnayan Samitis* to encourage organic linkage of SHGs with Gram Panchayats. The inclusion of SHG members in *Gram Unnayan Samiti*, the executive committee of *Gram Sansad* has been made

following the rule framed on the change of the West Bengal Panchayat Act, 1973, however, in practice, the committee is found to be less committed to the concern of the SHGs. Further, Gram Panchayats have been found to be more keen, competent and innovative in involving SHG members in implementing Government programmes especially where this kind of involvement has been instructed (NREG, Mid-day Meals, Pulse Polio) rather than incorporating their collective strength and judgement in enriching the decisions and functioning in addressing local issues, local problems and utilizing local resources. An important observation was that where SHGs as well as Gram Panchayats are equally nurtured, both of them can gain efficiency to initiate development action keeping the local context and concern in the focus.

- *Training and Capacity Building*: SHG movement has also improved the knowledge, Skill and capacity of rural women through various training programmes. Through these trainings, members are able to engage themselves in some economic activity and increase their income. These increased incomes often lead to control over such incomes and contribute to social and political empowerment.
- *Socio-Political Empowerment*: Apart from political participation, SHG movement are able to ensure socio-political empowerment of rural women. The SHG members were found more responsible in applying voting rights and decision-making than the non-SHGs. The local leaders also argued that SHGs are acting as a parallel power structure and highly influence the grassroots governance. However, lack of knowledge of PRIs, fear of losing ownership and exclusive hold over SHGs and fear of politicization work as contributing factors behind lack of proactive encouragement from PRIs.

Perception of Gram Panchayat Elected Members on SHG and Changing Scenario of Decentralisation in West Bengal

SHGs are playing a predominant role in bringing about change in the social and economic status of poor families in the village as well as contributing in the functioning of local Government in West Bengal. The linkages between Gram Panchayats and SHGs have increased due to the particular methodology the Government has adopted to support group members, extending capacity building support to SHGs irrespective of their promoting and supporting agencies, engaging SHGs in various development programmes irrespective of the promoting and supporting agencies, encouraging representation of SHGs in *Upa-Samitis* and making representation mandatory in *Gram Unnayan Samitis* to encourage organic linkage of SHGs with Gram Panchayats. This emerging strategy of SHG-PRI linkage has changed the scenario of decentralisation process in West Bengal.

Here, an attempt has been made to discuss some of the issues which relate to SHG and decentralisation that have been focused on and the Gram Panchayat member's responses to them. An effort was made to get their opinion on SHG and changing scenario of decentralisation in West Bengal.

Perception of the GP Members About the Importance of SHG-PRI Linkage for Strengthening the Decentralisation Process

In Birbhum district 40 per cent GP members strongly agreed and 32.50 per cent members agreed with the fact that the effective SHG-PRI linkage is important for strengthening the decentralisation

Table 6.33: Perception of the GP Members About the Importance of SHG-PRI Linkage for Strengthening the Decentralisation Process

District	*Gram Panchayat*	*Opinion of the GP Members (%)*			
		Strongly Agree	*Agree*	*Disagree*	*Strongly Disagree*
Birbhum	Jamna	40.00	30.00	10.00	20.00
	Hatia	33.33	40.00	26.67	6.67
	Koma	50.00	16.67	16.67	0.00
	Purandarpur	44.44	33.33	11.11	11.11
	District Average	**40.00**	**32.50**	**17.50**	**10.00**
Burdwan	Baidyapur	50.00	25.00	16.67	16.67
	Kalyanpur	46.15	23.08	23.08	7.69
	Majhergran	41.67	33.33	16.67	8.33
	Monteswar	38.46	38.46	15.38	0.00
	District Average	**44.00**	**30.00**	**18.00**	**8.00**

Source: Primary Data. *Note*: Figures in Percentage.

process. However, only, 17.50 per cent members disagreed and only 10 per cent strongly disagreed with this fact.

In Burdwan district the picture is quite similar. Here, 44 per cent and 30 per cent were found to be strongly agreed and only agreed with the fact that the effective SHG-PRI linkage for strengthening the decentralisation process. While, 18 per cent members disagreed and only 8 per cent strongly disagreed with the above mentioned fact.

So, the data clears that the GP members are well aware about the importance of SHG-PRI linkage for strengthening the decentralisation process. In our focused group discussion with GP members, majority of the present wanted to see SHGs as integral substructures of the Gram Panchayat acting together. They also argued that SHGs should be integrated into a broader vision of participatory local self-governance.

Perception of the GP Members about the SHGs as Parallel Power Structure of Panchayat

In Birbhum district 50 per cent GP members were strongly agreed and 32.50 per cent members were agreed with the fact that the SHGs

Table 6.34: Perception of the GP Members About the SHGs as Parallel Power Structure of Panchayat

District	*Gram Panchayat*	*Opinion of the GP Members (%)*			
		Strongly Agree	*Agree*	*Disagree*	*Strongly Disagree*
Birbhum	Jamna	60.00	30.00	10.00	0.00
	Hatia	40.00	46.67	13.33	0.00
	Koma	50.00	33.33	16.67	0.00
	Purandarpur	55.56	22.22	11.11	11.11
	District Average	**50.00**	**35.00**	**12.50**	**2.50**
Burdwan	Baidyapur	58.33	33.33	8.33	0.00
	Kalyanpur	53.85	30.77	15.38	0.00
	Majhergran	50.00	33.33	8.33	8.33
	Monteswar	53.85	30.77	15.38	0.00
	District Average	**54.00**	**32.00**	**12.00**	**2.00**

Source: Primary Data. *Note*: Figures in Percentage.

are becoming parallel power structure of Panchayat. However, only, 12.50 per cent members were disagreed and only 2.50 per cent strongly disagreed with this fact.

In Burdwan district, the picture is quite similar. Here, 54 per cent and 32 per cent were found to be strongly agreed and only agreed with the fact the SHGs are becoming parallel power structure of Panchayat. While only 12 per cent members disagreed and 2 per cent strongly disagreed with the above mentioned fact.

So, the data clearly indicates that over time SHGs have made them stronger and developed them as a parallel structure of Gram Panchayats in rural areas. The SHGs act as a vehicle for micro-finance and credit as well as a vehicle for women's empowerment and participation in various development issues. This emerging trend has changed the decentralisation picture of West Bengal.

Perception of the GP Members About the Women Empowerment in Political Space through SHG Involvement in Panchayat Activities

Regarding the opinion whether the SHG members now have access to greater political space, in Birbhum district 35 per cent GP members were strongly agreed and 45 per cent members were agreed with the

Table 6.35: Perception of the GP Members About the Women Empowerment in Political Space through SHG Involvement in Panchayat Activities

District	*Gram Panchayat*	*Opinion of the GP Members (%)*			
		Strongly Agree	*Agree*	*Disagree*	*Strongly Disagree*
Birbhum	Jamna	40.00	50.00	10.00	0.00
	Hatia	33.33	46.67	13.33	6.67
	Koma	33.33	50.00	16.67	0.00
	Purandarpur	33.33	33.33	22.22	11.11
	District Average	**35.00**	**45.00**	**15.00**	**5.00**
Burdwan	Baidyapur	33.33	50.00	16.67	0.00
	Kalyanpur	35.71	35.71	14.29	14.29
	Majhergran	25.00	41.67	25.00	8.33
	Monteswar	38.46	38.46	15.38	0.00
	District Average	**34.00**	**42.00**	**18.00**	**6.00**

Source: Primary Data. *Note*: Figures in Percentage.

fact that the SHGs are becoming parallel power structure of Panchayat. However, only, 15 per cent members were disagreed and only 5 per cent strongly disagreed with this fact.

In Burdwan district, the picture is quite similar. Here, 34 per cent and 42 per cent were found to be strongly agreed and only agreed with the fact the SHGs are becoming parallel power structure of Panchayat. While, 18 per cent members disagreed and only 6 per cent strongly disagreed with the above mentioned fact.

So, it is clear that the SHG movement has empowered women to enter the political space. A large number of SHG members in both of the district have been found either as Gram Panchayat member or member of *Upa-Samiti* or *Gram Unnayan Samiti*. During Focused Group Discussion, GP members also argued that SHGs promoted by Gram Panchayats provide greater political space for women. However, they also felt that over-time SHGs are not only being politicized but also treated as welcome development.

Perception of the GP Members About the Panchayat Sensitivity on SHGs

Regarding sensitivity and response issues in Birbhum district 50 per cent GP members strongly agreed and 37.50 per cent members were agreed with the fact that the SHGs are becoming parallel power structure of Panchayat. However, only 7.50 per cent members were disagreed and only 2.50 per cent strongly disagreed with this fact.

In Burdwan district, the picture is quite similar. Here, 50 per cent and 36 per cent were found to be strongly agreed and only agreed with the fact the SHGs are becoming parallel power structure of Panchayat. While only 12 per cent members disagreed and 2 per cent strongly disagreed with the above mentioned fact.

So, it is clear that the sensitivity and response of Gram Panchayats for rural people especially for the women have increased after SHG movement. However, political affiliation of GP leaders comes in the way of SHGs which are seeking linkages and support with their Gram Panchayats.

Perception of the GP Members About the Contribution of SHGs on Strengthening Local Self-Governance

Strengthening local self-governance is very important for effective

Table 6.36: Perception of the GP Members about the Panchayat Sensitivity on SHGs

District	*Gram Panchayat*	*Opinion of the GP Members (%)*			
		Strongly Agree	*Agree*	*Disagree*	*Strongly Disagree*
Birbhum	Jamna	60.00	40.00	0.00	0.00
	Hatia	46.67	46.67	6.67	0.00
	Koma	66.67	33.33	16.67	0.00
	Purandarpur	44.44	22.22	11.11	11.11
	District Average	**52.50**	**37.50**	**7.50**	**2.50**
Burdwan	Baidyapur	50.00	41.67	8.33	0.00
	Kalyanpur	50.00	35.71	7.14	7.14
	Majhergran	50.00	33.33	16.67	0.00
	Monteswar	46.15	30.77	15.38	0.00
	District Average	**50.00**	**36.00**	**12.00**	**2.00**

Source: Primary Data. *Note*: Figures in Percentage.

decentralisation. In West Bengal, SHGs are made a part of Local Self-Governance through incorporation in planning, implementation and monitoring process at grassroots level. Regarding this issue in Birbhum district 42.50 per cent GP members strongly agreed and 35 per cent members were agreed with the fact that the SHGs have contributed to strengthen Local Self-Governance. However, only, 17.50 per cent members disagreed and only 5.50 per cent strongly disagreed with this fact.

In Burdwan district, the picture is quite similar. Here, 44 per cent and 38 per cent were found to be strongly agreed and only agreed with the facts that the SHGs have contributed to strengthen local self-governance. While only 12 per cent members disagreed and 2 per cent strongly disagreed with the above mentioned fact.

So, it is clear from above discussion that SHGs in West Bengal have contributed a lot for strengthening Local Self-Governance as well as decentralisation process. FGD data also reveals that SHGs in West Bengal are sufficiently aware of Local Self-Governance processes and enthusiastic about Local Self-Governance. However, a better synergy between SHGs and PRIs in West Bengal will be difficult to achieve.

Table 6.37: Perception of the GP Members About the Contribution of SHGs on Strengthen Local Self-governance

District	*Gram Panchayat*	*Opinion of the GP Members (%)*			
		Strongly Agree	*Agree*	*Disagree*	*Strongly Disagree*
Birbhum	Jamna	50.00	40.00	10.00	0.00
	Hatia	40.00	33.33	20.00	6.67
	Koma	33.33	50.00	16.67	0.00
	Purandarpur	44.44	22.22	22.22	11.11
	District Average	**42.50**	**35.00**	**17.50**	**5.00**
Burdwan	Baidyapur	50.00	41.67	8.33	0.00
	Kalyanpur	42.86	35.71	14.29	7.14
	Majhergran	41.67	41.67	16.67	0.00
	Monteswar	38.46	30.77	23.08	0.00
	District Average	**44.00**	**38.00**	**16.00**	**2.00**

Source: Primary Data. *Note*: Figures in Percentage.

Perception of the GP Members about the Role of SHGs to Increase the Women Participation in Gram Sabha and Gram Sansad Meetings

Regarding people's participation in *Gram Sabha* and *Gram Sansad*, in Birbhum district 52.50 per cent GP members were strongly agreed and 32.50 per cent members were agreed with the fact that the SHGs have increased the people's especially women participation in *Gram Sabha* and *Gram Sansad* meetings. However, only, 12.50 per cent members were disagreed and only 2.50 per cent strongly disagreed with this fact.

In Burdwan district, the picture is quite similar. Here, 52 per cent and 40 per cent were found to be strongly agreed and only agreed with the facts that SHGs have increased the people's especially women's participation in *Gram Sabha* and *Gram Sansad* meetings. While, only 8 per cent members disagreed with the above mentioned fact.

So, it also clears that the presence of SHGs in an area increases the attendance as well as participation of women in meetings of the *Gram Sansad* and *Gram Sabha*. However, FGD reveals that many

Table 6.38: Perception of the GP Members about the Role of SHGs to Increase the Women Participation in Gram Sabha and Gram Sansad Meeting

District	*Gram Panchayat*	*Opinion of the GP Members (%)*			
		Strongly Agree	*Agree*	*Disagree*	*Strongly Disagree*
Birbhum	Jamna	60.00	30.00	10.00	0.00
	Hatia	46.67	33.33	13.33	6.67
	Koma	50.00	33.33	16.67	0.00
	Purandarpur	55.56	33.33	11.11	0.00
	District Average	**52.50**	**32.50**	**12.50**	**2.50**
Burdwan	Baidyapur	58.33	33.33	8.33	0.00
	Kalyanpur	50.00	42.86	7.14	0.00
	Majhergran	50.00	41.67	8.33	0.00
	Monteswar	46.15	38.46	7.69	0.00
	District Average	**52.00**	**40.00**	**8.00**	**0.00**

Source: Primary Data. *Note*: Figures in Percentage.

had attended the *Gram Sansad* meeting but only as passive listeners and there are no *Gram Unnayan Samiti* meetings to identify and prioritize common needs and works and subsequently implement them. So, Gram Panchayat should focus on strengthening and more effective functioning of *Gram Unnayan Samitis* and this can be done through development of synergy between SHGs and Local Self-Governance.

Testing of Hypothesis Regarding Changing Status of Decentralisation in West Bengal

The role of Self-Help Groups in strengthening the decentralisation has emerged as an extremely important area of focus in West Bengal. The decentralisation process has been given a pivotal role in sustainable development and Self-Help Groups are being perceived as the building blocks of development process. This section wants to explore the role of SHG movement in strengthening the decentralisation process in rural Bengal.

To measure the effect of SHG movement on decentralisation process some variables have been identified to conduct the association test. The responses on different issues have been measured through the nature of response (Yes/No) expressed by the respondents for different statements. Association test has been done by using these data.

Method of Association Test

H_0 — Null-Hypothesis—this hypothesis is nullified the hypothesis.

H_1 — Alternative Hypothesis.

There are two types of error in testing hypothesis.

Error — I-Rejecting a null-hypothesis when it is true.
Error — II-Accepting a null-hypothesis when it is false.

Probability of type I error is known as the level of significance. This is also known as size of the critical region.

Qualitative data test or Chi-square Test (χ^2): χ^2 test of independence.

Table of Observed Frequency

Variable			*A*	
B		A1	A2	Total
	B1	AB11	AB12	AB11+AB12 =C
	B2	AB21	AB22	AB21+AB =D
	Total	**AB11+AB21=E**	**AB12+AB22=F**	**AB11+AB12+AB21+ AB22=GT**

H_0 — Variable A is independent of Variable B
H_1 — Variable A is dependent on Variable B

Table of Expected Frequency

Variable			*A*	
B		A1	A2	Total
	B1	C*E/GT=Q	C*F/GT=W	(Q+W)
	B2	D*E/GT=R	D*F/GT=P	(R+P)
	Total	**(Q+R)**	**(W+P)**	**GT**

k=2; l=2

Here, k = number of column, and
l = number of row
Degree of Freedom = (k–1) × (l–1)
= (2–1) × (2–1)
= 1

$$\chi^2_1 = (AB11-Q)^2/Q + (AB12-W)^2/W + (AB21-R)^2/R + (AB22-P)^2/P$$

After calculating Chi-square value, the value should be at 5 per cent or 1 per cent level of significance.

From the table we have to find out the value of χ^2 at 5 per cent or 1 per cent level of significance. These values are denoted in the table as $\chi^2_{.05,1}$ or $\chi^2_{.01,1}$ respectively.

If the null-hypothesis is rejected then the degree of association or odds ratio have to calculate or find out.

The estimated odds ratio is: m= (AB11*AB22)/(AB12*AB21)

Association Test

Political Participation of Villagers

Table 6.39: Observed Frequency of Political Participation of Villagers

Variable	*Respondent*	*Level of Participation*		
		Participated	*Not Participated*	*Total*
Political Participation	SHG Members	86	42	128
	Non-SHG Members	59	69	128
	Total	**145**	**111**	**256**

H_0 —SHG movement does not improve the political participation of villagers

H_1 —SHG movement improves the political participation of villagers

Table 6.40: Result Table of Political Participation of Villagers

Chi-Square value, χ^2_1	*Coefficient of Association, Ø*	*Odd Ratio*
11.59	0.208	2.39

Here, χ^2 Value = 11.59 at Degree of Freedom 1.

While, the $\chi^2_{.05,1} = 3.84$, $\chi^2_{.01,1} = 6.63$ are the χ^2 table value at 5 per cent and 1 per cent level of significance.

So, calculated $\chi^2_1 > \chi^2_{.05,1}$ and $\chi^2_{.01,1}$

Hence, H_0 is rejected and it denotes that SHG movement improves the political participation of villagers.

Coefficient of Association, Ø = 0.208, which indicates moderate association.

Odd Ratio = 2.39>1, which means that the villagers engaged in SHGs have 2.39 times higher political participation than the non-SHG villagers.

Participation in Gram Sansad Meeting

Table 6.41: Observed Frequency Participation in Gram Sansad Meeting

Variable	*Respondent*	*Level of Participation*		
		Participated	*Not Participated*	*Total*
Participation in Gram Sansad Meeting	SHG Members	75	53	128
	Non-SHG Members	41	87	128
	Total	**116**	**140**	**256**

H_0—SHG movement does not improve the participation of villagers in *Gram Sansad.*

H_1—SHG movement improves the participation of villagers in *Gram Sansad.*

Table 6.42: Result Table of Participation in Gram Sansad Meeting

Chi-Square value, χ^2_1	*Coefficient of Association, Ø*	*Odd Ratio*
18.22	0.25	3.00

Here, χ^2 Value = 20.14 at Degree of Freedom 1.

While, the $\chi^2_{.05,1}$=3.84, $\chi^2_{.01,1}$=6.63 are the χ^2 table value at 5 per cent and 1 per cent level of significance.

So, calculated $\chi^2_1 > \chi^2_{.05,1}$ and $\chi^2_{.01,1}$

Hence, H_0 is rejected and it denotes that SHG movement improves the political participation of villagers.

Coefficient of Association, Ø = 0.25, which indicates moderate association.

Odd Ratio = 3.00>1, which means that the villagers engaged in SHGs have participated *Gram Sansad* meeting 3 times higher than the non-SHG villagers.

Participation in Gram Sabha

Table 6.43: Observed Frequency Participation in Gram Sabha

Variable	*Respondent*	*Level of Participation*		
		Participated	*Not Participated*	*Total*
Participation in Gram Sansad Meeting	SHG Members	58	70	128
	Non-SHG Members	15	113	128
	Total	**73**	**183**	**256**

H_0—SHG movement does not improve the participation of villagers in *Gram Sabha*.

H_1—SHG movement improves the participation of villagers in *Gram Sabha*.

Table 6.44: Result Table of Participation in Gram Sabha

Chi-Square value, χ^2_1	*Coefficient of Association, Ø*	*Odd Ratio*
35.43	0.35	6.24

Here, χ^2 Value = 35.43 at Degree of Freedom 1.

While, the $\chi^2_{.05,1}$=3.84, $\chi^2_{.01,1}$=6.63 are the χ^2 table value at 5 per cent and 1 per cent level of significance.

So, calculated $\chi^2_1 > \chi^2_{.05,1}$ and $\chi^2_{.01,1}$

Hence, H_0 is rejected and it denotes that SHG movement improves the political participation of villagers.

Coefficient of Association, Ø = 0.35, which indicates moderate association.

Odd Ratio = 6.24>1, which means that the villagers engaged in SHGs have participated Gram Sabha meeting 6.24 times higher than the non-SHG villagers.

Decision-making Process

Table 6.45: Observed Frequency Decision-making Process

Variable	*Respondent*	*Level of Participation*		
		Make	*Don't Make*	*Total*
Decision-making Process	SHG Members	70	58	128
	Non-SHG Members	52	76	128
	Total	**122**	**134**	**256**

H_0—SHG movement does not improve the decision-making power of villagers.

H_1—SHG movement improve the decision-making power of villagers.

Table 6.46: Result Table of Decision-making Process

Chi-Square value, χ^2_1	*Coefficient of Association, Ø*	*Odd Ratio*
5.07	0.13	1.76

Here, χ^2 Value = 5.07 at Degree of Freedom 1.

While, the $\chi^2_{.05,1}$=3.84, $\chi^2_{.01,1}$=6.63 are the χ^2 table value at 5 per cent and 1 per cent level of significance.

So, calculated $\chi^2_1 > \chi^2_{.05,1}$ and $\chi^2_{.01,1}$

Hence, H_0 is rejected and it denotes that SHG movement improves the political participation of villagers.

Coefficient of Association, Ø = 0.13, which indicates very minimal association.

Odd Ratio = 1.76>1, which means that the villagers engaged in SHGs have taken decisions 1.67 times higher than the non-SHG villagers.

Sensitivity of Gram Panchayat

Table 6.47: Observed Frequency of Sensitivity of Gram Panchayat

Variable	*Respondent*	*Level of Participation*		
		Make	*Don't Make*	*Total*
Decision-making Process	SHG Members	63	65	128
	Non-SHG Members	57	71	128
	Total	**120**	**136**	**256**

H_0 —SHG movement does not improve the sensitivity of GP towards villagers.

H_1 —SHG movement improve the sensitivity of GP towards villagers.

Table 6.48: Result Table of Sensitivity of Gram Panchayat

Chi-Square value, χ^2_1	*Coefficient of Association, Ø*	*Odd Ratio*
5.07		

Here, χ^2 Value = 5.67 at Degree of Freedom 1.

While, the $\chi^2_{.05,1}$=3.84, $\chi^2_{.01,1}$=6.63 are the χ^2 table value at 5 per cent and 1 per cent level of significance.

So, calculated $\chi^2_1 < \chi^2_{.05,1}$ and $\chi^2_{.01,1}$

Hence, H_0 is accepted and it denotes that SHG movement does not improve the sensitivity of Gram Panchayat towards villagers.

Capacity Building of Villagers

Table 6.49: Table of Observed Frequency Capacity Building of Villagers

Variable	*Respondent*	*Level of Participation*		
		Make	*Don't Make*	*Total*
Decision-making Process	SHG Members	80	48	128
	Non-SHG Members	26	102	128
	Total	**106**	**150**	**256**

H_0— SHG movement does not improve the capacity of villagers.
H_1— SHG movement improve the capacity of villagers.

Table 6.50: Result Table of Capacity Building of Villagers

Chi-Square value, χ^2_1	*Coefficient of Association, Ø*	*Odd Ratio*
46.94	0.39	6.53

Here, χ^2 Value = 46.94 at Degree of Freedom 1.

While, the $\chi^2_{.05,1}$=3.84 , $\chi^2_{.01,1}$=6.63 are the χ^2 table value at 5 per cent and 1 per cent level of significance.

So, calculated $\chi^2_1 > \chi^2_{.05,1}$ and $\chi^2_{.01,1}$

Hence, H_0 is rejected and it denotes that SHG movement improves the capacity of villagers.

Coefficient of Association, Ø = 0.39, which indicates better association.

Odd Ratio = 6.53>1, which means that the villagers engaged in SHGs have built capacity 6.53 times higher than the non-SHG villagers.

Hence, in this context of a broader vision of decentralised governance based on open direct participative democracy Self-Help Groups are being perceived by many as neighbourhood sub-structures who are an integral part of the institutions and processes of local self-governance that communities use to fulfil their aspirations for ensuring basic services and entitlements rather than purely as a civil society institution which can engage representative 'government' to be responsible, accountable and efficient in delivering various services to its citizens including Self-Help Groups within its jurisdiction.

The SHGs pay the most important role in the new approach of local governance in West Bengal in which emphasis has been given on decentralised community engagement along with more flexible and democratic way to deal with community problems and requirements. Self-Help Groups (SHGs) that have carved out new arenas for different forms of socio-political engagement. SHGs encompass the full range of indivisible, interdependent and interrelated rights (i.e. civil, cultural, economic, political and social rights). It has enhanced women involvement, especially of marginalised section, in local governance and has increased the quality and legitimacy of democratic decision-making. SHGs empower the rural women and prioritize the building and strengthening of a People's institution. SHGs create a sense of ownership of development processes through strategies of empowerment among the rural women. SHGs increase the degree of community participation in grassroots governance. Over time SHGs have made them stronger and developed them as a parallel structure of Gram Panchayats in rural areas. The SHGs act as a vehicle for microfinance and credit as well as a vehicle for women's empowerment and participation in various development issues. This emerging trend has changed the decentralisation picture of West Bengal. The SHG movement has empowered women to enter the political space. However, they also felt that over time SHGs are not only being politicized but also treated as welcome development. The sensitivity and response of Gram Panchayats for rural people especially for the women have increased after SHG movement. However, political affiliation of GP leaders comes in the way of SHGs which are seeking linkages and support with their Gram Panchayats.

Finally, the Self-Help Groups became an interface between the development process and the number of Government and elected institutions at the grass-roots level, particularly the Panchayati Raj Institutions. The efficacy of these Self-Help Groups (SHGs) has been considerably enhanced through a symbiotic relationship with the Panchayati Raj Institutions.

Socio-cultural and Political Constrains

West Bengal is one of the States which have achieved success to some extent in implementing decentralised plans and programmes. It has devolved many powers to the PRIs and recently to SHGs. However, there are some factors, which affect the strengthening mechanism of decentralisation process at grassroots-level. In the present study an attempt has made to recognize the important issues which are responsible for restricting effective decentralisation as well as strengthening local self-governance structure. First, focused group discussions were conducted with the villagers to identify the major challenges or constrain which are hindering the decentralisation process on the three major perspectives, i.e. personal, political and administrative. This exercise had recognized 5 major constrains for each perspectives. In the second phase respondents were asked to give score to the predetermined constrains. The highest score was 5 and lowest score was 1. On the basis of this data statistical analysis have been done to provide rank to each constrains within each three perspectives. Here degree of variability has been measured through calculating the Coefficient of Variation (CV). The Coefficient of Variation (CV) is used to compare the consistency of measurement or reliability. The smaller the Coefficient of Variation (CV), the higher is the consistency or reliability.

Coefficient of Variation = (Standard Deviation/Arithmetic Mean) × 100

Table 6.51: Major Constrains or Challenges Recognized during FGD

Personal constrains	*Social Constrains*	*Administrative Constrains*
Lack of Education	Lack of Community Support	Lack of Leadership Skill among the Group Leaders
Lack of Exact Idea about Panchayat System	Lack of Mutual Trust among the Group Members	Inefficient Group Leader
Lack of Interest	Political Interference	Lack of Initiatives at Government Level
Lack of Initiatives	Family Rituals or Norms	Lack of Bureaucratic Willingness
Lack of Support from Family Members	Lack of Voice	Lack of proper Monitoring

Personal Constrain

Personal constrains are related to the knowledge attitude and perception of individual person. These are directly or indirectly linked with the particular person, his/her family and the society he/she belongs. These constrains are very crucial for effective decentralisation because these emerges from the individual or household levels and often ignored by the development agencies. Here some crucial personal constrains are identified and ranked as per the respondents.

Table 6.52 very clearly indicates the scenario of personal constrains in both of the district and interestingly major constrains are same. Lack of family support is the major constrain in both of the district, because it has the smallest coefficient of variation as well as highest consistency. Lack of interest and lack of initiatives come second and third respectively in both of the districts. Lack of education and lack of idea about *Panchayats* are minimal factors in this case.

Table 6.52: Personal Constrain

Personal Constrains	*Birbhum*				*Burdwan*			
	Mean	*SD*	*CV*	*Rank*	*Mean*	*SD*	*CV*	*Rank*
Lack of Education	3.352	1.350	40.271	5	3.047	1.441	47.288	4
Lack of Exact Idea about Panchayat System	3.227	1.365	42.299	4	3.367	1.430	42.468	5
Lack of Interest	3.031	1.323	43.629	2	2.578	1.401	54.340	2
Lack of Initiatives	3.063	1.327	43.340	3	2.680	1.430	53.377	3
Lack of Support from Family Members	2.680	1.346	50.226	1	2.508	1.364	54.373	1

Source: Primary Data.

Social Constrains

Social constrains are related to social issues like awareness, mobility, rituals, family, social customs etc. This is a area which create a very strong barrier for rural women to participate in the democratic process as well as affecting the decentralisation process.

Table 6.53: Social Constrains

Social Constrains	*Birbhum*				*Burdwan*			
	Mean	*SD*	*CV*	*Rank*	*Mean*	*SD*	*CV*	*Rank*
Lack of Community Support	3.352	1.343	45.109	4	3.047	1.348	41.764	3
Lack of Mutual Trust among the Group Members	3.227	1.416	44.213	3	3.367	1.328	38.296	2
Political Interference	3.031	1.369	39.296	2	2.578	1.305	37.370	1
Lack of Voice	3.063	1.399	45.807	5	2.680	1.396	50.038	5
Family Rituals or Norms	2.680	1.339	38.875	1	2.508	1.331	44.956	4

Source: Primary Data.

Table 6.53 indicates the Coefficient of Variation of responses for different constrains regarding social issues. The smaller Coefficient of Variation, means higher the consistency or reliability. It means the factor have low Coefficient of Variation is most responsible for hindering the decentralisation process or the major constrain. The data clearly indicates that in Birbhum district Family rituals or norms comes first to restrict the women from participating in the decentralisation process. Political interference, lack of trust, lack of community support and lack of voice come next respectively. However, in Burdwan district Political interference is the major constrain for successful promotion of decentralisation.

Administrative Constrain

The Strengthening decentralisation process is highly dependent on the effective and efficient Government. Hence, administrative constrain indicates issues related to the attitude and perception of Local Self-Governance which includes Government officials, members, leadership issues and sensitization process.

Table 6.54: Administrative Constrain

Administrative Constrains	*Birbhum*				*Burdwan*			
	Mean	*SD*	*CV*	*Rank*	*Mean*	*SD*	*CV*	*Rank*
Lack of Leadership Skill among the Group Leaders	3.352	1.343	45.125	4	3.047	1.315	47.293	5
Inefficient Group Leader	3.227	1.362	48.432	5	3.367	1.290	43.331	4
Lack of Initiatives at Government Level	3.031	1.344	39.200	1	2.578	1.308	41.270	2
Lack of Bureaucratic Willingness	3.063	1.359	41.723	3	2.680	1.335	38.047	1
Lack of Proper Monitoring	2.680	1.306	40.487	2	2.508	1.371	41.596	3

Source: Primary Data.

Table 6.54 clearly indicates in both of the district lack of Government initiatives, lack of bureaucratic willingness and lack of monitoring, i.e. the frequent sensitization are the major constrains at administrative-level as these three factors have relatively high coefficient of variation. Leadership is also an issue but it can be diluted through the training and capacity building.

The above discussion indicates that the major constrains are lack of awareness and interest among the villagers, busy schedule of villagers, lack of proper coordination among the villagers and Gram Panchayat, political biasness, lack of Promotional Agencies, lack of Government initiatives, lack of bureaucratic willingness and lack of monitoring, i.e. the frequent sensitization, lack of Transparency, lack of Initiatives from elected members, political conflict etc.

References

Dreze, J., and Sen, A. (1995), *India Economic Development and Social Opportunity,* New York: Oxford University Press.

Law Department (Legislative), (2004), The West Bengal Panchayat (Gram Panchayat Administration) Rules, (2004), Kolkata, WB: Law Department (Legislative).

Law Department (Legislative), (2007), The West Bengal Panchayat (Gram Panchayat Accounts, Audit and Budget) Rules, (2007), Kolkata, WB: Law Department (Legislative).

Law Department (Legislative), (2009), West Bengal Act XLI of 1973: The West Bengal Panchayat Act, 1973 (As modified up to the 31st May, 2009), Kolkata, WB: Law Department (Legislative).

Law Department (Legislative), (2010), West Bengal Act VIII of 2010: The West Bengal Panchayat (Amendment) Act, 2010 (As modified up to the 13st May, 2010), Kolkata, WB: Law Department (Legislative).

Ministry of Law and Justice (Legislative Department), Government of India (GoI), (2005), The National Rural Employment Guarantee Act: *The Gazette*, Legislative Department, GoI, New Delhi, India.

Ministry of Panchayati Raj (MoPR), Government of India (GoI), (2006), Backward Regions Grant Fund: Programme Guidelines, MoPR, GoI, New Delhi, India.

Ministry of Rural Department (MoRD), Government of India (GoI), (2000), Panchayati Raj in India—Status Report 2000, MoRD, GoI, New Delhi, India.

Panchayat and Rural Development Department (P&RD Department), Government of West Bengal (GoWB), (2008), *Annual Administrative Report* 2008-09, P&RD Department, GoWB, Kolkata, WB.

Panchayat and Rural Development Department (P&RD Department), Government of West Bengal (GoWB), (2010), *Information on West Bengal Panchayats: Their Members and Functionaries*, P&RD Department, GoWB, Kolkata, WB.

Panchayat and Rural Development Department (P&RD Department), Government of West Bengal (GoWB), (2008), *SRD Annual Report* 2007-08, P&RD Department, GoWB, Kolkata, WB.

Panchayat and Rural Development Department (P&RD Department), Government of West Bengal (GoWB), (2009), *Roadmap for Panchayat in West Bengal: A Vision Document*. P&RD Department, GoWB, Kolkata, WB.

Panchayat and Rural Development Department (P&RD Department), Government of West Bengal (GoWB), (2011), SRD Project Completion Report 2011 (ARIES Project Code: 107904-101 and 107904-102), Kolkata, WB: P&RD Department, GoWB.

Paul, S.K. (2013), Decentralised Planning: Experience of West Bengal Panchayats, in Himadri Sinha and Anant Kumar (Eds.), *Governance of Commons and Livelihood Security*, Ranchi: Xavier Institute of Social Service.

Paul, S.K. and Mitra, A. (2015), Strengthening Local Self-Government in Rural West Bengal through SHG: A Study in the District of Burdwan, West Bengal, In Singha Roy, S. and Maitra, S.N. (Ed.), *Development and Politics in India,* Department of Political Science and History, Chandidash Mahavidyalaya.

The West Bengal Panchayat Act, 1973.

The West Bengal Panchayat (Amendment) Act, 1992.

The West Bengal Panchayat Amendment Act, 1994.

The West Bengal Panchayat (Amendment) Act, 2003.

The West Bengal Panchayat (Amendment) Act, 2010.

7
Conclusion and Recommendations

The decentralized governance has been considered as a mechanism of local self-government for promoting healthy and sustainable development. It is expected to facilitate effective people's participation, enhance degree of transparency and ensure greater accountability. Decentralized governance is assumed to provide more effective and competitive delivery of services at the grassroots level. Being closer to the people, decentralized governance is assumed to meet needs and preferences of the people. Hence, the decentralisation of power and decision-making processes from National and State to Local Bodies has become a major trend globally. The establishment of strong and accountable systems of governance at grassroots level will encourage a more equitable distribution of State-provided resources, which can be directed towards poor and vulnerable groups. An underlying hypothesis here is that democratic participation will yield strong mechanisms of accountability, which in turn, will improve the distribution of benefits to groups that are traditionally marginalized by market and state.

India is not an exception to this trend. India has been experimenting with the decentralized governance process for quite some time. Over time it has been realised that centralised decision-making at National and State-levels to be unsuitable for local conditions and policies need to be customized to the need of the local communities and should reflect the diversity embedded in these communities and situations faced by them. So, that, the local self-governance has become the arm of the Government that lies closest to the communities as well as increase the community access to resources. The grassroots initiatives from different States of India provide insights into the participation of local communities in decentralized decision-making and local self-governance.

Following the same trend, West Bengal has been one of the forerunners in installing a three-tier Panchayati Raj Institutions (PRIs) for rural local governance in India. The present generation Panchayats in the State started its journey in 1978, i.e. 15 years ahead of the 73rd Amendment of the Constitution of India. Ever since their inception, the State has demonstrated strong commitment to rural decentralisation by ensuring regular elections to PRIs, entrusting them with increasing responsibility of implementing various rural development programmes and making the development bureaucracy part of PRIs. The State also ensured adequate representation of the socially backward classes—Scheduled Castes (SCs), Scheduled Tribes (STs) and women—in PRIs for their involvement in the process of socio-economic development.

Further, the active involvement of grassroots women in local governance and decentralisation process has been promoted in West Bengal through Self-Help Groups (SHGs), in turn builds ownership over local developments as well as the leadership capabilities of women. The SHGs advocate for effective functioning of the decentralisation process in West Bengal, by enabling women and marginalized communities to engage in the participatory planning and local self-governance.

Keeping view on the above mentioned perspectives the present study was planned. The purpose of the study has been to enumerate the role of PRIs and SHGs in strengthening decentralisation process in rural West Bengal. The objectives of the study are:

1. To study the role of PRIs and SHGs for strengthening rural decentralisation.
2. To enumerate the way of the preparation and implementation of micro-level plans and people's participation in the planning process.
3. To study the perception and attitude of the elected members of PRIs in regard to devolution and delegation of powers to grassroots level.

4. To study the efficacy of SHG members *vis-à-vis* non-SHG members in decentralisation process.
5. To find out the changing scenario of decentralisation in PRIs after the SHG movement.
6. To study the socio-cultural and political constraints, which are hindering for strengthening the decentralisation process.
7. To suggest some appropriate policy measures for making effective micro-level plans as well as implementing mechanisms.

The present study has been carried out in the districts of Birbhum and Burdwan of West Bengal. Districts Birbhum and Burdwan have been selected on the basis of relatively backward and advanced district as in HDI and high SHG concentration respectively. According to Human Development Report (2005) Birbhum and Burdwan are ranking 13 and 5 in HDI respectively. The Burdwan district is far advanced than the Birbhum in case of agricultural development, educational development, infrastructure, public services, communication etc. Two Blocks have been taken on the basis of highest SHG concentration and lowest SHG concentration from each of the district for the field study. From each block, two Gram Panchayats have been taken on the same way, i.e. the concentration of highest SHGs and lowest SHGs. So, as a whole, eight Gram Panchayats have been studied. This study relies mainly on primary data. Multi-Stage Purposive sampling has been used for sample selection. The data were collected from three different groups of respondents: (1) Elected Members of Gram Panchayat, (2) SHG Office Bearers, and (3) Non-SHG Villagers. Respondents were interviewed with a view to collecting information on their awareness, perceptions and participation and their views on how local self-governance can be strengthened and sustained. In addition Focused Group Discussions were also conducted with the respondent to cross-check the data generated during field survey. On the basis of the information generated the predetermined objectives were enumerated and analysed. Here, in this chapter an attempt has been made to highlight the major findings and recommend some policy measures for effective decentralisation through Panchayati Raj Institutions (PRIs) and Self-Help Groups (SHGs) in West Bengal.

Major Findings of the Study

Decentralized Planning Process

1. West Bengal has a practical methodology for participatory planning which attempts to balance the need for participation with the requirements of rational planning. The *Gram Unnayan Samiti*, *Gram Sansad* and *Gram Sabha* are the primary institutions of planning process in West Bengal.
2. The general body meeting is a vital mechanism available to Gram Panchayat for discussing the overall planning and budgeting process and the whole workflow of the Gram Panchayat. The study clearly indicates that the average number of General Body meetings and *Upa-Samiti* meetings held in Burdwan district were more than the Birbhum district. It indicates that the Gram Panchayats of Burdwan district is more efficient in terms of holding the General Body meetings and *Upa-Samiti* meetings than the Gram Panchayats of Birbhum district. It also indicates that the better status of both functional and administrative decentralisation of Gram Panchayats of Burdwan district than the Birbhum district.
3. Some of the Gram Panchayats of Birbhum district and Burdwan district are unable to organize both half-yearly and annual *Gram Sansad* meeting in 2011-12 financial year due to political unrest. Likewise the lack of fund, poor planning and lack of accountability of various projects/schemes could not be implemented which created widespread public grievance resulting in public unrest in meetings deeming meetings ineligible to get counted.
4. The *Gram Sabha* meeting acts as a platform for information exchange and hence is an effective mechanism to enhance transparency and participatory process in the Gram Panchayat governance system. All the sampled Gram Panchayats of the present study were successfully organized *Gram Sabha* in the two respective financial years.
5. The present study reveals that in Birbhum district only 2 Gram Panchayats (50%), i.e. Hatia and Purandarpur Gram Panchayts were able to form GUS at all *Gram Sansads* and in Burdwan district except Kalayanpur other three sampled GP (75%) were able to form *Gram Unnayan Samiti* at all *Gram Sansads*.

6. However, the effectiveness of these *Gram Unnayan Samities* in both of the districts is a big question. In spite of formation majority of the *Gram Unnayan Samiti* were found ineffective and in action only in registers. So, the purpose and functioning of *Gram Unnayan Samiti* in effective decentralized planning is now somehow diluted.
7. Another interesting factor revealed from the field study that the Government has allocated a very marginal fund to *Gram Unnayan Samiti* and due lack of fund *Gram Unnayan Samiti* could not take developmental initiatives, resulting lack of good effective developmental work at grassroots level.
8. The present study shows very low level of people's participation in *Gram Sansad* meeting, which is not desirable in decentralisation process. It has also found that the most of the GS meeting were dissolved for the first time due to lack of coram.
9. In Burdwan district people's participation is comparatively higher than Birbhum district. The lowest and highest average total coram of Burdwan district was 7 per cent and 22.25 per cent respectively, which are quite higher than the Birbhum district.
10. In Burdwan district total attendance are fulfilling the coram but female attendance is not up to the target that is 33 per cent. It shows the same picture in Birbhum district like Burdwan district.
11. Female attendance as well as total attendance in both Birbhum and Burdwan districts is not satisfactory and also not so hopeful for decentralisation process. It clearly indicates that the minimum criteria mentioned in the *Gram Sansad* meeting norms which is attendance of 10 per cent voter for coram along with one-third women participation has not been fulfilled in majority of *Gram Sansad* meetings in both of the districts.
12. The study reveals very low participation in *Gram Sabhas* compared to the total number of voters of a particular Gram Panchayat. Both Birbhum and Burdwan districts are averagely fulfilling the norms of Coram.
13. However, in case of female attendance majority of the sampled Gram Panchayats of both of the district are miles away from the target. The average total attendances of

Birbhum district for two respective years are 5.53 per cent and 7.62 per cent. In Burdwan district average total attendances of two respective years are 7 per cent and 8.47 per cent.

14. In case of female attendance, the average female attendances of Birbhum district for two respective years are 21.65 per cent and 27.07 per cent. Following the same trend Burdwan district also shows the similar kind of picture with having 24.23 per cent and 29.75 per cent female attendance for two respective years.
15. The *Gram Sabha* norm for female attendance which is one-third of the total attendance has not been fulfilled in majority of cases in both of the district.
16. An interesting fact has been revealed during the verification process that the majority of the female attending *Gram Sabha* and *Gram Sansad* are engaged with Self-Help Groups. However, they have attended the meeting for their own interest. So, incorporation of SHGs in PRI system along with their capacity build have increased the female participation in *Gram Sabha* and *Gram Sansad* as well as empowering them to actively participate in the decentralized planning process.
17. Another fact has been found that to maintain the record on paper about the coram or to avoid the show cause from the higher authority regarding low participation the ruling party members and officials of the respective Gram Panchayat are sometimes making fake attendance sheet by putting false signature in the *Gram Sabha* and *Gram Sansad* meeting. One or two persons put lots of signature as per voter list on behalf of original person.
18. The reasons behind the low level of people's participation are many like, lack of awareness and interest among the villagers, busy schedule of villagers, lack of proper coordination among the villagers and Gram Panchayat, Political Biasness, lack of promotional agencies, distant meeting venue, lack of transparency, lack of initiatives from elected members, political conflict etc.
19. The most important step towards devolution of power and resources to the panchayat bodies was taken long back in West Bengal. The GoWB has taken a step forward by making

provision for *Gram Sansad* (a village meeting) apart from *Gram Sabha* (groups of village meeting).

20. The Gram Panchayat has to place the deliberation, recommendation and suggestion in the annual meeting of the *Gram Sansad*, the supplementary budget of the Gram Panchayat for the preceding year. The Gram Panchayat also has to discuss the report on the work done during the previous year and the work proposed to be done during the following year. Based on the discussion and recommendation Panchayat level plans are finalized for budgeting and execution.
21. Budgeting is also a crucial part of decentralized planning. Since, many of the components of planning, implementation as well as expenditure by the Panchayats are scheme based, the practice of proper budgetary control has not yet received enough attention, rather observance of only the scheme guidelines and maintaining scheme based fund utilization became the sole criteria.
22. However, when the fund is credited to a Panchayat, any expenditure has to be duly authorized by the competent authority and actual expenditure should be subject to budgetary control. The target is to ensure that each Standing Committee/*Upa-Samiti* will have positive contribution in preparation of budget and will exercise due budgetary control on expenditure related to its domain of activities and appropriate management practices will be followed for proper application of fund.
23. In the existing decentralized planning process, *Gram Sabha* incorporates the plans in the Gram Panchayat Annual Action Plans on the basis of priority as recommended by the *Gram Sansad*. Incorporation of the higher percentage of *Gram Sansad* plan in Gram Panchayat Annual Action plan indicates high level of decentralisation. Similarly, higher level of execution of plan indicates high level of efficiency at Gram Panchayat level.
24. The study shows that in 2011-12 financial year, average 11.25 number of schemes were taken by the each *sansad* of Birbhum district. Out of those, only 52.22 per cent schemes were included in Gram Panchayat Annual Action Plan. Out of them, 59.22 per cent schemes were executed. In the same year, average 14.38 numbers of schemes were taken by the

sansads of Burdwan district. Out of them 59.13 per cent *Sansad* schemes included in the annual action plan, and 64.71 per cent schemes executed from the Annual Action Plan.

25. In 2012-13 financial year, average 12 numbers of schemes were taken by the each *Sansad* of Birbhum district. Out of those, only 57.29 per cent schemes were included in GP annual action plan. Out of them, 61.82 per cent schemes were executed. In the same year, average 14.88 numbers of schemes were taken by the *Sansads* of Burdwan district. Out of them 65.55 per cent *Sansad* schemes included in the Annual Action Plan, and 69.23 per cent schemes executed from the Annual Action Plan.
26. Study clearly indicates that the Gram Panchayats are incorporating *Gram Sansad* level plans in their Annual Action Plan but the percentage is not up to the mark (<60%). It also reveals that the status of decentralized planning is quite better in Burdwan district than the Birbhum as well as the Gram Panchayats of Burdwan district are more efficient that that GPs of Birbhum district in case of plan implementation. Less inclusion of *Gram Sansad*-level plan also indicates the strong role of Gram Panchayat members and officials in formulation of Annual Action Plan. Gram Panchayat members and officials play crucial role in decision-making process of scheme selection as well as their execution.
27. While analysing the Annual Action plan an interesting fact has been revealed that the majority of the schemes of Annual Action Plan are under MGNREGA programme as it has comparatively bigger budgetary allocation than the other programmes. As a demand driven programme MGNREGA needs a bunch of schemes that is why maximum *sansad* schemes under MGNREGA are included in the Annual Action Plan.
28. Further, it has also revealed that the GPs of Birbhum district have more number of supplementary plans in Annual Action Plan than the Burdwan district. This indicates stronger level of grassroots governance in Burdwan district than the Birbhum district.
29. The average collection of Own Fund is more in Burdwan district than Birbhum district in two financial years. It has also found that the percentage expenditure of own fund is

high in Burdwan district than the Birbhum district. However, average expenditure of own fund in Burdwan district was very low in 2011-12 financial year. Higher collection of own fund as well as high percentage of expenditure indicates better level of financial decentralisation.

30. The study clearly indicates that the fund flow and percentage of expenditure are increased in the second financial year in both the districts. However, the percentage of expenditure under 3rd State Finance Commission was quite low in 2011-12 financial year in both of the districts. The average percentage of expenditure in 2011-12 financial year was 69.94 per cent in Birbhum district and 18.89 per cent in Burdwan district. The reason behind the low expenditure was the political unrest rater the administrative failure. The State election in 2011-12 hampers the development process in both the districts.
31. In 2012-13 financial year the average expenditure under 3rd State Finance Commission was increased in both of the districts. In Birbhum district the average expenditure was 89.35 per cent and in Burdwan district it was 91.23 per cent. So, both political and administrative stability improve the level of local governance in both of the districts.
32. The study reveals that in Birbhum district the fund flow has increased while expenditure has decreased in 2012-13 financial year. In Birbhum district average expenditure under 13th Central Finance Commission fund were 82.96 per cent and 51.11 per cent in 2011-12 and 2012-13 financial years respectively.
33. While in case of Burdwan district both the fund flow and expenditure have increased in successive years. The average expenditure of Burdwan district was 22.01 per cent and 56.56 per cent in 2011-12 and 2012-13 financial years respectively. It has been found that delayed transaction of fund from the Central and State Governments to PRIs is one of the major reasons behind low percentage of expenditure under 13th Central Finance Commission.
34. It has been found in the study that the maximum expenditure is done by the Panchayats under MGNREGS. In the 2011-12 and 2012-13 financial years average expenditure under

MGNREGS in Birbhum district was 95.60 per cent and 99.68 per cent whereas in Burdwan district 94.36 per cent and 99.54 per cent. So, in both of the districts the average expenditure has increased in the successive years.

35. It has been found that, Burdwan district is relatively advanced district. The scope of work under MGNREGs in Burdwan is lesser than the Birbhum district in various aspects. Infrastructure development of Burdwan district is already in a better position and that is why, the scope for infrastructure development is less in Burdwan than Birbhum district.
36. Financial Autonomy Ratio (FAO) is one of the important indicators to analyse the status of fiscal decentralisation. It is calculated by the share of Gram Panchayat's Own Fund (Tax & Non-Tax) in Gram Panchayat's total (include all funds) expenditure. The Financial Autonomy Ratio (FAO) shows the extent of reliance on own sources of funds which lead to autonomy. In this case the top ranker is the Gram Panchayat with the highest FAO. Higher FAO means higher financial sustainability of a Gram Panchayat.
37. Higher autonomy may be appreciated but it could also mean that the flow of Government and other funds are inadequate for the development of a particular Gram Panchayat.
38. The study clearly indicates that Financial Autonomy Ratio (FAO) is much higher in Gram Panchayats of Burdwan district than the Birbhum district. Average FAO of Burdwan district was also much higher in two successive financial years than the Birbhum district, i.e. 10.53 (2011-12) and 7.03 (2012-13) respectively.
39. The share of Gram Panchayat Own Fund in total expenditure is comparatively higher in Burdwan district than the Birbhum district. It means Gram Panchayat of Burdwan district has better financial autonomy than the Birbhum district.

Socio-Economic Features of the Elected Gram Panchayat Members of Sampled Gram Panchayat

40. The district-wise average percentage of caste composition among the Gram Panchayat members of the selected Gram Panchayat of both Birbhum and Burdwan districts has shown almost similar picture. The General Caste and Scheduled

Caste people are holding maximum representative than Scheduled Tribe and OBC representation in the local Government. However, in case of female participation cumulative participation of both Scheduled Castes and Scheduled Tribes women are more than the General Caste women in Burdwan district compared to Birbhum district. Although, individually participation of Scheduled Castes women is high in Birbhum district while participation of General Caste women is comparatively high in Burdwan district.

41. The study also reveals that the percentage of female representation in Birbhum and Burdwan districts are 42.50 per cent and 36 per cent respectively. So, it is clear that in case of district average, the Birbhum district has higher female representation than the Burdwan district. Although, it is clear from the study that percentage of female members of all selected Panchayats are maintaining the prescribed percentage of the Constitution of India.
42. The data indicates that the educational status of both Birbhum and Burdwan districts have slightly different picture especially in case of female education. Most of the representative's educational status is varying in between primary and higher secondary level. The per cent of representatives with higher education are very minimal. However, in case of higher education, Burdwan district is standing in slightly higher position than the Birbhum district. The data on education also indicates widening gender gap in educational status which leads to poor access to knowledge, skill and attitude among the female members.
43. The female representatives are economically unstable comparison to the male members. Majority of the female representation are housewives, i.e. engaged in unproductive domestic activities. Economic independence put them forward to the psychological advancement as well as greater acceptance in the family and society. Economic independence makes women more empower both socially, politically and economically. But, it has been found from the table that a significant number of female representatives belong to either less stable income group or totally economically dependent group. Because of less stable economic group or economic

insufficiency, the female representatives remain dependent to their husband or family, economically and as well as psychologically.

44. As per overall scenario, in Birbhum district 77 per cent seats are occupied by the Left Front, 10 per cent are from TMC, 8 per cent are from BJP and 5 per cent are Independent candidates. However, in Burdwan district, 94 per cent members are from Left Front and only 6 per cent are from TMC. In case of political power structure of the Gram Panchayat members, it has found that all selected eight Gram Panchayats are ruled by the Left Front.
45. Another important fact has been revealed that no female member from selected Gram Panchayats are elected as independent candidate, while in Birbhum district 5 per cent male representatives were elected as independent candidate. It appears that female members may be only elected under political banner or may not be enough confident to fight independently.
46. It has been seen that the political party plays a major role to bring the members (both male and female) into the politics. In case of female members, their husbands play a vital role for that. One more interesting fact is that the frequency of self-motivated female members is almost zero in both the districts.
47. Similarly, there is no male member motivated by their wives. It clears the fact of male domination in the grassroots politics and as well as in the Gram Panchayats. The actual facts behind the improvement in female representation at Gram Panchayat-level is due to provision of 33 per cent women reservation under 73rd Constitutional Amendment Act, 1992. In some cases, the husbands, who were earlier the representative of the respective *Sansads* motivate their wives to contest in the election to restore their power.
48. The percentages of previously elected male and female representatives of Birbhum district are 21.74 per cent and 11.76 per cent respectively and in Burdwan district the percentages are 28.13 per cent and 16.67 per cent respectively. However, male and female representatives associated with political parties in Birbhum district are 56.52 per cent, 17.65 per cent and in Burdwan district are 68.75

per cent and 27.78 per cent respectively. So, it reveals from the discussion that in both the districts, the frequency of previously elected members and political association are high in case of male than in the female members.

Awareness Levels of the Elected Gram Panchayat Members

49. The awareness-level on PRI related issues among the male and female members of Birbhum district is less than the members of Burdwan district. Although, the awareness-level among the female is remarkably low in both of the Birbhum and Burdwan districts than the male members. This reveals the male domination picture in the Gram Panchayats. Although after 73rd Constitutional Amendment Acts the awareness as well as participation have been inceased among the women representatives in Gram Panchayat.
50. The formation of budget is a crucial indicator like planning process to judge the awareness level of GP members. It appears that 52.17 per cent male members and 29.41 per cent female members of Birbhum district are aware about the Budget making process. In Burdwan district this picture is showing much better shape than Birbhum. Here, 68.75 per cent male members and 38.89 per cent female members know the budget making process.
51. Prioritization of schemes or sector-wise scheme selection is very important for the development of a particular area. But till now the percentage of members who can select proper scheme and prioritize them are very low in both Birbhum and Burdwan districts. In Birbhum district 60.87 per cent male Gram Panchayat members and 17.65 per cent female Gram Panchayat members are able to select scheme whereas, in Burdwan district 68.75 per cent male members and 27.87 per cent female members are able to do so.
52. Although 86.96 per cent male members and 58.82 per cent female members in Birbhum district and 87.50 per cent male members and 61.11 per cent female members in Burdwan district are well aware about various developmental schemes.
53. After planning and getting the sanction of the budget, proper implementation of the selected schemes at the village-level is very important characteristics of decentralisation process.

In Birbhum district, 86.69 per cent male Gram Panchayat members and 58.82 per cent female Gram Panchayat members know the process of execution of the selected schemes, whereas, 87.50 per cent male Gram Panchayat member and 66.67 per cent female Gram Panchayat members know the process of implementation of the schemes at the village-level in Burdwan district.

54. So, it has been observed from the discussion that the awareness level among the male and female members on decentralisation process related issues of Birbhum district is less than the members of Burdwan district. Although, the awareness-level among the female is remarkably low in both of the Birbhum and Burdwan district than the male members.
55. Another factor has been revealed on this issue is that at present the planning and budgeting process have became more centralized rather than decentralized as the level of participation at planning and budgeting process went low. The Gram Panchayat administration is giving an external pressure to develop plans which somehow dilute the actual needs of the villages. The political engagement is also hampering the entire process as it only focuses on fulfilling the political agenda rather than developing the areas.
56. The GP members are very positive about the importance of decentralized governance at grassroots level and this strong argument made it very clear that decentralisation is a must factor for sustainable development at grassroots level.
57. In spite of having high focus of GP members on decentralisation process, the Gram Panchayats have shown less focus on proper decentralisation. The political and bureaucratic prejudice is also a strong factor diluting the entire process.
58. The *Gram Unnayan Samiti* (*GUS*) is more effective in Burdwan district than the Birbhum district in preparation of micro-level plans. It has also revealed from the FGD that Burdwan district has shown special focus for effective management of the *Gram Unnayan Samiti* than the Birbhum district and which facilitated the GUS for showing efficiency. However, recent political interest has been diluting the role and effectiveness of *Gram Unnayan Samiti* at grassroots level

and made it only a living structure rather a effective institution.

59. Gram Panchayat elected members are well aware of the fact that people's participation is very essential for effective decentralisation. However, in practice they have found bound to political parties and the GP officials.
60. The political influence on planning and implementation of micro-level plans is a real fact in West Bengal and this study has no exception. It has been found that the planning and implementation process is highly influenced by the political parties in both of the district.
61. The Gram Sabha is a crucial organization for effective implementation of decentralisation process and devolution of power to local people. It is very essential for rural people to argue their right and strengthening the grassroots governance. However, over the year the main agenda of *Gram Sabha* is being diluting and emerging as a platform for political agenda and conflict.

Efficacy of SHG and Non-SHG Members in Decentralisation Process

62. Awareness and perception level of rural people especially the rural women is one the most important variable which highly influences the grassroots governance as well as entire decentralized process.
63. The study indicates that in Birbhum district, 43.75 per cent sampled SHG members have good knowledge about Panchayat vote, 45.31 per cent and 10.94 per cent SHG members have average and poor knowledge about Panchayat vote respectively. In Burdwan district, 48.44 per cent sampled SHG members have well, 42.19 per cent have average and 9.38 per cent have poor knowledge about Panchayat voting. So, SHG members of each district have similar kind of knowledge level regarding Panchayat vote.
64. In Birbhum district, 23.44 per cent sampled SHG members have good knowledge about role of PRIs, while 53.13 per cent and 23.44 per cent sampled SHG members have average and poor knowledge about role of PRIs respectively. However, in Burdwan district, 26.56 per cent sampled SHG

members have well, 51.56 per cent have average and 21.88 per cent have poor knowledge about role of PRIs. So, SHG members of Burdwan district have better knowledge level than the Birbhum district regarding role of PRIs.

65. Caste Reservation System is an important issue of decentralized governance. The 73rd Constitutional Amendment Act, 1992 had a mandatory provision of Caste Reservation. So, it is expected that the villagers have good knowledge about Caste Reservation System. In Birbhum district, 26.56 per cent sampled SHG members have good knowledge about role Caste Reservation System, while 48.44 per cent and 25 per cent sampled SHG members have average and poor knowledge about Caste Reservation System respectively. However, in Burdwan district, 29.69 per cent sampled SHG members have well, 46.88 per cent have average and 23.44 per cent have poor knowledge about Caste Reservation System. So, SHG members of Burdwan and Birbhum district have moderate knowledge level on Caste Reservation System.

66. Women reservation is another mandatory provision of decentralisation process. It is also expected that women folk of rural areas specially the women engaged with SHGs have better understanding about women reservation system in PRIs. However, the data regarding the knowledge level about women reservation is not satisfactory. In Birbhum district, 21.88 per cent sampled SHG members have good knowledge about women reservation, while 50 per cent and 28.13 per cent sampled SHG members have average and poor knowledge about women reservation respectively. While, in Burdwan district, 25 per cent sampled SHG members have well, 51.56 per cent have average and 26.56 per cent have poor knowledge about women reservation. So, SHG members of Burdwan district have quite better knowledge about women reservation than the Birbhum district.

67. Regarding PRI structure, in Birbhum district 21.88 per cent sampled SHG members have good knowledge, while 51.56 per cent and 26.56 per cent sampled SHG members have average and poor knowledge about PRI structure respectively. Similarly, in Burdwan district, 23.44 per cent sampled SHG members have well, 50 per cent have average and 26.56 per

cent have poor knowledge about PRI structure. So, SHG members of both Birbhum and Burdwan districts have similar understanding about PRI structure.

68. In recent trend, SHGs are engaged in implementation of these programmes so SHGs should have good knowledge about these programmes. Ground realities have also supported this argument. Regarding Schemes under Gram Panchayat, in Birbhum district 28.13 per cent and 51.56 per cent sampled SHG members have good and average level knowledge respectively, while only 20.31 per cent sampled SHG members have poor knowledge about Schemes under Gram Panchayat. Similarly, in Burdwan district, 31.25 per cent sampled SHG members have well, 46.88 per cent have average and 18.75 per cent have poor knowledge about Schemes under Gram Panchayat. So, SHG members of both Birbhum and Burdwan districts have similar as well as better understanding about Schemes under Gram Panchayat.
69. In Birbhum district, 20.31 per cent sampled non-SHG villagers have good knowledge about Panchayat vote, 37.50 per cent and 42.19 per cent sampled non-SHG villagers have average and poor knowledge about Panchayat vote respectively. In Burdwan district, 23.44 per cent sampled non-SHG villagers have well, 37.50 per cent have average and 39.06 per cent have poor knowledge about Panchayat voting. So, non-SHG villagers of each district have almost similar kind of knowledge level regarding Panchayat vote.
70. In Birbhum district, 12.50 per cent sampled non-SHG villagers have good knowledge about role of PRIs, while 42.19 per cent and 45.31 per cent sampled non-SHG villagers have average and poor knowledge about role of PRIs respectively. However, in Burdwan district, 15.63 per cent sampled non-SHG villagers have well, 43.75 per cent have average and 40.63 per cent have poor knowledge about role of PRIs. So, non-SHG villagers of Burdwan district have better knowledge level than the Birbhum district regarding role of PRIs.
71. Regarding Caste Reservation System in Birbhum district, 17.19 per cent sampled non-SHG villagers have good knowledge about role of Caste Reservation, while 35.94 per cent and 46.88 per cent sampled non-SHG villagers have

average and poor knowledge about Caste Reservation System respectively. However, in Burdwan district, 14.06 per cent sampled non-SHG villagers have well, 34.38 per cent have average and 51.56 per cent have poor knowledge about Caste Reservation System. So, here non-SHG villagers of Birbhum district have better understanding on Caste Reservation System than the Burdwan district.

72. The data regarding the knowledge level about women reservation is not satisfactory in both the districts. In Birbhum district, 10.94 per cent sampled non-SHG villagers have good knowledge about women reservation, while 31.25 cent and 57.81 per cent sampled non-SHG villagers have average and poor knowledge about women reservation respectively. While, in Burdwan district, 14.06 per cent sampled non-SHG villagers have well, 32.18 per cent have average and 53.13 per cent have poor knowledge about women reservation. So, non-SHG villagers of Burdwan district have quite better understanding about women reservation than the Birbhum district.
73. Regarding PRI structure, in Birbhum district 12.50 per cent sampled non-SHG villagers have good knowledge, while 39.06 per cent and 48.44 per cent sampled non-SHG villagers have average and poor knowledge about PRI structure respectively. Similarly, in Burdwan district, 12.50 per cent sampled non-SHG villagers have well, 40.63 per cent have average and 46.88 per cent have poor knowledge about PRI structure. So, non-SHG villagers of both Birbhum and Burdwan districts have similar understanding about PRI structure.
74. Regarding Schemes under Gram Panchayat, in Birbhum district 25 per cent and 50 per cent sampled non-SHG villagers have good and average level knowledge respectively; while only 25 per cent sampled non-SHG villagers have poor knowledge about Schemes under Gram Panchayat. Similarly, in Burdwan district, 31.25 per cent sampled non-SHG villagers have well, 46.88 per cent have average and 18.75 per cent have poor knowledge about Schemes under Gram Panchayat. So, non-SHG villagers of both Birbhum and Burdwan districts have similar as well as better understanding about Schemes under Gram Panchayat.

75. The study clearly indicates that in both districts the knowledge level of villagers who engaged in SHGs are quite better than the non-SHG villagers. However, only in case of Government schemes and programmes under Gram Panchayat the awareness level were found similar.
76. The continuous exposure, mobility and capacity-building support to SHG members have helped them to improve their knowledge and awareness level about PRI related issues. Hence, the above discussion clearly indicates that the SHG movement has improved the knowledge and understanding of villagers about PRIs in West Bengal.
77. The *Gram Unnayan Samiti* is the lowest structure of grassroots governance in West Bengal. Every *Gram Sansad* has its own *Gram Unnayan Samiti* for planning, implementation, monitoring of Government programmes and ensure better service delivery to the rural people. The effective execution of *Gram Unnayan Samiti* depends on the participation of rural people in decision-making process. So, it is expected that the rural people have good understanding about the *Gram Unnayan Samiti* but the scenario is different in field.
78. The study reveals the actual scenario of the field. It clearly indicates that in Birbhum district, 20.31 per cent sampled SHG members have good knowledge about *Gram Unnayan Samiti*, 42.19 per cent and 35.94 per cent sampled SHG members have average and poor knowledge about *Gram Unnayan Samiti* respectively. In Burdwan district, 23.44 per cent sampled SHG members have well, 48.44 per cent have average and 28.13 per cent have poor knowledge about *Gram Unnayan Samiti*. So, SHG members of each Burdwan district have better understanding than the Birbhum regarding *Gram Unnayan Samiti*.
79. In Birbhum district, 32.18 per cent sampled SHG members have good knowledge about *Gram Sansad* related issues, while 48.44 per cent and 18.75 per cent sampled SHG members have average and poor knowledge about *Gram Sansad* related issues respectively. However, in Burdwan district, 34.38 per cent sampled SHG members have well, 51.56 per cent have average and 14.04 per cent have poor knowledge about *Gram Sansad* related issues. So, SHG

members of Burdwan district have better knowledge level than the Birbhum district regarding *Gram Sansad* related issues.

80. In connection to awareness-level on Gram Sabha related issues, in Birbhum district, 23.44 per cent sampled SHG members have good knowledge about Gram Sabha related issues, while 46.88 per cent and 29.69 per cent sampled SHG members have average and poor knowledge about Gram Sabha related issues respectively. However, in Burdwan district, 25.00 per cent sampled SHG members have well, 48.44 per cent have average and 26.56 per cent have poor knowledge about Gram Sabha related issues respectively. So, SHG members of Burdwan and Birbhum district have similar knowledge level on *Gram Sabha* related issues.
81. The data regarding the knowledge level about women reservation have not found satisfactory. In Birbhum district, 18.75 per cent sampled SHG members have good knowledge about planning and budgeting process, while 43.75 cent and 35.50 per cent sampled SHG members have average and poor knowledge about planning and budgeting process respectively. While, in Burdwan district, 21.88 per cent sampled SHG members have well, 46.88 per cent have average and 31.25 per cent have poor knowledge about planning and budgeting process. So, SHG members of Burdwan district have quite better knowledge about planning and budgeting process than the Birbhum district.
82. In Birbhum district 20.31 per cent sampled SHG members have good knowledge, while 50 per cent and 29.59 per cent sampled SHG members have average and poor knowledge about implementation process respectively. Similarly, in Burdwan district, 21.88 per cent sampled SHG members have well, 53.13 per cent have average and 25 per cent have poor knowledge about implementation process. So, SHG members of both Birbhum and Burdwan districts have similar understanding about implementation process.
83. The knowledge about income and expenditure is important for ensuring the transparency and accountability. Regarding income and expenditure details, in Birbhum district 15.63 per cent and 48.88 per cent sampled SHG members have good and average level knowledge respectively; while 37.50

per cent sampled SHG members have poor knowledge about income and expenditure details. Similarly, in Burdwan district, 17.19 per cent sampled SHG members have well, 48.44 per cent have average and 34.38 per cent have poor knowledge about income and expenditure details. So, SHG members of both Birbhum and Burdwan districts have low understanding about income and expenditure details, which is not very good for transparency and accountability of Gram Panchayats.

84. The study shows that, in Birbhum district, only 9.38 per cent sampled non-SHG villagers have good knowledge about *Gram Unnayan Samiti*, 39.06 per cent and 51.56 per cent non-SHG villagers have average and poor knowledge about *Gram Unnayan Samiti* respectively. Similarly, in Burdwan district, 12.50 per cent sampled non-SHG villagers have well, 50 per cent have average and 37.50 per cent have poor knowledge about *Gram Unnayan Samiti*. So, non-SHG villagers of each Burdwan district have better understanding than the Birbhum regarding *Gram Unnayan Samiti*. However, the percentage of villagers with good understanding about *Gram Unnayan Samiti* is very low in both of the district.

85. In Birbhum district, 18.75 per cent sampled non-SHG villagers have good knowledge about *Gram Sansad* related issues, while 50 per cent and 31.25 per cent sampled non-SHG villagers have average and poor knowledge about *Gram Sansad* related issues respectively. However, in Burdwan district, 23.44 per cent sampled non SHG villagers have well, 56.25 per cent have average and 20.31 per cent have poor knowledge about *Gram Sansad* related issues. So, non-SHG villagers of Burdwan district have better knowledge-level than the Birbhum district regarding *Gram Sansad* related issues.

86. In connection to awareness-level on *Gram Sabha* related issues, in Birbhum district, 14.06 per cent sampled non-SHG villagers have good knowledge about *Gram Sabha* related issues, while 48.44 per cent and 37.50 per cent sampled non-SHG villagers have average and poor knowledge about *Gram Sabha* related issues respectively. However, in Burdwan district, 18.75 per cent sampled non-SHG villagers have well,

53.13 per cent have average and 28.13 per cent have poor knowledge about *Gram Sabha* related issues respectively. So, non-SHG villagers of Burdwan district have better knowledge level on *Gram Sabha* related issues than the Birbhum district.

87. In Birbhum district, only 9.38 per cent sampled non-SHG villagers have good knowledge about planning and budgeting process; while 39.06 cent and 51.56 per cent sampled non-SHG villagers have average and poor knowledge about planning and budgeting process respectively. While, in Burdwan district, 12.50 per cent sampled non- SHG villagers have well, 50 per cent have average and 35.94 per cent have poor knowledge about planning and budgeting process. So, non-SHG villagers of Burdwan and Birbhum district have low understanding about planning and budgeting process.

88. In Birbhum district 10.94 per cent sampled non SHG villagers have good knowledge, while 46.88 per cent and 42.19 per cent sampled non-SHG villagers have average and poor knowledge about implementation process respectively. Similarly, in Burdwan district, 15.63 per cent sampled non-SHG villagers have well, 50 per cent have average and 34.38 per cent have poor knowledge about implementation process. So, non-SHG villagers of both Birbhum and Burdwan districts have low understanding about implementation process.

89. Regarding income and expenditure details, in Birbhum district only 7.81 per cent and 35.94 per cent sampled non-SHG villagers have good and average level knowledge respectively; while 56.25 per cent sampled non-SHG villagers have poor knowledge about income and expenditure details. Similarly, in Burdwan district, 10.94 per cent sampled non-SHG villagers have well, 39.06 per cent have average and 50 per cent have poor knowledge about income and expenditure details. So, non-SHG villagers of both Birbhum and Burdwan districts have low understanding about income and expenditure details, which is not very good for transparency and accountability of Gram Panchayats.

90. The study indicates that 71.88 per cent SHG members have visited Gram Panchayat office for at least once in Birbhum district while in Burdwan district it is 76.56 per cent.

91. Similarly, in Birbhum district 62.50 per cent SHG members know Gram Panchayat members while in Burdwan district 70.31 per cent SHG members know Gram Panchayat members.
92. Regarding training programme, 59.38 per cent SHG members in Birbhum and 65.63 per cent SHG members in Burdwan have taken trainings from Gram Panchayat.
93. The study shows, 43.75 per cent SHG member in Birbhum and 54.69 per cent SHG member in Burdwan opined that Panchayat is sensitive about the SHGs.
94. The study also reveals 45.3 per cent SHG member in Birbhum and 56.25 per cent SHG member in Burdwan opined that Panchayats give proper response to SHGs.
95. Similarly, 64.06 per cent SHG member in Birbhum and 71.88 per cent SHG member in Burdwan opined that they got additional support from *Gram Panchayat.*
96 So, it is clear that SHG members are getting attention from *Gram Panchayats* and this has changed the perception and attitude of SHG members and they participate more in governance related issues. This trend is good for strengthening the decentralisation process in West Bengal.
97. The study shows the perception and attitude level of non-SHG villagers on PRI related issues. Table 6.29 indicates that 59.38 per cent non-SHG villagers have visited Gram Panchayat office for at least once in Birbhum district while in Burdwan district it is 67.19 per cent. However, 54.69 per cent non-SHG villagers in both of the districts know Gram Panchayat members.
98. Regarding training programme, only 18.75 per cent non-SHG villagers in Birbhum and 21.88 per cent non-SHG villagers in Burdwan have taken trainings from Gram Panchayat.
99. The study shows, 42.19 per cent non-SHG villagers in Birbhum and 46.88 per cent non-SHG villagers in Burdwan opined that Panchayat is sensitive about them.
100. So, it is clear that in Birbhum district are getting comparatively low attention from Gram Panchayats and that is why the common villagers have lack of participation in the decentralisation process.
101. However, the study clearly indicates that Gram Panchayats have given special focus to SHGs than the common villagers.

It also becomes obvious that SHGs make rural women folk aware about their social responsibilities and thereby they create an atmosphere of congenial to the decentralized structure.

102. Further, various trainings at GP-levels are also helping SHG members to develop their capacity and engage themselves into the economic activities as well as increase their income. These increased incomes often lead to control over such incomes and contribute to social and political empowerment.
103. Study clearly indicates that the SHG members are participating in political as well as functional decentralisation process. They are taking part in decision-making process at grassroots level.
104. Study clearly indicates that the non-SHG villagers have poor participation in the decentralisation process. So, lack of participation and interest hampers the successful implementation of decentralisation process in West Bengal.
105. The villagers engaged in SHGs have better participation and perception towards decentralisation process. SHG movement has also improved the women participation in *Gram Sansad* and *Gram Sabha* meeting.
106. The data also indicates that SHG approach has successfully promoted improved political participation as well as representation among the rural women. SHG formation has developed a participatory political culture in West Bengal.
107. It also reveals that through SHG approach, the rural people especially the women folk become more aware of their demands and rights, on doing so they form group and make use of legitimate political channels to realize those demands.
108. The inclusion of SHG members in *Gram Unnayan Samiti*, the executive committee of *Gram Sansad* has been made following the rule framed on the change of the West Bengal Panchayat Act, 1973, however in practice, the committee is found to be less committed to the concern of the SHGs.
109. Gram Panchayats has been found to be more keen, competent and innovative in involving SHG members in implementing Government programmes especially where this kind of involvement has been instructed (NREG, Mid-day Meals, Pulse Polio) rather than incorporating their collective strength

and judgement in enriching the decisions and functioning in addressing local issues, local problems and utilizing local resources.

110. An important observation was that where SHGs as well as Gram Panchayats are equally nurtured, both of them can gain efficiency to initiate development action keeping the local context and concern in the focus.

Decentralisation and Self-Help Group (SHG) Movement

111. In recent time local self-governance has given its emphasis on decentralized community engagement, is touted for being a much more flexible and democratic way to deal with community problems and requirements in a right-based framework. The most important actor in this new approach of local governance has been Self-Help Groups (SHGs) that have carved out new arenas for these different forms of socio-political engagement.

112. SHG approach is based on a framework of rights and obligations. It works towards strengthening the capacities of rights-holders to make their claims, and of duty bearers to meet their obligations.

113. SHGs encompass the full range of indivisible, interdependent and interrelated rights (i.e. civil, cultural, economic, political and social rights). It has enhanced women involvement, especially of marginalised section, in local governance and has increased the quality and legitimacy of democratic decision-making.

114. SHGs develop capacities for the knowledge and awareness so that community can make claims and government can meet their obligations. The notion of capability is essentially one of freedom—the range of options a person has in deciding what kind of a life to lead.

115. SHG is an empowerment approach which prioritizes the building and strengthening of a people's institution. SHGs create a sense of ownership of development processes through strategies of empowerment among the rural women. It highly emphasized on large scale social, economic and political empowerment of women who are the actual stakeholders.

116. The critical feature of SHG approach is that it focuses on raising accountability and transparency in the development process.
117. Another important feature of SHG approach is that it increases the degree of community participation in grassroots governance. Fortunately, the participation has found to be active, free and meaningful. It gives specific attention to issues of discrimination, quality, equity and vulnerability.
118. In West Bengal, the active involvement of grassroots women in local governance through Self-Help Groups (SHGs), in turn builds ownership over local developments as well as the leadership capabilities of women.
119. SHGs advocate for effective functioning of the decentralisation process in West Bengal, by enabling women and marginalized communities to engage in the participatory planning and local self-governance. In the recent past SHGs have come out from its actual shape and play a key role in the grassroots governance. The Self-Help Groups became an interface between the development process and the number of Government and elected institutions at the grassroots level, particularly the Panchayati Raj Institutions. The efficacy of these Self-Help Groups (SHGs) has been considerably enhanced through a symbiotic relationship with the Panchayati Raj Institutions.
120. In West Bengal, Panchayati Raj Institutions (PRIs) have been given a pivotal role in poverty alleviation and Self-Help Groups are being perceived as the building blocks of development process. SHGs are being incorporated in the grassroots governance structure to improve the knowledge, perception and participation of rural women as well as to strengthen the rural decentralisation process. Here, an attempt has been made to analyse the values generated and added by the SHG movement to strengthening rural decentralisation.
121. The data generated from the survey and Focused Group Discussion reveal that SHG movement has been successful to bring some transformation in socio-political and economic sphere of rural women which in turn strengthen the rural decentralisation.

Perception of Gram Panchayat Elected Members on SHG and Changing Scenario of Decentralisation in West Bengal

122. The Gram Panchayat members are well aware about the importance of SHG-PRI linkage for strengthening the decentralisation process. In our focused group discussion with Gram Panchayat members, majority of the representatives want to see SHGs as integral substructures of the Gram Panchayat and acting together. They also argued that SHGs should be integrated into a broader vision of participatory local self-governance.
123. Over time SHGs have made them stronger and developed them as a parallel structure of Gram Panchayats in rural areas. The SHGs act as a vehicle for microfinance and credit as well as a vehicle for women's empowerment and participation in various development issues. This emerging trend has changed the decentralisation picture of West Bengal.
124. The SHG movement has empowered women to enter the political space. A large number of SHG members in both of the district have been found either a Gram Panchayat member or member of *Upa-Samiti* or *Gram Unnayan Samiti*. During Focused Group Discussion, Gram Panchayat members also argued that SHGs promoted by Gram Panchayats provide greater political space for women. However, they also felt that over time SHGs are not only being politicized but also treated as welcome development.
125. The sensitivity and response of Gram Panchayats for rural people especially for the women have increased after SHG movement. However, political affiliation of GP leaders comes in the way of SHGs which are seeking linkages and support with their Gram Panchayats.
126. SHGs in West Bengal have contributed a lot for strengthening local self-governance as well as decentralisation process. FGD data also reveals that SHGs in West Bengal are sufficiently aware of local self-governance processes and are enthusiastic about local self-governance. However, a better synergy between SHGs and PRIs in West Bengal will be difficult to achieve.

127. The presence of SHGs in an area increases the attendance as well as participation of women in meetings of the *Gram Sansad* and *Gram Sabha*. However, FGD reveals that many had attended the *Gram Sansad* meeting but only as passive listeners and there are no *Gram Unnayan Samiti* meetings to identify and prioritize common needs and works and subsequently implement them. So, Gram Panchayat should focus on strengthening and more effective functioning of *Gram Unnayan Samitis* and this can be done through development of synergy between SHGs and Local Self-governance.

Testing of Hypothesis Regarding Changing Status of Decentralisation in West Bengal

128. SHG movement improves the political participation of villagers. Coefficient of Association, Ø = 0.208, which indicates moderate association. Odd Ratio = 2.39>1, which means that the villagers engaged in SHGs have 2.39 times higher politically participated than the Non-SHG villagers.
129. SHG movement improves the participation of villagers at *Gram Sansad* meeting. Coefficient of Association, Ø = 0.25, which indicates moderate association. Odd Ratio = 3.00>1, which means that the villagers engaged in SHGs have participated *Gram Sansad* meeting 3 times higher than the Non-SHG villagers.
130. SHG movement improves the participation of villagers at *Gram Sabha*. Coefficient of Association, Ø = 0.35, which indicates moderate association. Odd Ratio = 6.24>1, which means that the villagers engaged in SHGs have participated *Gram Sabha* meeting 6.24 times higher than the Non-SHG villagers.
131. SHG movement improves the decision-making power of villagers. Coefficient of Association, Ø = 0.13, which indicates very minimal association. Odd Ratio = 1.67>1, which means that the villagers engaged in SHGs have taken decisions 1.67 times higher than the Non-SHG villagers.
132. SHG movement does not improve the sensitivity of Gram Panchayat towards villagers.

133. SHG movement improves the capacity of villagers. Coefficient of Association, Ø = 0.39, which indicates better association. Odd Ratio = 6.53>1, which means that the villagers engaged in SHGs have built capacity 6.53 times higher than the non-SHG villagers.

Socio-cultural and Political Constrains

134. There are some factors, which affect the strengthening mechanism of decentralisation process at grassroots level.

Major Constrains or Challenges Recognized During FGD

Personal Constrains	*Social Constrains*	*Administrative Constrains*
Lack of Education	Lack of Community Support	Lack of Leadership Skill Among the Group Leaders
Lack of Exact Idea About Panchayat System	Lack of Mutual Trust among the group members	Inefficient Group Leader
Lack of Interest	Political Interference	Lack of Initiatives at Government Level
Lack of Initiatives	Family Rituals or Norms	Lack of Bureaucratic Willingness
Lack of Support from Family Members	Lack of Voice	Lack of Proper Monitoring

135. The scenario of personal constrains in both of the district and interestingly major constrains are same. Lack of family support is the major constrain in both of the districts, because it has the smallest coefficient of variation as well as highest consistency. Lack of interest and lack of initiatives come second and third respectively in cases of both districts. Lack of education and lack of idea about Panchayats are minimal factors in this case.

136. In Birbhum district family rituals or norms come first to restrict the women from participating in the decentralisation process. Political interference, lack of trust, lack of community support and lack of voice come next respectively. However, in Burdwan district Political interference is the major constrain for successful promotion of decentralisation.

137. In both the districts lack of government initiatives, lack of bureaucratic willingness and lack of monitoring, i.e. the frequent sensitization are the major constrains at administrative-level as these three factors have relatively high coefficient of variation. Leadership is also an issue, but it can be diluted through the training and capacity building.

Recommendations

At Gram Panchayat Level

- The Central and the State Governments should give special consideration in the Five Year Plans of GP with respect to the development of villagers as well as development of the weaker sections.
- The Central and the State Governments may transfer the fund based on subject matter such as infrastructure development, promotion of education, health, agriculture, irrigation etc. but not on the scheme basis like MGNREGA, BRGF etc. which will increase only schemes instead of its success.
- Election is an important institution for democratic decentralised governance. It is a prime and fundamental mechanism of accountability. However, it has not been practiced regularly, freely, and fairly at the Panchayats level.
- Government of West Bengal (GoWB) has empowered two important institutions, namely *Gram Sansad* (Village Parliament) and *Gram Sabha* (at the Gram Panchayat-level) for ensuring people's direct participation in planning and monitoring, evaluating the activities of Gram Panchayat. But instead of holding the meeting in most of the Gram Panchayats used to send the report by providing false information about convening of the meeting. Decisions are taken in the political party meeting at the Gram Panchayat level. Therefore, there are still some issues regarding these institutions which need to be addressed to.
- Regarding accountability and transparency, people's participation must be ensured in planning and implementation. GS is only an effective mechanism of accountability of elected members to the people, if it is held regularly to ensure that all the records and documents

including audit report, income and expenditure account of the GP are placed in the meeting for discussion and publish as annual report of the GP for distribution among the electorate.

- The awareness levels of the villagers are very low. To enhance the awareness level of the villagers regarding their role, responsibilities and entire Panchayati Raj system, huge awareness generation campaign through camps, door to door campaign should be organized.
- The elected Gram Panchayat members are coming from the socio-economically poor groups. The level of education is very poor. Panchayati Raj operation needs very efficient and skilled persons to operate the decentralisation process. So, there should be some landmark for educational qualification for the elected Gram Panchayat members. Educational level may help them to understand the whole process of decentralisation.
- One-third women reservation is mandatory in each Gram Panchayat. But, it appears from the study that the active women participation is very much poor. Women members are working as dummy representatives. So, the capacity-building for the women regarding decision-making is very necessary. Capacity-building and hand-holding training can be arranged for the women representatives.
- The political party or party leaders are taking much more initiatives to motivate the rural people to join in the politics. Politicians are generally choosing their preferable candidate instead of capable person. Gram Panchayat official as well as villagers should take more initiative to elect capable person as a Gram Panchayat member instead of political attachment.
- Gram Panchayats need to be more efficient in planning and budgeting as well as implementation of development schemes.
- Regarding sustainability of development, State Government should encourage and empower GP to collect local tolls and taxes by facilitating more public utilities. Gram Panchayats should be more effective in own fund generation as well as improve the expenditure of funds.
- Government official should be more clean and authentic in

case of beneficiary selection. Upper level Government officials should incorporate with the local Civil Societies for proper implementation of the Government running schemes.

- To promote the people's participation in the planning and implementation process, Government official from the upper-tier should take participation in the *Gram Sabha* and *Gram Sansad* meeting and they have to take initiatives for proper execution of those meeting and they also have to take strong step against political biasness.
- Government has to give emphasis on people's partnership in the implementation of the scheme. Then only rural people can understand about their role and responsibilities.
- The Central and State Governments should take necessary action for timely fund flow.
- The State should initiates proactive steps to create environment for promotion of social capital by encouraging Self-Help Groups, NGOs, cooperative organisations by extending financial support. These should be made partners with Panchayats for better governance at local levels.

At SHG Level

- Lack of proper coordination among the SHGs and Gram Panchayat is one of the most important challenges revealed from this study. In some cases, Gram Panchayats show little originality in providing need based support to SHG members particularly for financial management and livelihood management. So, Gram Panchayats need to provide more support to SHGs regarding livelihood promotion and social development. The Government should take initiatives to strengthen SHGs as primary social group and ensuring the role of Gram Panchayats. The SHGs should be strengthened to articulate and demand their rights.
- Lack of promoting organization is also a reason behind poor participation of SHGs. It might not have been a weaker means to reflect people's preferences in such decision-making, if there was a good representation of the mass organizations. Unfortunately, there were no such organisations found in sampled Gram Panchayats. So, exploration and utilization

of services of non-governmental organizations or technical institutions for supporting SHGs and Gram Panchayats will be key strategy to strengthening local governance.

- Political and bureaucratic unwillingness is another cause of low participation from SHGs. Elected members as well as the officials of the respective *Gram Panchayats* are not taking initiatives to engage SHGs in all development processes. So, local political party as well as Government officials need to be more cautious to engage SHGs in the decision-making process. The Government should create more inclusive forum for community participation.
- The political prejudice has been revealed as strong factors in weakening the relationship between SHGs and PRIs. Political conflict between various political parties turned out into political clashes. It creates problem for those who are not interested in politics but interested in development process.
- Sometimes lack of awareness and interest among the SHG members are also hampering the coordination process. It has often found that members are more interested to enjoy the subsidy money rather than doing some economic activity as well as participating in the grassroots governance. So, the actual objectives are often diluted and participation of SHGs becomes decreased. So, a right-based approach can be promoted to enhance the engagement of SHGs in the local governance process.
- Another challenges of SHG approach is the realization of rights among the members. Rights can be ordained but their actualization is not the result of ordains. Lack of organization among the members makes it difficult to enforce the rights. Rights-based framework should be implemented through institutional mechanisms for decentralisation, because decentralisation facilitates direct accountability for outcomes of decisions taken.

Conclusion

West Bengal is one of the States which have achieved success to some extent in implementing decentralised plans and programmes. It has devolved many powers to the PRIs and recently to SHG for strengthening decentralisation and promoting sustainable development. Keeping this in view, this project had been planned with the broad objective to assess the role of PRIs and SHGs in strengthening decentralisation process in West Bengal. The major finding of the project have been summarized below:

West Bengal has demonstrated sustained commitment to decentralisation through vibrant Panchayati Raj Institutions (PRIs) which have been promoting strong participatory and pro-poor decentralized local governance for identifying and responding effectively to the development needs of the poorest and most marginalized rural women and men. PRIs also ensured adequate representation of the socially backward classes—Scheduled Castes (SC), Scheduled Tribes (ST) and women in PRIs for their involvement in the process of socio-economic development. In fact, Panchayati Raj Institutions play the main role for democratic decentralisation and development of the rural community. Panchayati Raj Institutions take a number of initiatives to promote better quality of life in rural society through planning from the below and by the people. It ensures people's participation in planning and implementation at the grassroots level. However, the political prejudice has been revealed as strong factors in weakening the decentralisation process in West Bengal.

Further, in recent times local self-governance has given its emphasis on decentralized community engagement, is touted for being a much more flexible and democratic way to deal with community problems and requirements in a right-based framework. The most important actor in this new approach of local governance has been Self-Help Groups (SHGs) that have carved out new arenas for different forms of socio-political engagement. Over time Self-Help Groups have come out from its actual shape and play a key role in the grassroots governance. The Self-Help Groups became an interface between the development process, Government and elected institutions at the grassroots level, particularly the Panchayati Raj Institutions. The efficacy of these Self-Help Groups (SHGs) has been considerably enhanced through a symbiotic relationship with the Panchayati Raj Institutions. The key to this is to integrate these existing groups with the democratically elected and empowered Panchayats when the required devolution of power, functions and authority to them took place. In West Bengal, establishment of a system through which the Self-Help Groups and the Panchayati Raj Institutions interface efficiently, has been experienced and successful because both these institutions have the same mandate and objectives, i.e. ushering people-centred development and through it to empower the disempowered. Operating in the spaces between formal Governmental structures and the community, these activities emphasize the growing importance of Self-Help Groups as a major agent for decentralized governance and sustainable development. In particular, it has enhanced women involvement, especially of marginalized section, in local governance and has increased the quality and legitimacy of democratic decision-making. Self-Help Groups create a sense of ownership of development processes through strategies of empowerment among the rural women. It highly emphasized on large scale social, economic and political empowerment of women who are the actual stakeholders. At the last we may conclude that PRIs and SHGs in the West Bengal have developed certain spaces for the rural people that create the range of social and political impact for strengthening decentralized governance, which is immense.

References

Dreze, J., and Sen, A. (1995), *India Economic Development and Social Opportunity:* New York: Oxford University Press.

Law Department (Legislative), (2004), The West Bengal Panchayat (Gram Panchayat Administration) Rules, (2004), Kolkata, WB: Law Department (Legislative).

Law Department (Legislative), (2009), West Bengal Act XLI of 1973: The West Bengal Panchayat Act, 1973 (As modified up to the 31st May, 2009), Kolkata, WB: Law Department (Legislative).

Law Department (Legislative), (2010), West Bengal Act VIII of 2010: The West Bengal Panchayat (Amendment) Act, 2010 (As modified up to the 13th May, 2010), Kolkata, WB: Law Department (Legislative).

Ministry of Law and Justice (Legislative Department), Government of India (GoI), (2005), The National Rural Employment Guarantee Act: The Gazette, Legislative Department, GoI, New Delhi, India.

Ministry of Panchayati Raj (MoPR), Government of India (GoI), (2006), Backward Regions Grant Fund: Programme Guidelines, MoPR, GoI, New Delhi, India.

Ministry of Rural Department (MoRD), Government of India (GoI), (2000), Panchayati Raj in India—Status Report 2000, MoRD, GoI, New Delhi, India.

Panchayat and Rural Development Department (P&RD Department), Government of West Bengal (GoWB), (2008), *Annual Administrative Report 2008-09*, P&RD Department, GoWB, Kolkata, WB.

Panchayat and Rural Development Department (P&RD Department), Government of West Bengal (GoWB), (2010), *Information on West Bengal Panchayats: Their Members and Functionaries*, P&RD Department, GoWB, Kolkata, WB.

Panchayat and Rural Development Department (P&RD Department), Government of West Bengal (GoWB), (2008), *SRD Annual Report 2007-08*, P&RD Department, GoWB, Kolkata, WB.

Panchayat and Rural Development Department (P&RD Department), Government of West Bengal (GoWB), (2009), *Roadmap for Panchayat in West Bengal: A Vision Document*. P&RD Department, GoWB, Kolkata, WB.

Panchayat and Rural Development Department (P&RD Department), Government of West Bengal (GoWB), (2011), SRD Project Completion Report 2011 (ARIES Project Code: 107904-101 &107904-102), Kolkata, WB: P&RD Department, GoWB.

Paul, S.K. (2013), Decentralised Planning: Experience of West Bengal *Panchayats*, in Himadri /Sinha and Anant Kumar (Eds.), *Governance of Commons and Livelihood Security*: Ranchi, Xavier Institute of Social Service.

Paul, S.K. and Mitra, A. (2015), Strengthening Local Self-Government in Rural West Bengal through SHG: A Study in the District of Burdwan, West Bengal, In Singha Roy, S. and Maitra, S.N. (Ed), *Development and Politics in India,* Department of Political Science and History, Chandidash Mahavidyalaya.

Bibliography

Annual Administrative Report, 2008-09, WB: P&RD Department, GoWB.

Alsop, R., Krishna, A. and Sjoblom, D. (2000), Are Gram Panchayats Inclusive? Report of a Study Conducted in Rajasthan and Madhya Pradesh, Background Paper No. 3 of the World Bank's unpublished *Overview of Rural Decentralisation in India*, Volume 3.

Altekar, A.S. (1997), *State and Government in Ancient India*, New Delhi: Motilal Banarasidass Publications.

Bardhan, Pranab and Mookherjee, D. (2000), *Decentralising Anti-Poverty Programme Delivery in Developing Countries*, De Ivery. Website:www.httpi/lglobetrotter.berkeley.edu/macarthur/inequallty/papers/decdelpov.pdf

Blair, H. (2000), Participation and Accountability at the Periphery: Democratic Local Governance in Six Countries, *World Development,* 28 (1): 21-39.

Blomkvlst, H. and Swain, A. (2001), Investing Democracy and Social Capital in India, *Economic and Political Weekly*, XXXVI (8).

Braun, Foachim Von and Ulrike, G. (2002), Does Decentralisation Serve the Poor, Ed. by Ahmed Ehtisham and Vito Tanzi, *Managing Fiscal Decentralisation*, London: Routledge.

Breton, A. (1996), *Competitive Governments: An Economic Theory of Politics and Public Finance*, New York: Cambridge University Press.

Cheema, G.S. and Rondinelli, D.A. (Eds.), (1983), *Decentralisation and Development: Policy Implementation in Developing Countries*, Beverly Hills: Sage Publications.

Cochran, W.G. (1977), *Sampling Techniques* (Wiley Series in Probability and Statistics), John Wiley & Sons.

Conyers, Daina (1983), Decentralisation: The Latest Fashion in Development Administration, *Public Administration and Development,* 3 (1).

Constitution of India, Directive Principles of State Policy, Article 40.

Crook, R.C. and Manor, J. (1998), *Democracy and Decentralisation in South Asia and West Africa,* Cambridge: Cambridge University Press.

Crook, R.C. and Sverrisson, A.S. (2001), "Decentralisation and Poverty Alleviation in Developing Countries: a Comparative Analysis or, is West Bengal Unique?" IDS Working Paper 130. Brighton: Institute of Development Studies.

Datta, P. (2011), *Of Rural Decentralisation and People's Participation: Three Decade Experience in West Bengal,* Kolkata: Dasgupta & Co.

Deshpande, S.V. and Venkatesha, Murthy, G.B. (2002), Pressures from Below: Decentralised Governance in Karnataka, *Economic and Political Weekly*, 4 May.

Dewey, C. (1972), Images of the Village Community: A Study in Anglo-Indian Ideology, *Modern Asian Studies*, Vol. 6, No. 3, pp. 291-328.

Director of Census Operations; 2001, Census of India.

Director of Census Operations; 2011, Census of India.

District Statistical Handbook—Birbhum, 2006, West Bengal.

District Statistical Handbook—Burdwan 2006, West Bengal.

Drèze, J., and Sen, A. (1995), *India Economic Development and Social Opportunity:* New York: Oxford University Press.

Drèze, J. and Sen, A. (1996), *India: Economic Development and Social Opportunity*, New Delhi: Oxford University Press.

Drèze, Jean and Sen, A. (2012), *India: Development and Participation,* New Delhi: Oxford University Press.

Friedman, H. (1983), Decentralised Government in Asia: Local Policy Alternatives for Decentralised Development, in Cheema and D. Rondinelli (eds.), *Decentralisation and Development*, Beverly Hills: Sage Publications.

Dutta, P. and Sen, P. (2009), *Good Governance and Development: Contexts and Concerns*, Kolkata: Progressive Publishers.

Furstenberg, F. and Hughes, M.F. (1995), Social Capital and Successful Development among At-Risk Youth, *Journal of Marriage and Family*, 57 (August).

Ghatak, M. and Ghatak, M. (2002), Recent Reforms in the Panchayat System in West Bengal: Towards Greater Participatory Governance, *Economic and Political Weekly*, 5 January.

Ghosh, R. and Pramanik, A.K. (1999), *Panchayat System in India, Historical, Constitutional and Financial Analysis*, New Delhi: Kanishka Publication.

Ghosh, B. (2000), *Status of Panchayati Raj in the States and Union Territories of India*, New Delhi: Indian Institute of Social Sciences and Concept Publishing Company.

Golooba-Mutebi, F. (2000), Reassessing Participation in Uganda, Paper Presented at the Conference, *New Institutional Economics, Institutional Reform and Poverty Reduction,* Development Studies Institute, London School of Economics and Political Science, 7–8 September.

Government of West Bengal, (1973), The West Bengal Panchayat Act, 1973, As modified up to the 1st November, Government of West Bengal.

Government of West Bengal, (1994), The West Bengal Panchayat Amendment Act, 1994, Government of West Bengal.

Conyers, D. (1983), Decentralisation: The Latest Fashion in Development Administration, *Public Administration and Development,* 3 (1).

Haque, S. (1997), Local Governance in Developing Nations: Reexamining the Question of Accountability, *Regional Development Dialogue*, 18 (2).

Harriss, J. (2002), *Depoliticizing Development: The World Bank and Social Capital,* London: Anthem Press.

Heller, P. (1996), Social Capital as a Product of Class Mobilisation and State Intervention: Industrial Workers in Kerala, India, *World Development*, 24(6).

Inman, R. and Rubinfeld, D. (1997), Rethinking Federalism, *Journal of Economic Perspectives*, 11(4).

Islam, Md. N. (2003), Decentralised Governance and Development: A Gandhian Vision, *Gandhi Prasanga*, V (2): 63-68.

Jha, S.N. (1999), *Introduction, in Decentralisation and Local Politics: Readings in Indian Government and Politics*, Ed. by S.N. Jha and P.C. Mathur; Sage Publications.

Jha, S. (2000), Fiscal Decentralisation in India: Strengths, Limitations and Prospects for Panchayati Raj Institutions, Background Paper No. 2, World Bank Unpublished *Overview of Rural Decentralisation in India*, Volume 3.

Johnson, C. and Start, D. (2001), *Rights, Claims and Capture: Understanding the Politics of Pro-Poor Policy*, ODI Working Paper 145. London: Overseas Development Institute.

Joshi, R.P. (1999), *Constitutionalization of Panchayati Raj: A Re-assessment,* Rawat Publications, Jawahar Nagar, Jaipur-4 (India).

Joshi, R.P. and Narwani, G.S. (2002), *Panchayati Raj in India: Emerging Trends Across the States*, Jaipur: Rawat Publications, India.

Law Department (Legislative), (2004), The West Bengal Panchayat (Gram Panchayat Administration) Rules (2004), Kolkata, WB: Law Department (Legislative).

Law Department (Legislative), (2007), The West Bengal Panchayat (Gram Panchayat Accounts, Audit and Budget) Rules, 2007. Kolkata, WB: Law Department (Legislative).

Law Department (Legislative), (2009), West Bengal Act XLI of 1973: The West Bengal Panchayat Act, 1973 (As modified up to the 31st May, 2009), Kolkata, WB: Law Department (Legislative).

Law Department (Legislative), (2010), West Bengal Act VIII of 2010: The West Bengal Panchayat (Amendment) Act, 2010 (As modified up to the 13th May, 2010), Kolkata, WB: Law Department (Legislative).

Ledyard, J.C. (1984), The Pure Theory of Large Two Candidate Elections, *Public Choice,* 44 (1): 7-41.

Leonard, D. and Marshel, D.R. (eds.), (1982), Institutions of Rural Development for the Poor: Decentralisation and Organisational Linkages. Berkeley: University of California and Institute of International Studies.

Litvack Jennie, Junaid Ahmed and Richard, B. (1998), *Rethinking Decentralisation in Developing Countries,* The World Bank, Washington, DC.

Luckham, R., Goetz, A.M. and Kaldor, M. (2000), *Democratic Institutions and Politics in Contexts of Inequality, Poverty, and Conflict: A Conceptual Framework*, IDS Working Paper 104, Brighton: Institute of Development Studies.

Maddick, H. (1963), *Democracy, Decentralisation and Development*, Mumbai: Asia Publishing House.

Mahapatra, B.P. (2012), *Local Self-Governing Institutions and Fiscal Decentralisation in India: From to Function*, RULNR, Abstract 2193836, Research Unit, CESS, Hyderabad, India.

Mahapatra, S. (2006), An Ally on Panchayati Raj, In (ed.) *Panchayati Raj Institutions in India: Issues and Challenges*, New Delhi: Discovery.

Maheswari, S.R. (1971), *Local Government in India*, New Delhi: Orient Longman.

Maheswari, S.R. (1979), *Few Perspectives on Rural Local Government in India: The Ashok Mehta Committee Report*, Asian Survey, Vol. XIX.

Maheswari, S.R. (1983), *Rural Development in India*, New Delhi: Sage Publications.

Mahipal, (1997), Panchayati Raj in India: Issues and Challenges, *Kurukshetra*, 97(8),

Manor, J. (1999), *The Political Economy of Democratic Decentralisation, Directions in Development Series*, Washington DC: World Bank.

Mathew, G. (1995), *Panchayati Raj: From Legislation to Movement*, Delhi: Concept Publishing Company.

Mathew, G. (2001), Panchayat Elections: Dismal Record, *Economic and Political Weekly*, 20 January.

Mathew, G. (2001), Panchayats Powerless in AP, *The Hindu,* 17 April 2001.

Mathur, K. (1988), Panchayati Raj, Democracy and Politics in India, A Paper Presented on ICSSR Seminar on India since Independence, December 26-30.

Ministry of Law and Justice (Legislative Department), Government of India (GoI), (2005), *The National Rural Employment Guarantee Act: The Gazette,* Legislative Department, GoI, New Delhi, India.

Ministry of Panchayati Raj (MoPR), Government of India (GoI), 2006: *Backward Regions Grant Fund: Programme Guidelines*, MoPR, GoI, New Delhi, India.

Ministry of Rural Development (MoRD), Government of India (GoI), 2000: *Panchayati Raj in India—Status Report 2000*, MoRD, GoI, New Delhi, India.

Mohapatra, B. (2001), Social Connectedness and Fragility of Social Capital: View from an Orissa Village, *Economic and Political Weekly*, XXXVI (8): 665-72.

Moore, M. and Putzel, J. (1999), *Politics and Poverty: A Background Paper for the World Development Report 2000/1*, Brighton: Institute of Development Studies.

Mukherjee, S. (1974), *Local Self-Government in West Bengal*, Calcutta: Dasgupta & Company (Private) Limited.

Mukhopadhyaya, A. (1977), *The Panchayat Administration in West Bengal: A Study of West Bengal's Unhappy Utopia*, Calcutta: The World Press Private Ltd.

Mueller, D.C. (1989), *Public Choice II*, Cambridge: Cambridge University Press.

Nambiar, M. (2001), Making the Gram Sabha Work, *Economic and Political Weekly,* 18 August.

Nicholson, N.K. and Russell, C.S. (1981), *Public Choice and Rural Development: The Proceedings of a Conference, Resource for the Future*, USA: University of California.

Oommen, M.A. (1999), Panchayat Finance and Issues Relating to Inter-governmental Transfers, in S.N. Jha and P.C. Mathur (eds.) (1999) *Decentralisation and Local Politics: Readings in Indian Government and Politics (2)*, London: Sage Publications.

Oppenheimer, J. (1981), Does the Route to Development Pass through Public Choice, in Russel, C.S. and Nicholson, N.K. (Eds.) *Public Choice and Rural Development*, Washington DC: Resources for the Future.

Ostrom, E. (1990), *Governing the Commons: The Evolution of Institutions for Collective Action*, Cambridge: Cambridge University Press.

Oates, Wallace, E. (1972), *Fiscal Federalism*, New York: Harcourt, Brace and Jovanovich.

Oates, W.E. (1999), An Essay on Fiscal Federalism. *Journal of Economic Literature*, 37 (3).

Panchayat and Rural Development Department (P&RD Department), Government of West Bengal (GoWB); 2008, *Annual Administrative Report 2008-09*, P&RD Department, GoWB, Kolkata, WB.

Panchayat and Rural Development Department (P&RD Department), Government of West Bengal (GoWB), 2010, *Information on West Bengal Panchayats: Their Members and Functionaries*, P&RD Department, GoWB, Kolkata, WB.

Panchayat and Rural Development Department (P&RD Department), Government of West Bengal (GoWB), 2008, *SRD Annual Report, 2007-08*, P&RD Department, GoWB, Kolkata, WB.

Panchayat and Rural Development Department (P&RD Department), Government of West Bengal (GoWB), 2009: *Roadmap for Panchayat in West Bengal: A Vision Document*, P&RD Department, GoWB, Kolkata, WB.

Panchayat and Rural Development Department (P&RD Department), Government of West Bengal (GoWB), (2011), SRD Project Completion Report 2011 (ARIES Project Code: 107904-101 &107904-102), Kolkata, WB: P&RD Department, GoWB.

Panth, A.S. and Bohra, O.P. (1995), Finance of PRIs, *The Indian Journal of Public Administrations*. Vol. 41, No. 1, January-March.

Paul, S.K. (2013), "Decentralised Planning: Experience of West Bengal Panchayats", in Himadri Sinha and Anant Kumar (Eds.), *Governance of Commons and Livelihood Security*, Ranchi: Xavier Institute of Social Service.

Paul, S.K., and Mitra, A. (2015), Strengthening Local Self-Government in Rural West Bengal through SHG: A Study in the District of Burdwan, West Bengal, in Singha Roy, S. and Maitra, S.N. (Ed.), *Development and Politics in India,* Department of Political Science and History, Chandidash Mahavidyalaya.

Planning Commission, Government of India (GoI), (1997), *Ninth Five Year Plan, 1997-2000*, GoI, New Delhi.

Prud'home, R. (1995), The Dangers of Decentralisation, *The World Bank Research Observer*, 10 (2): 201-20.

Putnam, R.L. and Raffaella, Y.N. (1993), *Making Democracy Work: Civic Tradition in Modern Italy,* Princeton, NJ: Princeton University Press.

Rahman, H.Z. (2001), Re-thinking Local Governance towards a Livelihoods Focus, *PPRC Policy Paper,* Dhaka: Power and Participation Research Centre.

Rangarajan, C. (2004), Fiscal Federalism: Some Current Concerns. *Indian Journal of Federal Studies*, (1).

Rao, G.B. (2000), Strengthening of Panchayats: Beyond Contractor's Role, Paper presented at the Workshop on *Role of Panchayati Raj Institutions in Natural Resource Management*, 2 and 3 February, New Delhi.

Rao, M.G. (2002), Fiscal Decentralisation in Indian Federalism, in Ehtisham, A. and Tanzi, V. (Eds.), *Managing Fiscal Decentralisation*, London: Routledge Publications.

Romeo, L. (1999), Systems Experimentation in Support of Decentralisation Reforms: Reflections on Local Development Funds, *Regional Development Dialogue* 20 (2): 134-57.

Rondinelli, Dennis, McCullough, J.S. and Jonald, R.W. (1989), Analyzing Decentralisation Policies in Developing Countries: A Political Economy Framework, *Development and Changes*, 20 (1).

Roy, Chowdhury, S. (1996), Rethinking Co-operation: Towards a Non-Essentialist Conception, *National Seminar on Rediscovering Co-Operation*, Institute of Rural Management. Anand (November): 1-10.

Salmon, P. (1987), Decentralisation as an Incentive Scheme, *Oxford Review of Economic Policy*, 36(4).

Sangita, S.N. (2002), Institute for Self-Governance of Community Forestry Resources: Experiences from Three Indian States, Bangalore: ISEC (IDPAD Project).

Schonwalder, G. (1997), New Democratic Spaces at the Grassroots? Popular Participation in Latin American Local Governments, *Development and Changes*. 28(1).

Sharkamsky, I. (1991), *Public Administration, Policy-making in Government Agencies*, London: Purples.

Singh, R. (1996), *Panchayati Raj Manual: A Socio-Historical cum Legal Perspective*, New Delhi: Anmol Publications.

Slater, R.P. and Watson, J.R. (1993), Decentralised Planning and the Anti-Poverty Programmes, Some Possible New Direction, in Hooja, Rakesh and B. Yerram Raju, (Ed.) *Decentrallsed Planning in Multilevel Framework*, New Delhi: Rawat Publications.

Smith, B. (1985), *Decentralisation: The Territorial Dimension of the State*, London: George Allen & Unwin.

Stephen, F.R. (2001), *An Empirical Study of Women in Local Self-Governance in Karnataka*, Search Publications, Bangalore.

Sundaram, K.V. (1997), *Decentralized Multi-level Planning, Principles and Practice: Asian and African Experiences*, New Delhi: Concept Publishing Company.

Tam, H. (1998), *Communitarianism: A New Agenda for Politics and Citizenship,* London: MacMillan & Company.

Tanzi, V. (1995), Fiscal Federalism and Decentralisation: A Review of Some Efficiency and Economic Aspects. In Michael Bruno and Boris P. (eds.), *Annual World Bank Conference on Development Economies*, Washington DC: The World Bank.

Tanzi, V. (2001), *Pitfalls on the Road to Fiscal Decentralisation*, Working Paper, No. 19, Washington DC: Carnegie Endowment for International Peace.

The Constitution (Seventy-Third Amendment) Act, 1992, Government of India.

The Gazette of India, Ministry of Law and Justice, September 7, 2005.

UNDP., (1997), Decentralized Governance Programme: Strengthening Capacity for People-Centred Development, Management Development and Governance Division, Bureau for Development Policy, September 1997.

UNDP, (2003), The Human Rights Based Approach to Development: Towards a Common Understanding Among the UN Agencies: UNDP, New York.

Vyasulu, V. (2000), *Decentralisation, Democratisation, Finances, and the Constitution: Reflections Based on Local Reality*, Paper prepared for the Panel on Decentralisation of the National Commission to Review the Working of the Constitution.

Wade, R. (1985), The Market for Public Office: Why the Indian State is not Better at Development, *World Development* 13(4): 467-97.

Webster, N. (1992), *Panchayati Raj and Decentralisation of Development Planning in West Bengal*, Calcutta: K.P. Bagchi & Company.

World Bank (1997), *India Achievement and Challenges in Reducing Poverty*, Washington D.C.: World Bank.

World Bank (1997), *World Development Report: The State in Changing World*, New York: Oxford University Press.

World Bank (2000) *Overview of Rural Decentralisation in India*, Volume I, Unpublished Report, World Bank.

World Bank (2000), *Overview of Rural Decentralisation in India.* Volume II: *Approaches to Rural Decentralisation in Seven States,* Unpublished Report, World Bank.

World Bank (2000), *Overview of Rural Decentralisation in India,* Volume III: *Background papers,* Unpublished Report, World Bank.

World Bank (2000), *World Development Report 2000/1: Attacking Poverty*, Oxford: Oxford University Press.

World Bank (2000), *Multi-State Study of Panchayati Raj Legislation and Administrative Reform*, Vol. 3, Background Paper 1: De Souza, Peter, New Delhi, India.

World Bank (2000), *Overview of Rural Decentralisation in India,* Vol. 1, September 27, New Delhi, India.

Woolcock, M. and Narayan, D. (2000), Social Capital: Implications for Development Theory, Research and Policy, *The World Bank Research Observer*, 15(2), 225-49.

Index